Xinjiang – China's Northwest Frontier

Xinjiang is the 'pivot of Asia', where the frontiers of China, Tibet, India, Afghanistan, Pakistan and Central Asia approach each other. The growing Uyghur demand for a separate homeland and continuing violence in Xinjiang have brought this region into the focus of national and international attention. With Xinjiang becoming the hub of trans-Asian trade and traffic, and also due to its rich energy resources, Uyghur Muslims of Xinjiang are poised to assert their ethno-political position, thereby posing serious challenge to China's authority in the region.

This book offers a new perspective on the region, with a focus on social, economic and political developments in Xinjiang in modern and contemporary times. Drawing on detailed analyses by experts on Xinjiang from India, Central Asia, Russia, Taiwan and China, this book presents a coherent, concise and rich analysis of ethnic relations, Uyghur resistance, China's policy in Xinjiang and its economic relations with its Central Asian neighbours.

It is of interest to those studying Chinese and Central Asian politics and society, International Relations and Security Studies.

K. Warikoo is Professor of Central Asian Studies at Jawaharlal Nehru University, India. He has authored several books on Kashmir, Central Asia and Afghanistan, and is the founding editor of the quarterly journal *Himalayan and Central Asian Studies*. His books *Religion and Security in South and Central Asia* and *Himalayan Frontiers of India* have been published by Routledge in 2011 and 2009 respectively.

Central Asia Research Forum
Series Editor: Shirin Akiner

Other titles in the series:

Sustainable Development in Central Asia
Edited by Shirin Akiner, Sander Tideman and John Hay

Qaidu and the Rise of the Independent Mongol State in Central Asia
Michal Biran

Tajikistan
Edited by Mohammad-Reza Djalili, Frederic Gare and Shirin Akiner

Uzbekistan on the Threshold of the Twenty-first Century
Tradition and survival
Islam Karimov

Tradition and Society in Turkmenistan
Gender, oral culture and song
Carole Blackwell

Life of Alimqul
A native chronicle of nineteenth century Central Asia
Edited and translated by Timur Beisembiev

Central Asia
Aspects of transition
Edited by Tom Everrett-Heath

The Heart of Asia
A history of Russian Turkestan and the Central Asian Khanates from the earliest times
Frances Henry Skrine and Edward Denison Ross

The Caspian
Politics, energy and security
Edited by Shirin Akiner and Anne Aldis

Xinjiang – China's Northwest Frontier

Edited by
K. Warikoo

Routledge
Taylor & Francis Group

LONDON AND NEW YORK

First published 2016
by Routledge
2 Park Square, Milton Park, Abingdon, Oxon OX14 4RN

and by Routledge
711 Third Avenue, New York, NY 10017

Routledge is an imprint of the Taylor & Francis Group, an informa business

© 2016 K. Warikoo

British Library Cataloguing in Publication Data
A catalogue record for this book is available from the British Library

Library of Congress Cataloging in Publication Data
Names: Warikoo, K. (Kulbhushan), 1951–
Title: Xinjiang : China's northwest frontier / edited by K. Warikoo.
Description: Milton Park, Abingdon, Oxon : Routledge, 2015. | Series: Central Asia research forum | Includes bibliographical references and index.
Identifiers: LCCN 2015040441 (print) | LCCN 2015049600 (ebook) | ISBN 9781138184916 (hardback) | ISBN 9781315644868 (ebook)
Subjects: LCSH: Xinjiang Uygur Zizhiqu (China)–History. | Social change–China–Xinjiang Uygur Zizhiqu–History. | Economic development–China–Xinjiang Uygur Zizhiqu–History. | Xinjiang Uygur Zizhiqu (China)–Relations–China. | China–Relations–China–Xinjiang Uygur Zizhiqu. | Xinjiang Uygur Zizhiqu (China)–Economic conditions. | Xinjiang Uygur Zizhiqu (China)–Politics and government.
Classification: LCC DS793.S62 X53715 2015 (print) | LCC DS793.S62 (ebook) | DDC 951/.6–dc23
LC record available at http://lccn.loc.gov/2015040441

ISBN: 978-1-138-18491-6 (hbk)
ISBN: 978-1-315-64486-8 (ebk)

Typeset in Times New Roman
by Wearset Ltd, Boldon, Tyne and Wear

Contents

Tables

Contributors

K. Warikoo, Professor of Central Asian Studies, School of International Studies, Jawaharlal Nehru University, New Delhi.

Ji Zhen Tu, Senior Researcher, Xinjiang-Central Asia Regional Development Research Center, Urumqi.

Qiu Yonghui, Director, Department of Contemporary Religions, Institute of Religions, Chinese Academy of Social Sciences, Beijing.

K.R. Sharma, former Professor and Head, Department of Chinese Studies, University of Delhi, Delhi.

Debasish Chaudhuri, associated with the Department of Chinese Studies, University of Delhi, Delhi.

Natalia Ablazhey, Professor, National Research University of Novosibirsk, Russia.

Kh. Umarov, Professor of International Economics, Dushanbe, Tajikistan.

A.M. Yessengaliyeva, Professor, Faculty of International Relations, L.N. Gumilyov Eurasian National University, Astana, Kazakhstan.

S.B. Kozhirova, Professor, Faculty of International Relations, L.N. Gumilyov Eurasian National University, Astana, Kazakhstan.

Evgeny Vodichev, Professor, National Research University of Novosibirsk, Russia.

Chen Xi, Assistant Professor at Xinjiang-Central Asia Regional Development Research Center, Urumqi.

Wang Jianming, Researcher at the Ethnic Minority Groups Development Research Study Institute, Beijing.

Wang Qinji, Deputy Director, Xinjiang-Central Asia Regional Development Research Center, Urumqi.

Fu Jen-Kun, Director, Graduate School of Central Asian Studies, Ching Yun University, Taiwan.

Acknowledgements

I acknowledge with thanks all the contributors to this book, for sharing their expertise, knowledge and experience through their chapters. I am particularly grateful to the Central Asian Studies Programme of Jawaharlal Nehru University, New Delhi for providing some financial assistance to facilitate my field study in Xinjiang in June 2011. I am also thankful to the director and faculty of the Ethnic Minority Groups Development Research Study Institute, Beijing, Xinjiang-Central Asia Regional Development Research Center, Urumqi and Mr Yasir of the Xinjiang Academy of Social Sciences in Urumqi for extending their cooperation during my field study in Xinjiang. Though the views expressed by Chinese scholars here are those of individuals, they are nevertheless those of informed individuals who have worked/are working in the region for a significant period, thereby providing information generally not available elsewhere.

1 Introduction

K. Warikoo

Xinjiang lies at the heart of Asia, bordering Mongolia in the northeast, the Central Asian Republics of Tajikistan, Kazakhstan and Kyrgyzstan in the west and north, Afghanistan and Jammu and Kashmir in the south and southwest, Tibet in the southeast and mainland China in the east. It covers a vast expanse of land which constitutes about one-sixth of the total area of the People's Republic of China and holds the distinction of being her largest province where Muslims are in majority. Owen Lattimore, the noted American scholar, has called it the 'pivot of Asia',[1] where the frontiers of China, Tibet, India, Afghanistan, Pakistan and Central Asia approach one another.

Different names have been applied to designate the area at different periods of history. Juwaini, the noted Persian scholar, described it as *Kichik Bukhara* or little Bukhara so as to distinguish it from the proper Bukhara. Mirza Haidar Dughlat, the celebrated author of *Tarikh-i-Rashidi*, called it as *Mashriqi Turkestan* (East Turkestan). In the time of Chagatay Khans it was known as *Moghalistan* and later the name of its famous city and capital – Kashghar – was applied to represent the whole of Tarim basin. Thus several European travellers described it as Kashgharia. It was also known as Alty-Shahr (land of six cities – Kashghar, Yangi Hissar, Yarkand, Khotan, Ush Turfan and Aksu).

The socio-economic life of the people of Xinjiang has been moulded by its peculiar geophysical features. While the lofty mountain ranges of Altyn Tagh, Kunlun, Karakoram, the Pamirs, Tianshan, Alatao and the Altai virtually encircle the region, the great Taklamakan desert to the east cuts it off from the mainland of China. Yet the region's commercial intercourse with the neighbouring countries – India, Afghanistan and Central Asia – continue unhampered through the numerous passes in the mountain ranges. Though sterile and devoid of any forest life, these mountains are the fountainhead of numerous rivers and streams which bring life to the otherwise desert-dominated country. Within the Kashgharia basin the Aksu Darya (river), Kashghar Darya, Yarkand Darya and Khotan Darya combine to form the great Tarim river, from which the southern part of Xinjiang has derived its name, the Tarim basin. Similarly the northern or Dzungaria basin is fed by the Yili (Ili), Manas and Urungu rivers. It is along the course of these rivers and streams that a number of large and small oasis-settlements have come into existence. Where there is water, there is life. Where the water connection ceases, barren desert reappears.

Apart from this striking contrast between these lush green oases and their barren surroundings, Xinjiang has many more physiographic peculiarities. Whereas southern Xinjiang (Tarim basin) lies at an elevation of about 3,000–4,000 feet above sea-level, the Turfan depression lying to its northeast is 500 feet below sea-level. This depression is neither drained by any river nor blessed by any rainfall. The people there adopted the ancient system of artificial underground irrigation channels (*karez*) for watering their fields. However, northern Xinjiang (Dzhungaria basin) has the advantage of receiving about ten inches of rainfall a year as compared to the more arid Tarim basin with only about four inches of rainfall. This factor facilitates the development of pastoral nomadism in north Xinjiang as against the predominance of sedentary population in the Tarim basin.

From the historical point of view, mainland China has had a tenuous relationship with its distant periphery in Xinjiang. While its Chinese connection dates back more than 2,000 years, Xinjiang remained under the effective control of imperial China only intermittently for about five centuries.[2] Long distance, the intervening Taklamakan desert and lack of adequate means of communication, as well as the shifting balance of power in the mainland, were the contributory factors for China's weak control over Xinjiang for a considerable period in history. Whenever the centre was strong in China, it exerted its control over Xinjiang. And whenever the centre was weak, local chieftains, Mongol Khans, Khojas, Muslim chiefs and warlords assumed control over their territorial strongholds. However, the chiefs of Hami and Turfan in the eastern part of Xinjiang, being in proximity to mainland China, maintained a sort of tributary relationship with the centre, while retaining their autonomy.

Chinese interest in Xinjiang originated out of the need to safeguard mainland China from foreign incursions. As such, this westernmost border region, then known as *Hsi Yu*, was regarded as a buffer zone against these attacks from beyond the Great Wall.[3] However, the imperial government never lost sight of the importance of fostering trade relations with the outlying Central Asian states, as it enabled China to 'civilize' the turbulent nomadic tribes and to extend the political influence over them. Central Asian chiefs and trading delegations were encouraged to visit China and were given costly presents and even subsidies in return for their 'gifts' for the Chinese emperor. This was a deliberate move aimed at bringing the outlying border states in the ambit of 'tributary relationship' with imperial China.[4] The Mings consistently followed this policy and they set up a separate Board of Rites to supervise the conduct of relations with Central Asia. The Qings perfected this system by establishing a full-fledged Court of Colonial Affairs (*Li-fan Yuan*) to look after the affairs of the Central Asian dependencies of Xinjiang, Mongolia and Tibet. The Qings considered the possession of Xinjiang as a prerequisite for safeguarding their position in Central Asia. They successfully used both the military and diplomatic means to ensure the occupation of Xinjiang. Social segregation of numerous oasis-settlements and their respective populations hindered the formation of a united resistance movement against the Qing authorities.[5] Besides, the Qing policy of permanent settlement of Manchus, Han Chinese civil and military personnel, traders, artisans and Chinese Muslims (Hui) along with their families in Xinjiang altered the ethnographic and demographic composition of Xinjiang and diluted the local Muslim resistance to Chinese rule.

The earliest recorded history of China's relationship with the outlying border states of Central Asia dates back to 138 BC when the Han emperor, Wu Ti (140–86 BC), sent a mission headed by Chang Chan to Central Asia with the object of forging an alliance with the Yuchi people against the Huns,[6] who were threatening the security of China's western frontiers. Having failed in their attempts to secure such support, the Hans pursued the forward policy of extending effective military control over the 'western regions'. China succeeded in subduing certain oasis-states of the Tarim basin during the later Han period (26–220 AD).

Soon after Chinese control lapsed until it was reimposed by the Tangs (618–907 AD). The Tangs established the *An-Hsi* Protectorate (Four Garrisons) to maintain their authority over these outlying principalities. Tang annals are stated to have recorded that this Protectorate was meant to govern Khotan, Tokmak, Sule and Kucha. Yet Kashghar and other small settlements in this area continued to be under the control of native princes though subject to the overlordship of China. Thus due to internal dissensions among the ruling class in China and also due to lack of communication between their subjects in this far distant region, the Chinese could hold it in their possession only intermittently. However, the petty independent chiefs used to send embassies to China periodically, which were also used for smuggling merchandise.[7] To quote Chavannes, 'nothing more is heard of Anhsi or "Four Garrisons" from 790–91 AD'.[8] Tang rulers are, however, believed to have exercised their firm control over Xinjiang during their period of supremacy.[9]

With the decline of Tang power and the rise of Islam between the eighth and tenth centuries, this region again slipped out of Chinese control. Before Islam was introduced into the country in the tenth century by its ruling prince Satuk Boghra Khan (944–1037 AD), Buddhism was the popular religion of the people. The allegiance of the Central Asian chiefs to the Chinese emperor depended upon the latter's power to enforce it. When the Mongol armies of Chengiz Khan overran Turkestan in the thirteenth century, Xinjiang became part of kingdom assigned to one of his sons, Changhtay. By the fourteenth century the Mongol power waned, with most of its leaders having embraced Islam. Now several local centres of power emerged under the leadership of Mughal Khans and the priestly class of Khojas. The infighting and dissensions among the successive Mughal Khans of Mongol descent paved the way for the rise to power of a priestly class of Khojas under Hidayatullah Afak in Kashgharia in the seventeenth century. It may be recalled that Khoja Makhdum-ul-Azim, a learned theologian of Bukhara, who claimed descent from the Prophet, had settled in Kashghar in the early fifteenth century. He was granted land and other privileges by the ruling

Mughal Khans. Thus came into being a line of Khoja feudals who controlled both their landed estates and their revenues. Being the hereditary religious officials and feudal nobles both at the same time, they exercised a good deal of control over the affairs of the country. The internal feuds among the ruling Mughal princes proved useful to these Khojas, who were by now eager to take over the reins of government. It was under these circumstances that Khoja Hidayat Allah, also named Khoja Afaq, wrested power in the seventeenth century. After the death of Afak, the Khojas too became divided into two warring factions, *Ak-Taghliqs* (white-capped Muslims) and *Kara-Taghliqs* (black-capped Muslims). Kashgharia witnessed perpetual strife between the rival factions of the Khojas, until after Zhungaria was wrested by the Chinese from the Kalmuks in 1755. By 1759, Kashgharia was under the control of the Qings. The dispossessed Khojas found asylum in the Kokand Khanate from where they seized every opportunity to foment trouble and rebellions against the Chinese rulers in Kashgharia. Even during such periods when China could not sustain its hold over the numerous oasis-states of Central Asia, it sought to bring them in the orbit of the 'nominal vassalage' system by fostering trade. The Silk Route, which passed through the oasis-states of the Tarim basin, provided a stable link to facilitate such communication between the mainland of China and the peripheral areas. The Mings sent several Chinese missions to distant cities of Central Asia such as Samarkand, Bukhara, Andkui, Herat, Shiraz and Isfahan,[10] to encourage the Central Asian states to send trade missions to China and also to gather political intelligence about the outlying territories. The Mings encouraged 'tributary relationships' with the principalities of Central Asia by offering trade concessions as a bait. Whereas private Chinese traders were generally prevented from going to Central Asia, the Mings admitted only such Central Asian merchants who would come as part of a diplomatic mission from a vassal state bringing 'tribute' to the emperor.[11] On their part, the Central Asian chiefs found it profitable to send such embassies bearing gifts, as this facilitated their commercial adventures in the 'Middle Kingdom' and also gave them Chinese presents in return, which were several times greater in value.

The farce of this 'tributary relationship' between Ming China and Central Asia becomes obvious from all available historical evidences. These 'tribute' missions would not only specify the gifts desired in exchange,[12] but the merchants often forged the official documents of their kings in which they offered 'cliental submission to the king of China'.[13] Even the Ming annals have recorded instances of the false claims made by such Central Asian trading missions. Similarly, we do not find any mention about the relations between the Moghul Khans of Central Asia with China in the *Tarikh-i-Rashidi* of Mirza Haidar Dughlat, though Ming official history *Ming Shih* is full of references to 'tribute' from the Moghuls. Therefore, it is not surprising to find Tamerlane and his son and successor, Sultan Shahrukh, having been enrolled as 'tributaries' in the Ming annals,[14] though both of them maintained diplomatic relations with China on equal footing and even challenged the Mings on several occasions. With the weakening of Ming vitality and increase of border threats from

Mongolia, the Chinese position in Central Asia became tenuous. Now trade came to be used as political concession to buy peace.

The period of Chinese rule in Xinjiang from 1760 to 1825 is stated to be un-interrupted by any such upheavals, resulting in relative peace and stability in the region. But it was soon plunged into disorder as a result of a series of Khoja rebellions, which subverted the Chinese authority, but for only limited periods. During their short-lived successes, Khoja leaders like Jahangir, Yusuf, Katta Tora and Walli Khan Tora set in motion a process of mass killings of Chinese soldiers, civilians and even innocent natives. Serious reprisals were organized to root out all traces of opposition with the arrival of Chinese reinforcements. Con-sequently, the local economy, particularly cottage industry and trade, suffered a severe setback. The Chinese policy of appeasement towards the neighbouring ruler of Kokand, who was provided with an annual subsidy[15] and other trading privileges in Kashgharia in exchange for his promise of restraining the Khoja exiles living in that Khanate, did not prevent Khoja Buzarg and his adjutant Yakub Beg from launching a successful offensive against the Chinese in the 1860s. It was in 1865 when Khoja Buzarg Khan with the aid of adventurous Yakub Beg rebelled against Chinese in Kashgharia and succeeded in overthrow-ing them. Yakub Beg's task was facilitated by the great Tungani insurrection that had rocked the Gansu province of China and also Chinese Turkestan, which resulted in wholesale killing of non-Muslim Chinese residents and soldiers. Buzarg Khan was soon displaced by the ambitions Yakub Beg, who assumed full control of Kashgharia by 1870. Throughout his rule, Yakub Beg remained busy suppressing small revolts by chiefs of different oases and an atmosphere of suspicion prevailed in the country owing mainly to the ruler's lack of trust in his nobles and subjects. People were forced to adhere strictly to the Islamic prin-ciples in all their daily habits, which they seemed reluctant to do.

It was in 1871 that Russia occupied Kuldja lying north of the Tian shan mountains, simultaneously making a promise to the Chinese government in Peking to hand it back to China as and when she re-occupied Kashgharia. In the meantime Chinese were making full-scale war preparations against Yakub Beg. Tso-Tsung Tang, Chinese Governor of Shansi and Gansu, occupied most of Zungaria by 1876. Kashgharia was taken without any difficulty in 1877, in which year Yakub Beg died.[16] The Chinese government soon entered into nego-tiations with the Russian government for the retrocession of Kuldja.[17] Now Chinese Turkestan was formed as a separate province after an imperial edict was issued on 18 November 1884, and it was renamed as Xinjiang.[18] Hitherto it had formed part of the Gansu province. Since then, China has maintained a firm hold on the province.

The nineteenth century formed a significant period in the history of Xinjiang in more than one respect. The country witnessed a series of uprisings and several changes of government. The Kashgharians lived with savage atrocities under the brief reign of Walli Khan Tora. They also saw the resurgence of Islamic funda-mentalism during the tough rule of Yakub Beg, the impact of which was finally washed away during the lax administration of his Chinese successors. This period presents an example of the colonial practices and exploitative methods employed by the Manchus and the local feudals, at the same time exposing the inherent weaknesses of the Chinese administrative structure. This weakness becomes more apparent from the type of relations which existed with the Khanate of Kokand. Apart from dominating the external trade of Kashgharia with the Central Asian Khanates and through them with Russia proper, the Khans of Kokand harboured political ambitions in the region. To achieve these ambitions they incited Khoja rebellions there. However, the incorporation of Kokand into the Russian empire eliminated this threat. But the approach of Tsarist Russia to the borders of Xinjiang turned the region into the centre of Anglo-Russian rivalry over Central Asia. The British Russophobes were so apprehensive of the Russian advance into Kashgharia and from there to India that the entire machinery of the British Empire was geared to ensure that Xinjiang remained a friendly buffer between British India and the Russian Empire in Central Asia. The British tried to woo Yakub Beg (the independent ruler of Kashgharia from 1865 to 1877) and forged a friendly alliance with him. For this purpose commercial relations between India and Kashgharia through Kashmir and Ladakh were promoted with a view to extending political influence in that region. But the British plans to dominate both the internal and external markets of Kashgharia did not succeed, as Yakub Beg practically adopted a policy of equidistance by proposing friendship with both the British and the Russians. However, trade between India and Xinjiang did not recede into the background as a result of the Chinese re-occupation of the area. In fact the British used every opportunity to render 'friendly' advice to the local Chinese authorities to counter the supposed Russian threat.

After the Chinese revolution of 1911 and the consequent extermination of Qing rule, Xinjiang entered into an era of warlordism which lasted until the mid-1940s. All the successive provincial leaders were Han Chinese – Yang Tseng-hsin (1911–28), Jin Shuren (1928–33) and Sheng Shih-tsai (1933–44), whose authoritarian policies acted as a catalyst for a series of Muslim uprisings that rocked Xinjiang from 1931 to 1949. By 1932 the Chinese authority in Xinjiang was successfully subverted by the Muslim rebellion of Dungans and Uyghurs. The Dungans besieged Urumqi, the headquarters of provincial administration. Khoja Niaz and Sabit Damulla set up a Muslim administration in Kashgar under the name of the 'Turkish-Islamic Republic of Eastern Turkestan'. Three Khotan-lik brothers, Abdullah Boghra, Noor Ahmadjan Boghra and Mohammad Amin Boghra, calling themselves Amirs, held power from Yangi Hissar to Khotan in southern Xinjiang under the title of 'Committee for National Revolution' later renamed as the 'Khotan Islamic Government'. In the wake of this serious political disorder in Xinjiang, Chinese and other non-Muslims, particularly the Hindu traders,[19] were massacred by the Muslim separatists. It was only in late 1934 that the Chinese provincial administration could crush these Muslim rebellions with Soviet military support. However, new centres of Muslim resistance emerged soon after. In 1937, General Mahmud leading the pan-Turkic and Islamic forces and General Ma Hu-shan, leader of the Dungans, realigned themselves in combined endeavour to oust the 'infidel' Chinese from the Xinjiang region. But they suffered crushing defeat at the hands of Chinese troops who received active military and aerial support from the Soviets. The establishment of the Turkic Islamic Republic of Eastern Turkestan (TIRER) between 1933 and 1934, which was based on the principles of Islamic *Shariah*, was an abortive attempt to establish an independent Islamic government in Xinjiang.[20] Efforts to set up the Independent Republic of East Turkestan in 1933 and 1944 ended in failure and Xinjiang was completely brought under control by the Chinese Communist forces in 1949.

Even before Xinjiang Uyghur Autonomous Region was formally founded on 1 October 1955, China took a unique step of designating over 50 per cent of Xinjiang land area as autonomous counties and prefectures in 1953–4 in recognition of their distinct ethno-cultural characteristics. China's policy of developing the underdeveloped regions was accompanied by the migration of Hans from the mainland to the sparsely populated northwest, which brought about structural changes in the region's demographic profile. The policies followed during the Great Leap Forward (1958–66) provided impetus to this process. Race relations between the Hans and the Turkic peoples in Xinjiang have been marked by mutual distrust and hatred. Uyghurs in Xinjiang continue to nourish aspirations of ethno-political independence and have not come closer to the Chinese national mainstream, notwithstanding the economic development due to increased Chinese/foreign investments and flourishing border trade. The large-scale Han migration further contributed to the resentment and discontent among the Uyghurs, leading to violence against Hans as well as the Chinese government.

With Iran's Islamic revolution in 1979, Mujahideen resistance in Afghanistan (1979–94), the rise of the Taliban (1994–2001), the independence of Muslim-majority Central Asian Republics on the direct borders of Xinjiang and the emergence of Al Qaeda and now ISIS which provided thrust to the radical Islamic forces in Xinjiang, the religious factor has assumed significance in the ongoing Uyghur separatism and violence. Though the 1980s and 1990s saw numerous violent incidents in Xinjiang, including bomb blasts, arson, racial attacks and hate campaign by the Uyghur separatists against Chinese rule, the past few years have witnessed an escalation in such violence and growing Uyghur resistance being spearheaded by East Turkestan Islamic Movement (ETIM), World Uyghur Congress, etc. The growing Uyghur demand for a separate homeland and violence have brought this region to the centre of national and international attention.

On its part, the Chinese government has been quite conscious of the threat and has succeeded in enlisting external support in its campaign against the separatists, religious extremists and terrorists, particularly after 9/11. Through the Shanghai Cooperation Organisation (SCO), China has persuaded the neighbouring Central Asian Republics, Russia and few other countries to take a common stand against the three evils of separatism, extremism and terrorism. On the other plane China has launched Great Western Development Programme aimed at bringing the non-Han people into the national mainstream and integrate them both in economic, educational, social and economic realms. With Xinjiang becoming the hub of trans-Asian trade and traffic and also due to its rich energy resources, the Muslims of Xinjiang are poised to assert their ethno-political position, thereby posing serious challenge to China in the region.

It is against this background that this book presents coherent and concise yet detailed analyses of ethnic relations, Uyghur resistance, China's policy in Xinjiang and its economic relations with its Central Asian neighbours in an integrated manner. Eminent academics and area specialists from India, Chinese Academy of Social Sciences (Beijing), Eurasian National University (Astana), Institute of Economic Studies, Tajikistan (Dushanbe), National Research University of Novosibirsk (Russia), Xinjiang Central Asian Regional Development Research Centre (Urumqi) and School of Central Asian Studies, Ching Yun University, Taiwan have contributed to this volume. The book provides a third view of Xinjiang from its neighbourhood, giving Indian, Central Asian, Siberian, Taiwanese and also Chinese perspectives on the developments in Xinjiang in modern and contemporary times.

This chapter, by K. Warikoo, has described the unique geographical setting, chequered history and politics of Xinjiang, at the same time as explaining the role of these factors in shaping the turn of events in Xinjiang in modern and contemporary times. The next chapter, also by K. Warikoo, explores the indigenous cultural heritage of Xinjiang in a historical perspective. It underlines the curious interplay of the geography and history of Xinjiang which has resulted in its ethno-cultural diversity with a rich and variegated cultural mosaic. It also highlights the salient features of China's cultural policy in contemporary times. In Chapter 3, Ji Zhen Tu, a local Chinese author (based in Xinjiang itself), discusses the main features of Xinjiang's industrial system, based on oil exploration, petroleum, coal, steel and non-ferrous metals.

Chapter 4, by K. Warikoo, makes a historical analysis of Qing policy in Xinjiang. It provides an insight into the Qing policy of military conquest, demographic expansion, political manoeuvring and trade concessions as the means to preserve their territorial gains in Xinjiang. This is followed by a chapter from Qiu Yonghui from the Chinese Academy of Social Sciences, Beijing, who provides an insight into the new thinking in China about China's nationalities policy, particularly towards the minorities. She points to the fears in China over the repeated disorders in Xinjiang and hence the need for rethinking the Chinese policies both in theory and practice.

In Chapter 6, K.R. Sharma, the noted China expert of India, makes a critical analysis of the ethnic problem in China and calls for dealing softly with the huge middle group of Uyghurs by providing them genuine autonomy. Chapter 7, by Debasish Chaudhuri, delves into the state-driven process of territorial, political and economic integration of Xinjiang into mainstream China, covering the period from the Republican Revolution in 1911, through the Warlord regimes, Guomindang's coalition experiments (1944–9) and subsequently under the People's Republic of China (1949 to present). In Chapter 8, Natalia Ablazhey from Novosibirsk (Siberia) focuses on the issue of Kazakh diaspora in Xinjiang and provides a historical perspective of the process of migration from Kazakhstan to Xinjiang and vice versa, during the past hundred years or so.

In the ninth chapter Kh. Umarov, the veteran economist from Tajikistan, provides an insider Central Asian view of the extent and pattern of economic cooperation between Xinjiang and the adjoining Central Asian Republics. Chapter 10, by A.M. Yessengaliyeva and S.B. Kozhirova from Kazakhstan, provides an insight into the fast growing cross-border trade between China and Kazakhstan, which has not only turned Xinjiang into a launching pad for Chinese penetration into Central Asia, but has also led to the development of China's northwestern region. In Chapter 11, Evgeny Vodichev of Novosibirsk (Siberia) explores the potential and prospects of cross-border interaction between Xinjiang and South Siberia, in pursuit of the Big Altai approach.

In the following three chapters, Chen Xi, Wang Jianming and Wang Qinji of Xinjiang of the Central Asia Regional Development Research Centre, Urumqi provide local Chinese perspectives on the social and economic development processes underway in Xinjiang besides shedding light on the Chinese religious policies in this frontier region. The book closes with two chapters by K. Warikoo (India) and Fu Jen-Kun (of Taiwan) making in-depth analyses of the ethnic-religious separatism in Xinjiang and China's response.

Notes

1 Owen Lattimore, *Pivot of Asia*. Boston, 1950.
2 Owen Lattimore, 'Xinjiang', in his *Studies in Frontier History: Collected Papers, 1928–58*. London, 1962, p. 184.
3 K. Warikoo, 'China and Central Asia: A Review of Ching Policy in Xinjiang, 1755–1884', in K. Warikoo and Dawa Norbu, *Ethnicity and Politics in Central Asia*. New Delhi, 1992, pp. 2–20.
4 Ibid.
5 Ibid.
6 J.F. Fletcher, 'China and Central Asia', in J.K. Fairbank, ed., *The Chinese World Order*. Cambridge, 1974, p. 207.
7 T.D. Forsyth, 'Introduction', in N. Prejevalsky, *From Kulja across the Tian Shan to Lake Lp Nor*. London, 1879, p. 15.
8 Cited in Aurel Stein, *Ancient Khotan*. Oxford, 1909, Vol. I, pp. 61–5.
9 Macartney, the British Indian government's Special Assistant resident in Kashgar during 1890s, secured scraps of Chinese manuscripts from sand-buried sites near Khotan bearing witness to the fact that Chinese money was current and Chinese officials collected taxes in Chinese Turkestan during the Tang period. See his *Xinjiang: The Chinese are Rulers over an Alien Race*. London, 1909, p. 5.
10 Fletcher, 'China and Central Asia', p. 207.
11 Ibid., pp. 207–8.
12 J.M. Amiot, *Memoires Concernent T Histoire, les sciences les arts, les moers, les usages & c des Chinois*. Paris, 1789. Cited in Fletcher, 'China and Central Asia', pp. 208, 347.
13 L.J. Gallagher, trans. *China in the Sixteenth Century: The Journals of Mathew Ricci, 1583–1610*. New York, 1953. Cited in Fletcher, 'China and Central Asia', p. 347.
14 Fletcher, 'China and Central Asia', p. 209.
15 During the process of Chinese re-occupation of the country, all but one son of its last Khoja ruler, Burhanddin, died. The sole survivor, Sadat Ali, who was popularly

known as Sarimsak, had sought refuge in the neighbouring Khanate of Kokand. His successors led the revolt against the Chinese in Kashgharia, receiving men and material support from their co-religionists in Kokand. In a bid to bribe the Kokand rulers, who supported the cause of the Khojas, the Chinese started subsidizing the Khan of Kokand – probably from 1813 – with 200 yambus (silver shoes) valued at about 3,660 pounds sterling. See H.W. Bellew, *History of Kashgharia*, 1875, p. 76; A.N. Kuropatkin, *Kashhgaria*, translated from Russian by W.E. Gowan. Calcutta, 1882, p. 137; V.S. Kuznetsov, 'Tsin Administration in Xinjiang in the First Half of the Nineteenth Century', *Central Asian Review*, Vol. 10, No. 3, 1962, pp. 271–84.

16 Yakub Beg is allegedly said to have died after having been administered poison by one of his servants. Some believe that he committed suicide after hearing news of the Chinese occupation of Ush Turfan.

17 It was followed by the Treaty of St. Petersburg signed between China and Russia on 24 February 1881.

18 An imperial edict issued on 18 November 1884 raised the status of Chinese Turkestan to a full-fledged province and the region was called Xinjiang (Hsin Chiang), literally meaning 'New Dominion'. Lattimore, *Pivot of Asia*, p. 50.

19 K. Warikoo, 'Muslim Migrations from Xinjiang to Kashmir'. *Strategic Analysis*, Vol. 14, No. 1, April 1991, p. 18.

20 Ibid., p. 29.

2 Cultural heritage of Xinjiang

K. Warikoo

Xinjiang Uyghur Autonomous Region of China is the only autonomous region of China in which the Muslim ethnic groups are in majority.[1] Whereas its physiography has contributed to the formation of its ethno-cultural peculiarities, Xinjiang's vital position as the crossroads of different cultures has been responsible for development of its unique cultural heritage. The Tien Shan range of mountains cuts the region into two distinct but unequal parts, the northern region being traditionally dominated by pastoral nomads and the southern region possessing numerous fertile oasis-settlements with well established agricultural and trading traditions. The people of the northern region, generally known as Dzungaria, have had closer cultural affinity with the Mongols living across the border in the east and with the Kazakhs in the west, both having strong commercial and nomadic connections. Similarly the Muslims of southern region of Xinjiang, also known as the Tarim basin, maintained intimate relations with the adjoining areas of Afghanistan, northern India and Central Asia due to their religious affinity and active trade contacts. As against this, the eastern part of Xinjiang (Hami and Turfan), being located on the main Silk Route and closer to the mainland of China, remained under the influence of Chinese culture. Such a curious interplay of geography and history of Xinjiang has resulted in its cultural diversity with different non-Han ethnic groups concentrated in their respective autonomous prefectures, each group therefore retaining its territorial base. Whereas the Muslim Uyghurs following a settled way of life are predominant in the southern part of Xinjiang, particularly in Kashghar, Khotan, Aksu and Turfan, the Muslim Kazakh nomads are concentrated in Iili and Hami prefectures in the north. Similarly the Muslim Kyrghyz nomads inhabit the Kizilsu Prefecture (adjoining the Kyrghyzstan Republic) and the Muslim Tajiks have been provided an autonomous County of Tashkurghan within the Kashghar Prefecture. As such Xinjiang presents a unique picture of ethnographic diversity with a rich and variegated cultural mosaic.

Since ancient times Xinjiang has been a meeting place of different peoples and their cultures. A network of overland trade routes, the most important being the Silk Route, connect Xinjiang to Central and South Asia. The Silk Route provided a stable communication link, thereby facilitating the multilateral exchange of commerce and culture between China, Central Asia, India, Afghanistan and the Mediterranean through the oasis-settlements of Xinjiang. The long distance trade encouraged urbanization and related institutions. This in turn stimulated the exchange of goods and ideas and led to regional inter-dependence between the different oasis-settlements of Xinjiang. The trading in different commodities was accompanied by an exchange of ideas, art forms and technologies of embroidery, carpet making, calligraphy, sericulture, agriculture, leatherware, metalware, etc. So much so that many areas along the trade routes turned into cosmopolitan trading centres each becoming famous for specific products and also for 'religious, particularly Buddhist institutions and festivals which generated pilgrimage parallel to trade'.[2] For instance, Khotan was famed for jade, carpets silk fabrics and also for numerous Buddhist monasteries, Buddhist pilgrim centres and a festival with car processions.[3] Kucha was known for gold, copper, iron, fine felts, carpets, etc. and also for extensive Buddhist cave monasteries and the *Panchvarsika Parisad*, the quinquennial Buddhist ceremony.[4] Whereas the Silk Route played a key role in the diffusion of knowledge and culture, the caravan traders and pilgrims acted as the instruments of this cultural exchange. Xinjiang was thus subject to varying degrees of cultural influences from China, India, Persia, Afghanistan and Tibet.

The discovery of Neolithic artefacts and pottery in Lopnor, Keriya and Aksu indicates the existence of settled community life in Xinjiang since remote antiquity.[5] The earliest Chinese references to this region are traceable in the historical records of the Han dynasty. Sima Qian (145–50 BC), the Chinese court historian, travelled extensively and recorded details about folklore, local customs and cultures.[6] His works contain references to Central Asia and when studied in-depth can throw important light on the culture and art forms then prevalent in Xinjiang. The *Memoir of the Western Region*, which is part of a larger work known as the *History of the Han Dynasty* compiled by Ban Gu (32–92 AD)[7] is another valuable reference source for understanding the society and culture of Xinjiang in ancient times. These Chinese annals have referred to the existence of well developed agricultural culture, the introduction of Buddhism and the art of writing in the oasis-states of Xinjiang during the Han period.[8] The 300 years of the Tang dynasty were most productive in terms of economic and cultural intercourse between Xinjiang and China. According to the Tang chronicles, the people of Xinjiang followed the Buddhist religion and were fond of music and dance.[9] The *Records of Music* in the *Sui Histories* show that some Central Asian musical instruments found their way to the mainland of China. With the development of agriculture in the oasis-states of Xinjiang trade also flourished, resulting in increased communication between agricultural settlers, pastoral nomads and their neighbours. A number of Chinese merchants and artisans followed the Silk Route to Xinjiang where they did business and made paper, metalware, gold and silver ornaments and jade articles. The Chinese influence began to be felt more during the Tang period (618–907 AD) when Chinese traders, adventurers and artisans introduced their knowledge of more productive agricultural methods, rice cultivation, silk production, mineral exploitation, jade quarrying and metalware, particularly casting of iron and other allied crafts, into Xinjiang.

Buddhist savants from India contributed to the spread of Buddhism in Central Asia and East Asia. One of the eminent scholars was Kumarajiva (344–413 AD) who broke political, geographical, cultural and linguistic barriers for the propagation of Buddhism. Son of a Kuchean princess, Jiva, and Kashmiri Brahman father, Kumarayana, Kumarajiva went to Kashmir with his mother and studied Buddhism for five years. On his return to Kucha, he stopped at Kashghar and studied Mahayana texts. On his return from Kashmir to Kucha, many Kashmiri missionaries accompanied Kumarajiva to propagate Buddhism.

The travelogues of Chinese travellers Fa Hien (fourth century AD), Che Mong (404 AD), Fa Yong and Tao-yo (420 AD) and more particularly Huien Tsang (seventh century AD) who travelled through Xinjiang, provide authentic accounts of the state of cultural development in this region before the advent of Islam. All these travellers found Buddhism prospering in the oasis-settlements of Xinjiang. They have testified to the existence of hundreds of Buddhist monasteries with thousands of monks and abundant usage of Sanskrit literature.[10] Huien Tsang mentions four important centres of Buddhism in Central Asia – Shan-shan (Kroraina), Khotan, Kucha and Turfan. Kashmir played an important role in introducing Buddhism to Khotan, which in turn played a key role in the transmission of Buddhism to China. Kucha was one of the most important centres of Buddhist learning. According to Huien Tsang, the famous Chinese pilgrim and monk who travelled to India from 629 to 645 AD, 'in Kucha there were more than 100 Buddhist monasteries with above 5,000 priests, who were adherents of the Sarvastivada school and studied in the language of India'.[11] From Kucha, Huien Tsang visited Aksu (Pohluka), where he found 'tens of monasteries with above 1,000 priests, all adherents of Sarvastivada school'.[12]

Huien Tsang came to India in 630 AD in search of Buddhist texts after an arduous journey across Central Asia. He spent 14 years of his life (630 to 644 AD) visiting Buddhist monasteries on the Silk Route. Knowing both Chinese and Sanskrit, Huien Tsang translated 77 texts into Chinese and took back a great corpus of Buddhist texts to China. His itinerary included Balkh, Kafiristan, Swat, Gandhara, Bamiyan, Baltistan, Darel, Gilgit, Kashmir, Poonch, Badakhshan, Ishkashim, Wakhan, Shignan, Pamirs, Yarkand, Khotan, Kucha, Loulan, etc. On his return journey to Central Asia, Huien Tsang found in Kashghar 'hundreds of Buddhist monasteries with over 1,000 priests all following Saravastivada school'.[13] In Yarkand there were 'some tens of Buddhist monasteries and about 100 priests, besides numerous stupas in memory of Indian arhats who had passed away'.[14] And in Khotan, 'the system of writing was found to have been taken from that of India. The people were Buddhists and there were above 100 monasteries, with over 5,000 priests, chiefly Mahayanists. Arhat Vairochana had come from Kashmir to propagate Buddhism here'.[15]

Several important places on the Silk Route system such as Kucha, Balkh, Bamiyan, Khotan, Kashghar, etc. developed into important centres of Buddhism when parts of Central Asia and northwestern India were integrated into a single kingdom under the Kushans. Khotan has been the most important commercial and Buddhist centre on the southern limb of Silk Route having had strong connections with India. Khotan has three main ancient sites – Ak Sepul, Yotkan and Malik Awat. Relics and artefacts found by Stein in Yotkan are now lying in the British Museum. However, some antiquities from Yotkan and some other sites are placed in a shabbily arranged local museum at Khotan. Major Buddhist sites in Xinjiang have been stripped of their treasures, which were carried away by foreign archaeologists to museums outside China. On a visit to a small local museum in Bachu (Maralbashi), one found antiquities discovered in the desert between Maralbashi and Aksu stored there. These relics included Buddhist figures, statues of a monkey god, wooden tablets with Brahmi inscriptions, etc. About 45 km further from Bachu, one saw remains of an ancient Buddhist site on the Tok Serai hills. There are still existing three or four stone images of Buddha (2' × 1'), though these have been defaced. Kucha was yet another important centre of Buddhism in Central Asia. On a visit to the famous Buddhist caves at Kumtura, Kyzyl and Kyzyl Gaha, one found paintings and frescoes of Buddha in different forms, monkey gods and a figure with a flute. Only 230 Buddhist caves out of the original 330 are still in tact in the Kucha complex. The British and German archaeologists have removed the paintings in these caves to their respective countries, and only eight caves are now open to public view. Cave No. 17 has elaborate murals depicting Indian characteristics. A statue of Kumarajiva is erected in the Kucha cultural complex, which is well maintained. These frescoes need to be reconstructed and preserved.

Korla, which is the new and modern oil city of Xinjiang, was an important trading centre having economic links with both China in the east and Central Asia in the west. On a visit to the local museum in the Korla town, this author found several Buddhist artefacts, an image of Tara which was excavated in Yenchi county of Korla and also several folios in Mongolian, Tibetan and Kharosthi scripts. There was one round stone with inscriptions of *Om Mane Padma Hum* still preserved here. In Turfan lie the ancient cities of Jiohe and Gaochang, where one can see the traces of an ancient Buddhist monastic establishment. In the famed Bezeklik caves of Thousand Buddha near the Flaming Mountains in Turfan, there are few remnants of the paintings of Buddha. Images of Buddha, monkey gods, etc. have now been recreated by the Chinese authorities to attract tourists. The local museum at Turfan contains some painted pots, two small Buddha statues and some mummies.

The propagation of Buddhism was accompanied by an extensive use of Indian arts-painting, sculpture, music, processions and dance. A curious example of the cross-cultural movement is provided in the manner the artists from Kizil in Xinjiang influenced and contributed to the art of Bamiyan and Hindu Kush in the second half of the seventh century AD.[16] The archaeological excavations conducted in the early twentieth century in Xinjiang, particularly at Yotkan, Dandan Uiliq, Niya, Loulan, Miran, Turfan, etc., have unearthed some of the remnants of ancient Buddhist shrines and stupas having rich treasures of Buddhist images, Brahami and Kharosthi manuscripts, wooden tablets and frescoes. Whereas Kharosthi script was current in southern Xinjaing from Khotan up to Loulan in the Lopnor area up to the third century AD, Brahami script came into vogue after the fourth century.[17] That the Buddhist works were written in Sanskrit and were studied by the Buddhist scholars and monks makes it clear that Sanskrit language was in vogue among the literary and cultural circles in this region.[18] It is established now that Buddhism was the popular religion in the oasis-states of Xinjiang from about the second century BC until the tenth century AD when Islam was established there by the ruling prince Satuk Boghra Khan (944–1037 AD).[19]

With the adoption of Islam as the state religion, the Uyghur culture came under the pronounced influence of Persian, Turkic and Arabic elements. The written form of Arabic script was now introduced as the official script and Arabic architectural style was employed in building shrines, *madrassas* and mosques. Persian music, dance and literature began to be enjoyed by the people. Even in the field of agriculture one finds that the technique of digging *Karizes* (underground canals) in Turfan was adopted under the Persian influence. Similarly new titles like *Mirab* (the officer in charge of irrigation), *Qazi* (religious magistrate), *Mullah* (referred to a person educated in Islamic law and religion) were introduced in the social hierarchy of Xinjiang. Local officials were conferred the titles of *Beg* and *Hakim* (Governor), terms that are of Turkish origin. Common Turkish names still used in Xinjiang included Mehmet, Izhak, Yusuf, Akmat, Abbas, Osman, etc., all reflecting the Islamic influence.[20] Similarly those who had the privilege to go on a pilgrimage to Mecca were called with pride and respect as *Haji*. The title of *Khoja*, which carried local prestige, was also common.[21] It was during the eleventh century that the famous Xinjiang linguist, Muhammad Kashgari, composed his *Divan Lughat-it-Turk*, the dictionary of Turkic words, phrases, poems and proverbs in Arabic script. It is gratifying to note that the Uyghur and Chinese editions of this work have been published. That the burial site of Muhammad Kashgari, which was discovered in Opal near Kashgar in 1981, has been declared as a protected cultural site and rebuilt at government expense,[22] reflects upon China's new policy of preserving the cultural heritage of its national minorities. Another famous work of the same period, *Qutaadgu Bilig* written by Yusuf Has Hajib of Balasagun in Arabic script, has been published in Uyghur and Chinese editions. By the end of eleventh century AD the Turkic language had become the lingua franca in the entire Tarim basin.[23] However, the spread of Islam in Xinjiang not only acted as a 'barrier against the westward spread of Confucianism and Chinese literature'[24] but also resulted in the obliteration of its rich Buddhist cultural heritage.

The cultural treasures of Xinjiang again suffered a setback in the early thirteenth century after its conquest by the Mongols. However, the Mongol Khans were quick to adopt the Turkish language and Muslim faith of the Uyghurs. Mirza Hyder Dughlat of the Dughlat tribe of the Mughals of Chaghtai line and a native of Kashgar composed a voluminous dynastic history of Mughal Khans of Turkestan known as *Tarikh-i-Rashidi*. It is the only available contemporary account of this branch of Mughals covering about 200 years from 1347 to 1542 AD.[25] Originally written in Persian, *Tarikh-i-Rashidi* has since been translated into English. The arrival of Khoja Makhdoom Azam, a learned theologian of Bukhara belonging to the Nakshbandi order, in Kashghar in about the fifteenth century AD paved the way for establishment of Khojas as a spiritual and temporal force in Xinjiang. The *wakf* (endowment) lands attached to the mosques and *madrassas* were also controlled by the Khojas and their trustees. Two sons of the first Khoja founded two rival sects of *Ak Taghliqs* (white-capped Muslims) and *Oara Taghliqs* (black-capped Muslims).[26] *Tazkira-i-Khwajagan*, a contemporary though sketchy account of the Khojas of Kashgar covering the years 1700 to 1756 AD, was written by Mohammad Sadiq of Kashgar, which is available in English through its translation by Robert Shaw.[27]

The Sunni Muslim Uyghurs of southern Xinjiang have been the followers of Nakshbandi order to which the Khojas of Kashghar belonged. They were fond of visiting numerous shrines that dot the oases. Several European travellers who visited the region during the nineteenth century found these shrines, particularly 'tombs of four Imams', *ziarats* of Imam Musa Qasim, Imam Jafar Sadiq, Kaptar-mazar, shrine of Ordam Padshah-all in Khotan, shrines of Hazart Afaq, Ak-mazar, Pojakhom Khoja, Abrazyk Qazi Khoja-all in Kashgar and tombs of Khoja Mohammad Sharif Pir, Altyn-mazar, shrine of *moi-mubarak* (Holy hair) and the sanctuary of Aftu-maidan-all in Yarkand, quite popular, attracting huge crowds of pilgrims. These shrines were looked after by a regular establishment comprising of a *Sheikh*, *Imam* and *Mutavalli* and other assistants, all of whom were fed and maintained by the offerings of pilgrims and revenue of wakf lands attached to each of these shrines.[28] Both Stein and Sven Hedin who visited the 'Pigeon's sanctuary' near Khotan during their travels in Xinjiang found thousands of pigeons housed in wooden buildings and maintained and fed by pilgrims' offerings. The local people believed these birds to be the offspring of a pair of doves which 'miraculously appeared from the heart of Imam Shakir Padshah who died fighting the Buddhists of Khotan'.[29] Similarly Robert Shaw, who visited Kashghar in 1868–9, found the popular shrine of Hazrat Afaq decorated with yak tails, flags and numerous huge horns of Ovis Poli.[30] Lansdell, who visited Xinjiang region in 1888, saw some Muslim Kyrgyz offering a piece of tallow at a stone image at Tokmen.[31] Younghusband was surprised to see the Muslims of Askoli near Moztagh pass offering a sacrifice of bullocks to a (supposed) deity at the summit of a mountain.[32] The curious custom of placing horns and skulls of mountain sheep and deer over the domes of shrines and mosques and the fluttering of yak tails and flags over their masts has been noted by all the foreigners who visited Xinjiang during the nineteenth century. This custom has been compared to that of similarly adorned monuments in the mountainous regions of India where they are called *Devis* and *Shato* by the Hindus and Buddhists respectively.[33] These un-Islamic features pointed to the continuance of the local pre-Islamic method of worshipping the traditionally hallowed spots. Aurel Stein, after corroborating the topographical information provided by earlier Chinese travellers like Huien Tsang with the archeological data collected in the course of his excavations in the region, concluded that many of these Muslim *ziarats* marked the position of early Buddhist shrines and that the popular legends attached to them often retained clear traces of earlier Buddhist tradition related by the Chinese pilgrims.[34] Stein also found the Muslim Uyghurs at various places revering stone images, which custom he traced back to the Buddhist times. A similar view was held by the renowned Soviet Orientalist, V. Bartold. According to him, the Buddhists were exhaustively persecuted as idolators but their monasteries (*viharas*) were inherited by the Muslims and transformed into theological schools (*madrassas*) and mosques.[35] Recent excavations by the Chinese archeological group from the Xinjiang Autonomous Regional Bureau of Cultural Relics at the shrine of Opal near Kashghar revealed many pre-Islamic relics, pieces of Buddhist sculpture and hundreds of Sanskrit folios,[36] thereby corroborating what has been stated above. At Hazrat Afak Khoja's shrine, situated about 5 km away from Kashghar, which was built around 1639–40 and constructed in Uyghur style, one finds extensive usage of Swastika and lotus symbols in tile work on the exterior of this shrine. It was declared as a Special Protective Site of Historical Relic of China on 13 January 1988.[37] During a visit to the shrine in June 2010, this author found a Muslim priest with some of his devotees lighting a lamp and performing some traditional rituals and lighting lamps.

The *Twelve-Muqams*, a classical musical tradition of the Uyghurs, has evinced global interest due to its importance as a symbol of Uyghur cultural identity and its linkages with the *muqamat* traditions in Central Asia. Known as the 'mother of Uyghur music', the *Twelve-Muqams* has large sets comprising of sung poetry, stories, dance tunes and instrumental sections. Recording of music along with notation and lyrics of the *Twelve-Muqams* was completed in 1955 and the music score of the *Twelve-Muqams* was published in 1960, thus turning the rich oral tradition into a textual heritage. Subsequently, in the 1980s, a Muqam research institute and a Muqam art troupe were established in the Xinjiang government. In 2005 the Xinjiang Uyghur Muqam Arts of China was approved by UNESCO as 'Masterpieces of the Oral and Intangible Heritage of Humanity'.

Similarly, the local epic traditions such as the famous Kyrgyz epic *Manas* of about 500,000 lines, *Janger*, an epic of Mongols and *Gesar* have been collected, edited, translated and published. The Uyghur literary classics *Rabiya and Seidi* and *Farhad and Sherin* and the Kazakh long poem *Selihe and Semen* have been edited and translated into Chinese and published.

Local folklore is rich in oral folklore genres: *nakhsha*, *bayt* and *qoshaq* (songs), *lapar* (humorous song and dance performances), *tepishmaq* (riddles), *maqal-tamsil* (proverbs, sayings), *chochak* (tales), *rivayat* (legends), *apsana* (myths), *latifa* (humorous anecdotes). Efforts have been made to collect and publish local literature, folklore, poetry, narratives and history. *Bulaq*, the journal of classical literature published in Urumqi since 1980, has brought to light over 20,000 pages of articles and literary works in Uyghur. *Miras* (Heritage) is another popular journal about Uyghur literature, folklore and folk art, published by the Xinjiang Uyghur literary and art academy from Urumqi since 1983. Other publications include *Tangritagh*, a bi-monthly literary journal published in Urumqi since the 1980s, *Tarim*, a monthly literary journal published since the 1950s, *Uyghur Khalq dastanliri* (a collection of *dastan*, prose and poetry narratives) published in Urumqi since 1981 and *Uyghur Khalq nakhshiliri* (a collection of folk songs with musical transcriptions) published in Urumqi since 1980s.

In the post-1949 period, the Communist Chinese government followed a calculated policy of encouraging local folklore, song and dance ensembles, regional festivals and ethnic games as part of their policy to promote the formation and consolidation of numerous cultural identities. The Arabic script, which was allowed to be used by Uyghurs for some time, was replaced in 1958 by a modified Latin script based on Chinese pin-yin system.[38] At the same time new scripts based on the Chinese system were devised for several ethnic languages, which did not have a script of their own. During the Cultural Revolution, local religion and culture suffered heavily. Harsh Chinese policy towards religion and culture was liberalized in 1978. Uyghur books in Arabic script began to be published in Xinjiang in 1981. The official use of Arabic script was revived in 1982, in deference to the wishes of Uyghurs.[39] The development of educational communication facilities and the interaction of Hans and Uyghurs of Xinjiang in contemporary times also resulted in the creation of a new generation of Uyghurs who are influenced by Chinese language, literature, arts, in short by all aspects of Chinese daily life. A large number of Chinese words have penetrated the Uyghur language. Notwithstanding the impact of Chinese, the Uyghurs in Xinjiang have not wavered from their adherence to their faith, tradition, culture and way of life. So much so, there have been voices of dissent[40] from Uyghur academics, intellectuals and littérateurs on various issues of the history, culture and society of Xinjiang.

China and its people have, throughout history, been conscious of its historical and civilizational importance. Xinjiang has been embedded in Chinese memory and consciousness since ancient times, as various Chinese annals have recorded numerous episodes of China's forays and feats in this remote northwestern outlying border area. Chinese cultural policy in Xinjiang has the following main features:

1   To preserve, sustain and promote all those objects, historical and cultural sites and episodes in Xinjiang's history which demonstrate China's administrative and political jurisdiction in this area.

2   Accordingly numerous sites in Xinjiang which have been ascribed cultural and national importance are appropriated and presented as treasured part of ancient Chinese civilization and its presence in Xinjaing.

3   To promote Uyghur shrines and tourist spots as places of cultural tourism, which attract both Chinese tourists from the mainland and also from Hong Kong, Taiwan, etc., besides the Uyghur pilgrims.

4   Xinhua Book Store in Kashgar and Urumqi are housed in well organized multi-storey buildings, with books in Chinese accounting for the majority of the stock. However, books in Uyghur, Kazakh, Kyrgyz, Mongolian and Xibe are also available in substantial quantities. These books are mainly translations of Chinese works, local literature, etc.

5   Uyghur handicrafts such as brassware, musical instruments, knives, wooden articles, as well as dance, are promoted. Typical Central Asian bazaars (local markets) are functioning and catering to the needs of the local people, in every town and city in Xinjiang. The Central Asian bazaars in Kashgar and Urumqi have developed as centres of international trade with adjoining countries in Central Asia and trade with adjoining countries in Central Asia and South Asia (Pakistan and Afghanistan).

6   Uyghur music and dance is promoted at the national level, in a bid to bring it nearer to the mainstream and also to create better social and cultural understanding between the Uyghur and Han communities. One Uyghur athlete, Adil, has been performing his rope walk every day in the National Stadium at Beijing, drawing applause from the audience. Uyghur girls and boys also perform their dance in several forms at intervals at the National Stadium. Even after the 2008 Beijing Olympic Games, the National Stadium presents a lively atmosphere every day, with thousands of visitors, particularly during holidays.

7   Chinese cuisine has been introduced into Xinjiang in a big way. Apart from the Hui Muslim restaurants (which follow Chinese food style), a number of Chinese hotels and restaurants are opening everywhere. Quan Ju De, the famous roast duck restaurant of Beijing, has opened a branch in Urumqi, which is the exact replica of the original one in Beijing. Peking ducks served in the Urumqi restaurant are brought in from Beijing. This is the unique Chinese way of Sinicizing the local food.

As such Xinjiang presents a classical example of the synthesis of different cultures – Chinese, Indian, Persian and Turkish, and different religions – ancient nature worship, Buddhism and Islam. This rich and composite cultural heritage was cemented by the ideological and religious force of Buddhism and Islam, by aristocratic lineages of Chinese, Kushans, Arabs, Turks, Mongols and others, by the high mobility of statesmen, scholars, divines, artisans, craftsmen and traders. The movement of trade and ideas and the reciprocal cultural influences enriched the horizons of human development and left a deep imprint on the political, economic and social life in the entire region. The Chinese government set up the Oriental Languages Department of Beijing University as early as 1949, and also established the Central Institute of Nationalities for the study of minority cultures.

UNESCO, which has initiated a project on Silk Routes – the routes of dialogue – needs to initiate work on the project of preparing a cumulative catalogue of artefacts, manuscripts, etc. which were excavated by the Western archeologists such as Aurel Stein (UK), Albert Grundwel and Albert von le Coq (Germany), Paul Pelliot (France), Sven Hedin (Sweden), L. Warner (United States), Count Otani (Japan), etc. in Xinjiang and which are presently scattered in different museums throughout the world. Steps need to be taken to identify and preserve the literary and artistic works and cultural monuments that are still in existence in Xinjiang. On the basis of the findings of archaeologists, a catalogue of the same needs to be prepared and published. Old classics in Chinese, Brahami, Kharosthi, Turkic, Persian and Uyghur that have been found in Xinjiang or produced there need to be microfilmed and published possibly with English translations.

The preservation and promotion of indigenous ethno-cultural identities in Xinjiang, including both oral and written treasures of epics, literature, traditions, folklore, festivals, music, dance, shrines and *mazars*, will not only fulfil the ethno-cultural aspirations of the non-Han minorities in Xinjiang, but will also be useful to the Chinese authorities in dealing with the rising tide of Islamist extremism in Xinjiang.

Notes

1 Yuan Qing Li, 'Population Change in the Xinjiang Autonomous Region (1949–1989)'. *Central Asian Survey*, Vol. 9, No. 1, 1990, p. 49.
2 D.E. Klimburg-Salter, *The Silk Route and the Diamond Path*. Los Angeles, 1982, p. 25.
3 Ibid.
4 Ibid.
5 Jack Chen, *The Sinkiang Story*. New York, 1977, p. 4. Geng Shamin, 'On the Fusion of Nationalities in the Tarim Basin and the Formation of the Modern Uighur Nationality'. *Central Asian Survey*, Vol. 3, No. 4, 1984, p. 2.
6 Cui-yi Wei, 'Ancient Chinese Historical Records about Central Asia'. *Central Asian Survey*, Vol. 5, No. 2, 1986, p. 82.
7 Ibid., p. 83.
8 Shamin, 'Fusion', p. 2.
9 Ibid., p. 3.
10 P.C. Bagchi, *India and Central Asia*. Calcutta, 1955, pp. 46–7.
11 Thomas Watters, *On Yuan Chwang's Travels in India, 629–645 AD*. Edited by T.W. Rhys Davids and S.W. Bushell. 2nd edition. New Delhi, 1973, p. 60.
12 Ibid., pp. 64–5.
13 Ibid., p. 290.
14 Ibid., p. 293.
15 Ibid., p. 295.
16 Klimburg-Salter, *Silk Route*, pp. 114–15.
17 Bagchi, *India and Central Asia*, pp. 46, 92.
18 Ibid., pp. 93–4.
19 Ibid., pp. 31, 45.
20 Linda Benson, 'Chinese Style, Turkic Content: A Discussion of Chinese Transliteration of Turkic Names'. *Central Asian Survey*, Vol. 7, No. 1, 1988, p. 88.
21 Ibid., p. 89.
22 Kahar Barat, 'Discovery of History: The Burial Site of Kashgari Mahmud'. *AACR Bulletin*, Vol. 2, No. 3, Fall 1989, pp. 9–11.
23 Shamin, 'Fusion', p. 10.
24 M.I. Siadkovsky, *The Long Road: Sino-Russian Economic Contacts from Ancient Times to 1917*. Moscow, 1974, p. 36.
25 Mirza Hyder Dughlat, *The Tarikh-i-Rashidi*. Translated by E.D. Ross and edited by N. Elias. London, 1895, pp. 2–8.
26 K. Warikoo, 'Chinese Turkestan during the Nineteenth Century: A Socio-Economic Study'. *Central Asian Survey*, Vol. 4, No. 3, 1985, pp. 74, 109.
27 See R.B. Shaw, *The History of the Khojas of Eastern Turkistan*, summarized from the Tazkira-i-Khwajagan of Muhammad Sadiq Kashgari. Calcutta, 1897.

28 Warikoo, 'Chinese Turkestan', p. 93.
29 M.A. Stein, *Sand-Buried Ruins of Khotan*. London, 1903, vol. 1, pp. 194–5; Sven Hedin, *Through Asia*. London, 1898, vol. 2, p. 745.
30 Shaw, *History*, p. 61.
31 H. Lansdell, *Chinese Central Asia*. London, 1893, Vol. 1, p. 121.
32 F.E. Younghusband, *The Heart of Continent*. London, 1904, p. 176.
33 Warikoo, 'Chinese Turkestan', p. 93.
34 M.A. Stein, 'Note on Buddhist Local Worship in Muhammadan Central Asia'. *Journal of the Royal Asiatic Society*, 1910, p. 839.
35 See V. Bartold, *Turkestan down to the Mongol Invasion*. London, 1928.
36 Barat, 'Discovery of History'.
37 Shaw, *History*.
38 Ildiko-Beller-Mann, 'Script Changes in Xinjiang', in S. Akiner, ed., *Cultural Change and Continuity in Central Asia*. London, 1991, p. 74.
39 Ibid.
40 For instance Turghun Almass in his three books *The Uighurs*, *A Short History of Xiongnii* (Turks) and *The Literature of the Uighurs*, written and published between 1986 and 1989, has described Uyghurs as an 'indigenous nation' independent of China and created an ideological basis to link them to Turkic and Islamic peoples in terms of their race, religion, culture and history.

3 Energy and natural resources in Xinjiang

Ji Zhen Tu

Xinjiang is not only rich in resources and energy, but their exploration process is also advantageous. The quality of these rich reserves of oil, natural gas, coal, wind and water energy is much higher. Xinjiang has huge mineral reserves; currently there are 138 categories of the discovered minerals. In recent years, the Chinese government has invested huge funds in the development of Xinjiang's resources and its impact has been profitable.

Xinjiang's oil resources are estimated to be 2.086 billion tons, accounting for 30 percent of Chinese continental oil resources. Natural gas resources are 1,010.3 trillion cubic meters, accounting for 34 percent of Chinese continental natural gas resources. The reserves of oil shale are estimated to be 2,200 million tons, and the oiliness rate is 9–13 percent. The oil and natural resources are mainly situated in Gobi, desolate sands and hinterland of deserts, where the weather is much worse, and transportation is difficult. The geological structure of the oil-yielding area is much complex, as the oil layers are buried deep. But the performance of raw oil is much better, which is generally lower in sulphur content and freezing point. So it is the best material to produce high-quality lubricants, highway bitumen, high-ranking refrigerant, medicines, cosmetics, etc. Heavy-grade oil reserves of Xinjiang are listed at the top in China due to its quality. Distribution of Xinjiang's oil and gas resources is basically on the north-oil, south-gas pattern. There are several categories of crude oil such as heavy oil, light oil, concentrated oil, dense oil, etc. Heating value of natural gas is higher, and its water contents are lower.

Coal reserves of Xinjiang rank first in China, and its quality is very fine. According to the estimates by the Xinjiang Geological Minerals Bureau, Xinjiang's gross coal reserves within 2,000 m vertical depth are 2.19 trillion tons, accounting for 47.4 percent of the estimated gross national resources. These are listed first among all the provinces and autonomous regions of China. The accumulated explored reserves are 9.71 billion tons, and other reserves are 9.50 billion tons. Coal is distributed/discovered in over half of the counties and cities in Xinjiang and the area of the coal rocks spans about 310,000 square kilometers. There are 133 coal producing areas whose coal reserves are explored, including 36 super-big coal fields, among which the coal resources of the Yongur and Turpan-Hami Basins exceed 50 billion tons, thus being ranked among the top ten world coal conglomeration basins. Currently four coal basins are formed in Turpan-Hami, East Yongar, Yili and Kubai. Xinjiang's coal has fine quality. Sulphur content is less than one percent, ash content is lower than 10 percent, phosphorus content is also lower, while its heat value is higher, and the proportion of high-quality coal is higher. Second, the shallow coal layer is easy to explore, which can even be exploited openly. Third, it has lower gas content and safety coefficient is higher. Fourth, Xinjiang has all categories of coal, including long-flame coal, gas coal, coking coal, etc., capable of meeting numerous demands of industry, power and people's daily life. Fifth, there are numerous and thick coal layers, reaching even tens of layers, and the thickness of the main exploitation layer is generally between three and 20 meters, and even exceeding 180 meters.

Wind energy resources rank second in China. The reserves of Xinjiang's wind energy, that is, at the height of ten meters, are 872 million kilowatts, accounting for 20.8 percent of the national storage, thus being second largest in China. The area of the "Nine Wind Areas," such as Dabaicheng, Small Grass Lake, 13 Houses, is 778,000 square kilometers. Average annual wind power density is equal to or greater than 150 watt/square meter. Annual efficient wind speed time is 5,600–7,300 hours and technological explorative amount is 120 million kilowatts. Moreover, the quality of the wind energy is good, the wind frequency distribution is reasonable and devastating cyclones are rare.

Xinjiang is rich in water energy resources with an annual runoff of surface water being 8.82 billion cubic meters. Surface water consumption per capita is 5,146 cubic meters, which is about 2.25 times higher than the national average level. The explorative groundwater is 2.51 billion cubic meters, and glacier reserves account for 50 percent of the whole country. There are 721 rivers in Xinjiang, the bigger ones include Tarim River, Hetian River, Yili River, etc. The entire length of the Tarim River is 2,180 kms, the fourth longest river in China. There are more than 100 lakes here, whose total area is over 10,000 square kilometers. There are several lakes with economic value, such as Bositeng Lake, Sailimu Lake, Manas Lake, etc. There are over 7,300 glaciers, covering an area of more than 5,800 square kilometers, and gross water reserves are over 24 billion cubic meters. The glacier resources are mainly distributed in the Altai, Tianshan, Kunlun and the Pamir mountain areas. The reserves of water energy resources are 38.178 million kilowatts and the total explorable large-scale hydro power stations throughout the region is 4,370,000 kilowatts. Since Xinjiang is located in the hinterland of the European-Asian continent, the weather is arid, and the water resources are heavily influenced by seasonal factors. The time-space distribution is much imbalanced, and the surface water vaporization is big, resulting in the deficiency of water resources in some places.

Energy development and utilization in Xinjiang

Currently, an industrial system suited to Xinjiang's characteristics, that is, dominated by oil exploitation, petroleum and petrifaction, with coal, spinning, steel and non-ferrous metals being the backbone, has come into existence in Xinjiang, and 32 national and regional industrial parks have been established.

Oil and gas exploration

There is strong oil and natural resources exploration in an area of 1,660,000 square kilometers of the territory of Xinjiang, with the area of sediment rock available for oil and gas exploitation being about 901,000 square kilometers, accounting for 54 percent of the area in the whole of Xinjiang. It is mainly distributed in the Three Basins, that is, Yongar, Tarim and Turpan-Hami, to form the "Three Oil Fields." Keramay is the biggest oil field and was constructed in 1950s in the Yongar Basin in the north of Xinjiang. After 50 years' efforts, the Xinjiang Oil Management Bureau has found 28 oil and gas fields, including 19 oil fields and nine gas fields. Xinjiang has set up three oil fields – Keramayi, Dushanzi and Zepu – which have got 56 production installations that have been in the top technological level all over the country. Annual natural gas production is 1,800 million cubic meters. Annual one-time raw oil processing capacity has reached 5,950,000 tons. There are more than 210 accumulated productive oil and petrifaction products, out of which more than 20 are exported to Japan, Thailand, Malaysia, etc. The Tarim oil field lies in the Tarim Basin in the south of Xinjiang, whose estimated oil reserves are 1.08 billion tons, and its natural gas reserves are 8.4 trillion cubic meters. It is considered the hopeful strategic relay region for the Chinese petroleum industry. After the establishment of the Tarim Oil Exploitation and Exploration Department in April 1989, risk exploitation bidding was implemented, and more than ten foreign companies from the United States, Japan, etc., and several exploitation teams from Daqing, North China and other domestic oil fields, were invited to form 45 deep well drilling teams. Later on, 34 oil and gas fields were explored in Lunnan, Hetian River, etc., out of which 15 have been put into exploration, and 4,800,000 tons of annual raw oil productivity was established. The Turpan-Hami oil field is located in the Turpan-Hami Basin, in the east of Xinjiang, with estimated oil reserves of 1,600 million tons, and natural gas reserves of 36.50 billion cubic meters. Here exploration started in the 1990s and after several years' efforts, a new-type oil and gas field has grown rapidly. With the exploration of 16 oil and gas fields, five oil and gas containing structures were discovered. The accumulated explored oil and gas is the equivalent of 291.62 million tons, and the annual productivity of 3,600,000 tons of crude oil has been established.

In recent years, the country has invested huge funds in the exploitation and exploration of oil and natural gas in Xinjiang, and the accumulated explored oil reserves are 2,590 million tons and natural gas reserves are nearly 1 trillion cubic meters. In 2008, crude oil production reached 27.22 million tons, showing an increase of 6.7 times from 1978, by 40 percent from 2001. Xinjiang has become the second crude oil production area in China. By 2012, the crude oil production touched 34.00 million tons. Natural gas production in 2008 was 2.40 billion cubic meters, showing an increase of 9,230 times since

1953, 95 times since 1978, and 4.7 times since 2001. It is ranked first in China. By 2012, the natural gas production reached 3.50 billion cubic meters. With the exploration of Xinjiang's oil and natural gas, and the cooperation between China and West Asian countries in relevant fields, the pipeline transportation construction has developed rapidly in Xinjiang. It possessed more than 4,000 kilometers of oil and gas transmission pipelines in 2008, and an oil and gas pipeline network connecting northern, southern and eastern Xinjiang has come into existence.

In the past 12 years, since the implementation of the Western Development Strategy, the country has invested 120 billion yuan (including 28 billion yuan by Xinjiang) in the "Eastern-Transmission of Western-Gas" Project, which has been put into use, starting from the Lunnan area, Tarim, Xinjiang, passing through Gansu, Ningxia, Shanxi, Henan, Anhui, Jiangsu up to Shanghai, and its total length is 4,200 kilometers. The annual gas transmission in the early stage has been 12 billion cubic meters, and the project can realize stable gas supply for 30 years, which is a key project of the Western Development Strategy.

With the advancement of science and technology and perfection of oil exploitation and exploration technologies, more and more oil and gas resources in Xinjiang will be explored, enabling it to become an important strategic area in twenty-first-century China's oil and gas resources exploration. It will be one of the main oil and gas production areas in the world.

Coal resources development

Abundant coal reserves are the advantageous resource with high attraction and potential in the new industrialization process in Xinjiang. In recent years, a group of big companies and groups, such as Luneng, Shenhua, Luan, joined the development of Xinjiang's coal power generation and coal chemical industry. In January 2010, Heilongjiang Longmei Group, the largest coal company in Northeast China, promised to invest 60 billion yuan in the development and production of coal and coal chemical industry in Xinjiang in the coming ten years. A comprehensive coal development base of over tens of millions of tons is being prepared for construction, accompanied by the implementation of coal power generation, coal chemical industry and other comprehensive development projects. Currently, the "one major, double wings" railway construction, "eastward-transmission of western-power" electricity network construction and building of other infrastructure for the coal industry are being implemented. The advantage of coal resources is being applied for the benefit of industry and economy at an accelerated pace. Xinjiang's raw coal yield increased from 180,000 tons in 1949 to 67.63 million tons in 2008. Power generation increased from less than one million kilowatts in 1949 to 4.89 million kilowatts in 2008. The coal power and coal chemical industry dependent on coal resources are flourishing. Coal fields containing tens of millions of tons are mined one after another. By the year 2012, coal productivity reached 150 million tons, while the coal chemical industry will reach a certain productive stage.

Wind resources development

The wind resources utilization started much earlier in Xinjiang. No. 1 Dabaicheng Wind Power Plant was completed in 1989, the first wind power plant in China. After 20 years of development, five out of nine wind power areas in Xinjiang have been put into operation. By the end of 2007, Xinjiang's wind power assembling scale reached 279,000 kilowatts. Since the second half of 2008, as a result of the international macroeconomic situation, Xinjiang's power supply load increased slowly and the traditional electricity industry suffered losses. But wind power has developed well. Along with the construction of large wind power projects, the assembly scale of wind power in Xinjiang has been expanding. In December 2008, the ceremony for the completion of the first phase of the Mayitasi Wind Power Plant project and the commencement of its second phase was held in Emin County. In January 2009, the Altai Golden Wind Buerjin Wind Power Plant, with an investment of 400 million yuan and 495,000 kilowatts of assembly capacity, began generating power. The prospects of wind power in Xinjiang are great as wind power has become the investment hotspot, relying on its abundant wind resources. Xinjiang's wind power market will attract more and more wind power firms both from home and abroad. The investment prospects of wind power in such key wind resource areas as Dabaicheng, Ala Shankou and Tacheng are bright. It is estimated that the accumulated assembly capacity of Xinjiang's wind power will exceed ten million kilowatts by 2020.

Water resources exploration

This mainly reflects in the strengthening of adjustment and control over water resources. Since the establishment of the People's Republic of China, total investment in Xinjiang's water conservation has been over 20 billion yuan. Several projects have been established on the main rivers. There are 485 reservoirs with total capacity of over six billion cubic meters, which is about 162 times and 200 times of those in the year 1949 respectively. In recent years, the government invested more than ten billion yuan in the comprehensive treatment of Tarim River. This project was completed in 2008, putting an end to 30 years of over 300 kms of dry river. Moreover, a group of modern large water conservation projects, such as Kezier Reservior in Aksu and the Wuluwati Irrigation Hinge in Hetian, and a large group of main and branch canals, along with the leakage proof project, were completed. Thus water exploration, capacity of reservoirs and efficient irrigation area increased rapidly in the whole region. The benefit of the reservoirs has been immense. The irrigated area is nearly 20,000 mu, most of which is the sustainable harvest area. The area of water available for fish farming is 800,000 mu. Some reservoirs also provide for the water consumption of cities and industry at the same time.

Benefits of resources exploration

China has been sticking to the principle of macro exploitation, macro exploration and big investment, trying to transform the resources advantage into the economic advantage, through rapid economic development of Xinjiang and exploration of its resources. The exploitation and exploration of oil, natural gas and coal resources not only meets the demand of Xinjiang's economic and social development, but further drives the development of machinery, transportation, communication, construction, power, water conservation, chemical industry and other industries, along with the creation of some local industries related to the "vegetable baskets" and "rice bags" projects. Growth of the third industry stimulated the generation of employment, urbanization process moved forward, and the new type of oil and petroleum chemical industry cities on the south and north of the Tianshan Mountains, such as Keramay, Dushanzi, Kurla, Kucha, Zepu, are flourishing, resulting in huge changes in Xinjiang's urban and rural scenario.

Since 1989, the Chinese government has invested more than 1 billion yuan in the construction of gas field exploration, relevant pipelines and gas stations. About 78 million yuan were invested in 2008. About 300,000 households in 23 cities and counties of five prefectures in southern Xinjiang, that is, Kurla, Hetian, Atushi, Aksu, Moyu, Luopu use clean and cheap natural gas now. This puts an end to the practice of "cutting red poplar for fuel" by the residents in the countryside. The natural gas heating in Urumqi increased by ten million cubic meters in 2010. Over 250 boilers are being transformed in order to reduce pollution levels. Seventy percent of the towns and cities in Xinjiang use natural gas now.

The Hetian region, where the Uyghurs account for over 95 percent of the population, achieved all-round natural gas promotion and utilization in power, heating, auto, catering and civil fields in 2006. Hetian is the first middle-size city in China realizing the overall natural gas heating, resulting in the saving of over 100,000 tons of raw coal annually. During the course of oil and gas exploitation and exploration, the Central Oil and Petroleum Companies also shoulder social responsibilities for the benefit of the nationalities in Xinjiang. For example, the Tarim oil field in southern Xinjiang opens its market to the locality, and its total investment in Xinjiang has reached 36 billion yuan, creating such rich cities and counties as Kurla, Kucha and Qiemo. Moreover, nearly three billion yuan were invested directly to help the poor regions in southern Xinjiang to build roads, extend wires, dig water wells, build schools, etc. The Turpan-Hami Oil Field follows a policy of co-construction between the oil field and the local environment, driving the development of the local economy. They purchase more than 5.58 billion yuan of materials from the locality, accounting for 30 percent of the total oil field investment. In over 50 projects which are joint ventures with the locality, nearly 100 million yuan have been invested. Its tax contribution amounts to two billion yuan. Funds are provided for the local reservoirs, roads, poverty alleviation disaster management, water transformation and sickness prevention and cure, etc. All these steps help in creating a good social environment for the development of the oil field.

Xinjiang's gross industrial yield increased by 4.3 billion yuan after the completion of the first phase of the "eastward-transmission of western-gas" project. Its added industrial value increased by 26.8 percent, fiscal income increased by one billion yuan, driving 3 percent of Xinjiang's GDP growth. In May 2010, the Central Committee of the Communist Party of China held a conference on Xinjiang to discuss issues of development and the reform of the resources tax. From 1 June 2010, the tax rate of 5 percent according to the price has been introduced. As a result of the new tax policy, the financial income of Xinjiang would increase to four billion yuan every year. To conclude, the resources are abundant in Xinjiang and their exploration and utilization have developed immensely, benefiting the local people.

4 Xinjiang under the Qings

K. Warikoo

It was only under the Qings (1644–1911 AD) that Xinjiang was finally absorbed within the Chinese empire. The process of their expansion into Xinjiang was gradual but continuing. The Qings pursued a calculated policy of military conquest, demographic expansion, political manoeuvring and trade concessions as the means to preserve their territorial gains. The Qings not only contributed to the territorial expansion of Chinese empire but also initiated the process of Sinification of the western border region of China. No understanding of the history of Xinjiang in modern times, particularly the contemporary political and ethnic issues, is possible without getting an insight into the Qing policies in this area. It is in this context that an attempt is hereby made to examine the Sino-Xinjiang relations under the Qings with particular reference to their policy as was practised then.

Qing conquest of Xinjiang, 1755–9

By the time the Manchu Qing empire was established in China in 1644 AD, several small independent principalities had come into existence in Central Asia. Initially the Qings did not make any alteration in the Ming policy of fostering trade-cum-tributary relations with the Central Asian states. As Fletcher states, 'during this time Qing relations with Central Asia proper (Eastern and Western Turkestan) were restricted to the traditional blend of "tribute" and trade, with merchants sometimes coming directly from Central Asia and sometimes coming as part of Oyirad "tribute" embassies'.[1] But the emergence of a powerful Oirat-Dzungar Khanate of Western Mongols in the 1670s–80s presented a fresh challenge to the Chinese prestige in Central Asia. In 1688, the *Oirats* attacked the *Khalkha* – the Eastern Mongols – following which the *Khalkha* leaders sought refuge in China which gave it readily.

By 1689 AD, Galadan, the leader of Western Mongols, had succeeded in incorporating the Khanates of Hami, Turfan and Kashgaria (the southern part of Xinjiang) within his kingdom. From the 1690s onwards there ensued a bitter and long struggle between the Dzungar Khanate and the Qings for supremacy in Central Asia. Galadan's efforts to secure the support of the Dalai Lama in the Sino-Dzungar wars posed another threat to the Chinese position in Central Asia.

Realizing the implications of the Dzungar–Tibet alliance, the Qings established their effective presence in Tibet in 1727–8 when a permanent garrison and an Imperial Resident (*Amban*) were stationed at Lhasa. The Qings sought to overcome the problem of Dzungar threat by following the old Chinese policy of 'using barbarians to regulate barbarians'.[2] In pursuit of this dictum, the *Khalkha* (Eastern Mongols) were successfully played against the *Oirats* (Western Mongols). Several other factors such as the Russian inroads into a large part of Kazakh territory, Qing domination over the *Khalkha* Mongols and Tibet and internal strife among the Dzungars, contributed to the weakening of the Dzungar Khanate.

The death of Galadan Tsering in 1745[3] and the subsequent internecine struggles and civil wars among the Dzungars provided an excellent opportunity to the 'Chieng Lung Emperor of China to eliminate for ever the Dzungar threat to China'.[4] When one of the Western Mongol faction leaders, Amursana, sought Chinese military support in the autumn of 1745 in a bid to reclaim the Dzungar throne,[5] the Qings responded to his request immediately. That the Qings had already made up their mind to attack Dzungar Khanate becomes obvious from an edict issued in mid-1754 by the Qing emperor, in which he dwelt upon his plan of intervention in the internecine struggle of the *Oirats*. It stated:

> Their tribes (the Oirats) have been fighting each other for the past several years. And they are having trouble with the Kazakhs, which is what is sowing discord (among) their people. This is the opportunity we must use. If we lose it without planning (anything else), their position will gradually grow stronger within a few years.... Next year I intend sending troops in two directions and reaching Ili.[6]

By August 1755 the Qing army had defeated the *Oirats*. Amursana was recognized as Prince of the first degree (*Qinwang*) and made second in command of the army (*Fu Jiangiun*). In doing so Qings wanted to divide the once strong Dzungar Khanate into four units under four different Khans each subordinated to the Middle Kingdom. The policy had been clearly stipulated earlier in an edict dated March 1755 which stated: 'This time we have sent troops specifically to pacify the Dzungars. In future we shall grant the title of Khan to Amursana and three other Oirats.'[7] Obviously the Qing policy did not suit Amursana, who aspired to be the lone and supreme authority over the Dzungar Khanate like his predecessor. He soon launched a struggle against the Qing troops. The years 1756–7 witnessed intense fighting between the two sides, until the *Oirats* were finally defeated in 1757 by the Qings.[8] In their struggle against the *Oirats*, the Qings employed their usual tactics of playing one local faction against the other. This time they enlisted the support of Mongol feudal lords and even the Lamaist clergy.[9]

All available contemporary accounts of the Qing military expedition to Dzungaria are unanimous in the view that the Qing army indulged in large-scale massacre of the insurgents and even the local civilian population of Dzungaria.[10]

Some estimates put the numbers of killed as more than one million people.[11] Even modern Chinese historians admit that 'this victory was won by the most ruthless, almost total extermination of the population of Dzungaria'.[12] The Qing victory over Dzungaria was commemorated by erecting two monuments in Ili with inscriptions in Chinese, Manchu, Oirat and Tibetan languages. One of the passages read as under:

> Oh, ye people of Dzungaria!... For generations in turn you have turned out to be thieves. The mighty ones have robbed the indigent ones, and those many assembled have oppressed those who were few.... Now the DaiQing (Qing) nation was supported by Heaven. It was not at all the might of men.[13]

After having finally subjugated Dzungaria (northern parts of Xinjiang), the Qings focused their attention on the southern oasis-states in Kashgharia or *Alty Shahr*, which shared common Islamic culture and a sedentary way of life with the people of Western Turkestan. The principalities of Turfan and Hami situated in the northeastern part of Xinjiang, due to their proximity to China and closer trade relations, had already established the 'tributary' relationship with the Qings in 1644 and 1649 AD.[14] The Khojas who gained supremacy in Kashgaria in the early seventeenth century under the leadership of Khoja Hidayatullah, popularly known as Hazrat Afak, got divided into two rival factions, *Ak Taghliqs* (white-capped Muslims) and *Qara Taghliqs* (black-capped Muslims), soon after his death. When, in 1756–7, the Qing army was engaged in military operations against the Dzungars, they found two Khoja brothers being held as hostages by the *Oirats* in order to ensure Kashgharia's subservience to the Dzungar Khanate.

The Qings freed the Khoja brothers, invested them with tributary status and provided them military assistance to seize power from the rival Khoja faction then ruling Kashgharia. But once the Khoja brothers had gained control over Kashgharia, they turned the tables on the Qings. When in early 1757 the Qing court sent a mission to secure 'tribute' from the Khoja brothers, they massacred members of the mission and declared independence of Kashgharia.[15] The Qings took nearly a year to launch an offensive against the Khojas, as they wanted to consolidate their position in Dzungaria and also to enlist support of the feudal nobility of various oasis-states of Eastern Turkestan during the intervening period. In an imperial edict dated 3 February 1758 the Qings laid responsibility for the Khoja rebellion on Khoja Jihan, whereas his brother Khoja Burhan-ud-Din was offered a reward for apprehending and handing over his brother to Qings.[16] The Khojas did not fall in this trap and continued their struggle jointly. Another edict issued on 5 March 1758 called upon the Begs of Yarkand, Kashghar, Kucha, Aksu and Khotan to assist the Qing troops in apprehending the Khoja rebels.[17] The Qings did succeed in securing cooperation from the feudal nobility of certain oasis-states, such as Kucha and Wusha.[18] The Qing army, which was dispatched on 10 February 1758 by the Emperor Chien Lung, took about a year to finally exterminate the last traces of Khoja resistance in Kashgharia.[19] Whereas the Khoja brothers are reported to have been killed while fleeing towards Badakhshan, the *Ak Taqhlik* line of Khojas survived only after moving westwards to Kokand.

The newly acquired territories of Dzungaria, Eastern Turkestan and also the principalities of Hami and Turfan were now incorporated in the Qing empire and the area was redesignated as Xinjiang (New Dominion) in 1768. The annexation of Xinjiang enhanced the political prestige of the Qings in Mongolia, Tibet and other Central Asian states. Now the Khan of Kokand too recognized the Chinese supremacy in Central Asia and offered 'tribute' to the Qing court. Notwithstanding the huge expenses of maintaining the vast territory of Xinjiang, China achieved long-term strategic gains in Central Asia. The possession of Xinjiang not only served as the first line of defence against foreign intrusions but also facilitated the process of Chinese consolidation in Mongolia and Tibet.

Policy of indirect administration

Though the Qings did not formally bring the newly acquired territory of Xinjiang within the provincial structure of China, its redesignation as Xinjiang (New Dominion) indicated their desire to hold this frontier territory perpetually. *Li-fan Yuan* (the Court of Colonial Affairs) continued to be responsible for all matters relating to Xinjiang, Mongolia and Tibet and also for the supervision of relations with other Central Asian states. Originally established by the Qings in 1638 AD to conduct and regulate China's trade and tribute relations with the Central Asian states, *Li-fan Yuan* now assumed the role of actual administration of Xinjiang, Tibet and Mongolia.[20] This imperial institution was now strengthened and organized into various bureaus, each of which looked after the judicial matters, translation of documents from Central Asian rulers, training of students in the Central Asian languages, postal stations, watch towers, registration of adult males, grant of annual subsidies to princes, etc.[21] The Qings preferred to govern Xinjiang indirectly through the traditional indigenous feudal institutions using the local headmen, *Begs* and princes as instruments of local rule. Though working under the overall supervision of thin upper stratum of Manchu bannermen and Chinese bureaucracy, the native *Begs* were made directly responsible for maintenance of general law and order, collection of taxes, matters relating to trade, justice, etc.

For the sake of administrative convenience, Xinjiang was divided into two administrative divisions, Dzungaria or *Tien Shan Pei-lu* (Northern Circuit) and Kashgharia or *Tien Shah Nan Lu* (Southern Circuit), which was in conformity with the geographical and ethnic diversity of the region. The civil and military administration of both these divisions was placed under the supreme command of a Military Governor (*Chiang Chun*) who had his headquarters at New Kuldja in the Ili basin.[22] *Chiang Chun* was assisted by a Military Lieutenant Governor (*Tu Tung*) stationed at Urumqi, with his jurisdiction over the Dzungaria, Hami and Turfan areas. Besides, there were three councillors (*Khan Ambans*) at New Kuldja, Tarbagatai and Kashghar.[23] The two principal divisions of Dzungaria and Kashgharia were further subdivided into various circles each placed under an Imperial Resident (*Amban*) who in turn looked after his circle through the native *Begs*. The posts of *Chiang Chun*, *Tu Tung*, *Khan Amban* and *Amban* and other top official positions were reserved for bannermen.

The highest *Beg* official was the *Hakim Beg* whose duty was to oversee the civil administration of major cities. There were about 35 *Hakim Begs* each in charge of different oasis-cities of Kashgharia. Under *Hakim Begs* there were 34 categories of lesser *Begs* like treasurer, tax collector, village headman, irrigation commissioner, labour commissioner, judicial officer, chief of the night police, 1,000 man unit commander, 100 man unit commander, etc.[24]

While making appointments of these *Beg* officials, the Qing authorities ensured that they were not posted in their native places. By following this 'law of avoidance' the Qings sought to minimize the risks of local nobility using political power and territorial base for any rebellious activities. Thus the *Begs* could stay in their office subject to the will of the higher Chinese authorities. In practice, however, the imperial officers were transferred regularly and the local *Begs* would continue to remain in office unless removed for some special reason. However, the *Begs* were obliged to pay obeisance to the Chinese emperor and also to dress in Chinese fashion. The indigenous officialdom (*Begs*) and clergy were exempt from taxes. Similarly the *Akhunds* and imams, though deprived of their political powers, continued to discharge the functions of 'native judiciary and provided the organization and leadership' of the religious and cultural life in Kashgaria.[25] The tax-free status of the *wakf* (religious endowment) land and other properties attached to mosques, places of pilgrimage (*Ziarats*) and tombs was retained.[26] The Qings did not interfere in the religious practice of Muslims. Nor was their system of administration of justice tampered with. But the Muslim officers could not try the cases of Chinese, Manchu or Buddhist Kalmuks. In this way the Qings followed a policy of non-interference towards the Muslims of Kashgaria.

The Qings did not make any alteration in the existing feudal structure of local administration. They concerned themselves with the task of maintaining ultimate control, the actual job of governing being left to the *Beg* officials. The Qings followed a deliberate policy of segregating the natives of Kashgharia from increased contacts with the Han Chinese population. The Chinese civil and military personnel and traders resided in separate walled settlements, which were built at a considerable distance from the native settlements. These came to be known as *Yangi Shahr* (new City) and *Qalay-i-Shahr* (City Fortress). While following a policy of conciliation towards the Muslims of Kashgharia, sufficient safeguards were taken to minimize the possibility of their collective political action against the Qings. Whereas curbs were imposed on the political activities of the Muslim clergy, the local officialdom of *Begs* was subordinated to the overall control of Qing officers. As part of their policy of 'using barbarians against the barbarians' the Qings bestowed special favours on the 'loyal' factions among the local nobility and clergy. The *Qara Taghliq* faction of Khojas received preferential treatment against the *Ak Taghliqs*.

Similarly the Muslim chiefs of Hami and Turfan were treated exceptionally well. They enjoyed greater autonomy and authority, which was the reward for their voluntary submission and loyalty to the Qings even before the Chinese conquest of Dzungaria.[27] But the Khans of Hami and Turfan had no jurisdiction over the Chinese settlers who, like their counterparts in Northern or Southern Circuits, came under the charge of the Military Lieutenant Governor at Urumqi. In short, the Qing policy of administration in Xinjiang was designed to maintain peace and tranquility in this strategic border region involving least possible economic burden on the imperial government.

Policy of agrarian-military settlements

Notwithstanding their policy of pacification towards the Muslims of Kashgharia, Hami and Turfan, the Qings took simultaneous steps to encourage the agrarian and military settlements in Xinjiang. The region was treated as the outlying military dependency of China and the expenditure involved in the maintenance of Chinese bureaucratic apparatus and military garrisons was desired to be met out of the local resources. In the words of Fletcher, 'the imperial government expected its Inner Asian dependencies (Mongolia, Xinjiang and Tibet) to be self-supporting'.[28] In pursuit of this policy the Qings laid emphasis on increased agricultural production by improving irrigation facilities, reclamation of wastelands and setting up of new military-agrarian settlements. Though the traditional taxation system of land-tax, *Kharaj* (one-tenth of the harvest in kind) was not changed, 50 per cent tax in kind was levied on farmers cultivating government land.[29] The Qings sought to exploit the economic potentialities of Xinjiang to the maximum possible in order to meet all the grain requirements of the Chinese officials and military forces locally.

After their occupation of Xinjiang, the Chinese treated it as an area fit for agrarian-military settlements and the place of exile for criminals, political prisoners and fugitives who were moved here along with their families. Apart from the Qing officialdom comprising the Military Governor, Lieutenant Governor, *Khan Ambans* and *Ambans* (all of whom were bannermen) that governed Xinjiang, the area was garrisoned by troops (10,000–23,000 in number) consisting mainly of bannermen from Jehol and China proper, but also nomads from Inner Mongolia, Manchurian tribal peoples (Sibos, Solons and Deghurs) and Han Chinese from Gansu and Shansi.[30] These garrison troops were not only stationed for unspecified periods but permanently settled in Xinjiang along with their families. The strength of these military garrisons had risen to more than 98,000 persons (including their dependents) by the beginning of the nineteenth century.[31]

Numerous military-agricultural settlements were established in Ili, Urumchi, Barkul, Tarbagatai and Kur Karasu districts (Dzungaria division) and Hami, Turfan, Karashahr, Aksu, Kucha, Khotan and Sairam districts (Kashgharia division).[32] But the main garrison force was stationed at Ili and Urumchi in the Dzungaria circuit whereas the presence of Chinese troops in Kashgharia was kept to the minimum. To quote Fletcher, 'the imperial authorities focused their attention on the defence and development of the Tien Shan Northern Circuit and regarded Altishahr mainly as a huge tax-farm to support the army'.[33] But the local tax receipts were never enough to cover the expenses incurred to maintain the huge military force and bureaucratic apparatus in Xinjiang. Though the granaries of Xinjiang garrison were reported to be full by 1800 AD, yet 'something like 12,000,000 silver *taels* had to come each year from China proper for Xinjiang to meet its expenses'.[34] Hence the need to reclaim more and more wastelands for increasing agricultural production and beef up the local revenue receipts.

Dzungaria region, which was almost entirely depopulated during 1750s and which possessed vast expanses of land, provided a suitable place for settlement of people from outside. The Qings encouraged the Manchus, Sibos, Solons and Chahars and Han Chinese to set up permanent military-agrarian settlements in Dzungaria. Similar military settlements were set up in Hami, Turfan and Kashgharia too. Dzungaria was also peopled by the Han Chinese traders, craftsmen and other settlers, exiles and convicts, Chinese Muslims (Dungans) from Gansu, Shansi and China proper and also the Muslims of Kashgharia (who later came to be known as *Taranchis*).

All these settlers received land free from government and were required to pay fixed taxes both in cash and kind which generally amounted from 10 to 20 per cent of the harvest.[35] Every military or civilian settler was required to grow food for himself and three Qing soldiers.[36] But towards the end of the eighteenth century the Qings found to their dismay that these military settlements had not attained self-sufficiency. This was largely due to the inexperience of Manchu soldiers in agricultural operations. In order to fulfil the food grain requirements of the Xinjiang forces, it became imperative for the Chinese to make optimum use of the arable and waste land resources. So in 1802, a large canal was dug in New Kuldja to facilitate the creation of new agrarian settlements for Manchu troops.[37] They were, however, allowed to hire their land to Muslim tenant farmers (*Taranchis*) from Kashgharia, in order to keep them in continuous military training. But these bannermen, though treated as hereditary proprietors of land, were not entitled to lease, sell or mortgage the same.[38] As was anticipated, the *Taranchi* cultivators, on account of their vast experience in the sedentary way of life, could grow enough food for the use of Chinese military and civilian personnel.[39] In the beginning about 6,000 families of *Taranchis* (about 34,000 persons) had been settled in the Ili valley and their number increased to about 8,000 families (50,000 persons) by the end of the eighteenth century.[40] Though the *Taranchi* settlers were placed under the administrative control of a Muslim *Hakim Beg* at Kuldja, their movement was restricted within their settlements.[41]

In short, the Qings laid the foundation of the Sinification of Xinjiang. They took a series of administrative and political steps to facilitate the permanent settlement of Manchus, Han Chinese civilian and military personnel, political fugitives and criminal convicts, traders, artisans and Chinese Muslims (Huis) along with their families in Xinjiang, thereby redrawing its ethnographic and demographic map. According to Fletcher, 'by the turn of the nineteenth century, hundreds of thousands of Chinese Muslims and non-Muslim Han Chinese'[42] were settled there. The Qing policy of setting up military-agrarian settlements was designed to secure long-term political and economic gains. This policy yielded the desired results as it ensured the permanent physical presence of the Qings, dilution of Muslim resistance and increased the agricultural productivity in Xinjiang. But the high rate of taxes that were imposed to secure finances for providing irrigation facilities and agricultural implements to the new settlers created deep discontent among the peasantry. The forcible bondage of new settlers to lands allotted to them and the exploitation by the local and Chinese officialdom, also contributed to armed Muslim uprisings against the Qings from the 1820s to the 1860s.

Muslim rebellions and re-establishment of Chinese power

The late eighteenth century was marked by the general decay of the Qing empire. This was mainly due to the deterioration in the standards of military-bureaucratic apparatus, shortfall in the country's finances, intense exploitation of peasants and oppression of ethnic minorities. The problem of common people was accentuated by the rampant corruption among the officialdom, usury and unlawful duties levied by the officials for personal profit. High offices and ranks were sold at a high premium. Xinjiang was no exception to this state of affairs. In fact the problem was further compounded in this frontier region due to the deterioration in the quality of Qing officials and troops posted there. The officials went there with the desire of amassing as much wealth as was possible within their span of official tenure in Xinjiang.

At the same time the local population found the 'Manchu overlordship increasingly distasteful'[43] as they had to bear the brunt of high taxes that were levied to meet the rising expenses of military garrisons. The dispossessed Khojas assumed the leadership of the disaffected Muslims and thus started a series of armed Muslim uprisings against the Chinese authorities. The Khoja leaders like Jahangir, Mohammad Yousuf, Katta Tora and Walli Khan Tora succeeded in subverting the Qing rule during the first half of the nineteenth century, but only for limited periods. The Khans of Kokand, who harboured political ambitions in Kashgaria and wanted to have their monopoly over its external trade, also accentuated the problems for the Chinese by extending open support to the resistance movement led by Khojas. The Qings tried to purchase peace from the Kokand ruler by granting him a sizeable subsidy in exchange for his promise to restrain the Khoja fugitives living in his Khanate. In the year 1832 the Qing authorities had relented before the Kokandi demand to station a tax collector and agent (*Aksakal*) in Kashghar. They also allowed the Kokandi merchants to trade duty-free in Kashgharia.[44]

The Qing policy of appeasement towards the neighbouring ruler of Kokand, who was provided with an annual subsidy and other privileges in Kashgharia in exchange for his promise of restraining the Khoja exiles living in that Khanate, did not prevent Khoja Buzarg Khan and his ambitious lieutenant, Yakub Beg, from launching a successful offensive against the Chinese authorities in 1864. By this time the Qing power in Central Asia had touched the lowest point, which was in total contrast to the phenomenal increase of Russian influence in this region. Qings were too preoccupied with the Opium war, Taiping Rebellion (1851–64), Tungan uprisings in Shanxi and Gansu to offer any organized resistance and send reinforcements to salvage the imperial authority in Kashgharia.[45] The religious resurgence and disaffection among the local Muslims made the task of Khoja Buzarg Khan and Yakub Beg much easier. Buzarg Khan was soon dispossessed by the wily Yakub Beg who assumed full control over Kashgharia by 1870. Meanwhile the growing European pressure on China exacerbated Qing difficulties in Central Asia.

The Russian expansion in Central Asia including their occupation of Ili and increased Russian commercial and political interest in the affairs of Xinjiang led to active Chinese policy towards the border region. The Qings considered Xinjiang as the first line of defence against foreign intrusions. Though the incorporation of Kokand into the Russian empire had eliminated the source of foreign abetment to the Khoja rebellions, the Qings were now confronted with the problem of increasing Russian and British influence in Central Asia. Encouraged by the successes achieved by the Chinese general and military strategist, Tso Tsung Tang, against the Taipings and Tungan rebels of Shanxi and Gansu, the Qings entrusted to him the task of re-establishment of Chinese power in Xinjiang. By the year 1879 Tso's troops had recovered nearly all of Xinjiang.

The Qings now entered into negotiations with the Russians for retrocession of Ili. After prolonged talks the two sides reached a compromise and signed the Treaty of St. Petersburg on 24 February 1881.[46] Now the Qings changed their policy of treating Xinjiang as a military dependency. It was brought within the regular administrative structure of China and made a full-fledged province. An imperial edict to this effect was issued on 18 November 1884. To quote Fletcher, 'wary of the Russian threat and determined to eliminate Kashgaria's constant disorders, the Qing court abolished the rule of the Begs and integrated Eastern Turkestan into the administration of China proper'[47] by incorporating it as a full-fledged province. Now Xinjiang was treated as part and parcel of the Chinese empire and its local administration was organized on the same lines as was the case in other provinces of China.

Conclusion

Occupying a pivotal position in Central Asia, Xinjiang presented a unique picture of geographic and ethnographic diversity. The Tien Shan range of mountains cut the region into two distinct but unequal parts – Dzungaria basin to the north and Kashgharia or Tarim basin to the south. Whereas the Dzungaria region was mainly dependent on pastoral economy, the Kashgharia division, possessing numerous fertile oasis-settlements, had a well developed agricultural economy. The *Oirat* (Mongol) population of Dzungaria had closer political and cultural affinity with the people of Mongolia to the east. They also had closer physical interaction with the

Kazakh nomads in the west, both having strong commercial and nomadic connections. Similarly the Muslims of Kashgharia maintained close ties with the adjoining Central Asian Khanates of Kokand and Bukhara in the west due to their cultural affinity and active trade contacts with the people of those Khanates. As against this, the principalities of Hami and Turfan, which were located in the northeastern part of Xinjiang on the main Silk Route, maintained close political and trade relations with the Chinese due to their geographical proximity to China proper. In other words, the geo-political orientation of Xinjiang was more inclined towards Mongolia and Western Turkestan than to China in the east. The process of integration of this border area with the mainland of China became further complicated due to the absence of proper means of communication and the intervention of the vast Taklamakan desert between the two regions.[48]

This westernmost border region, then known as *Hsi Yu*, was regarded as a buffer zone against the attacks from beyond the Great Wall. However, the imperial government never lost sight of the importance of fostering trade relations with the outlying Central Asian states, as it enabled China to civilize the turbulent nomadic tribes and also to extend her political influence over them. Central Asian chiefs and trading delegations were encouraged to visit China and were given costly presents and even subsidies in return for their 'gifts' for the Chinese emperor. This was a deliberate move aimed at bringing the outlying border states in the ambit of 'tributary relationship' with imperial China. The Mings consistently followed this policy and they set up a separate Board of Rites to supervise the conduct of relations with the Central Asian states. The Qings perfected this system by establishing a full-fledged court of Colonial Affairs (*Li-fan Yuan*) to look after the affairs of the Central Asian dependencies of Xinjiang, Mongolia and Tibet.

The emergence of a powerful Dzungar Khanate in the seventeenth century presented an immediate threat to the Chinese imperial interests in Central Asia. So the Qings considered the possession of Xinjiang as a prerequisite for safeguarding their position in Central Asia. They successfully used both the military and diplomatic means to ensure the occupation of Xinjiang. Whereas all elements of resistance from the Dzungars and Muslims of Xinjiang were crushed by resorting to brutal force, they also whipped up inter- and intra-ethnic discord among various groups with a view to prevent the formation of any united front against the Qings. So much so, the Chinese Emperor Chien Lung proudly listed the success of the military campaign in Xinjiang (1755–9) as one of his 'ten perfect achievements'.

Soon after their conquest of Xinjiang, the Qings followed a policy of liquidation of all elements of opposition in order to instill fear among the local people. In this process Dzungaria suffered severe human and material losses. The Khoja leaders of Kashgharia who used to act as the rallying points for local resistance movement were eliminated and some of them sought refuge in the adjoining Khanate of Kokand. Besides, the permanent settlement of numerous military colonies in Xinjiang ensured the effective military presence of the Qings. At the same time the Qings did not think it prudent to dislodge the indigenous and traditional Uyghur, Kyrgyz and Kalmuk (Mongol) bureaucratic substratum, under which the native *Begs*, headmen, princes or chiefs were delegated all local authority, even permitting them to govern by Islamic laws. In this manner the Qings ensured the loyalty of the local officialdom and clergy, who 'developed a vested interest in Qing rule'.[49] The Qings used the contradictions between and in the different nationalities and kindled ethnic discord, in a bid to sustain their authority in the region. Accordingly numerous favours were bestowed on *Qara Taghliq* faction of the Khojas as against the *Ak Taghliqs* who had been in the forefront of the Khoja uprisings. Similarly, the chiefs of Hami and Turfan were accorded special treatment for their loyalty. The Qings succeeded in curbing the political powers of the local clergy without seriously offending the religious sentiments of the Muslims of Kashgharia.[50] They also followed a policy of isolation from the local population in order to avoid any possible inter-ethnic clashes between the Chinese military or civilian settlers and the local Muslims. The Chinese traders, artisans, soldiers and officials shut themselves inside newly built mud-fortified townships in every district.[51]

The social segregation of numerous oasis-settlements and their respective populations hindered the formation of united resistance movement against any oppression by the Qing authorities or their subordinate *Beg* officials.[52] Though the Chinese authorities did not alter the traditional tithe system of land taxes, the actual duties realized from agriculture and trade were much higher due to arbitrary and corrupt exactions of the native bureaucracy. Fixed sums were farmed out to *Hakim Begs* or *Begs* of respective circles or sub-circles for collection. The Qings thus avoided any direct involvement in the collection of taxes. In case of a revolt or some opposition, the people's anger was soothed by fixing the responsibility on the native officials.

All these factors contributed to general peace and increased agricultural productivity in Xinjiang during the period of Qing rule. This period also witnessed the consolidation of Qing power in Xinjiang and the spread of 'Han Chinese influence, culture and population'.[53] But with the decadence of the Qing power, the growing European pressure on China and the recurrence of non-Han rebellions against the imperial government, the Qing hold over peripheral areas became weak. So much so, Yakub Beg, a Kokandi adventurer, established an independent and Islamic state of Kashgharia (1865–77). But once the Qings had suppressed the Muslim uprising in Shanxi and Gansu provinces of China, full attention was given to the re-occupation of Xinjiang. It was now incorporated as a full-fledged province of China. With this the 'Qing relations with Central Asia came to an end'[54] as the Central Asian states of Eastern Turkestan and Western Turkestan had ceased to be independent, the former being part of China and the latter part of Russia.

Notes

1 J.F. Fletcher, 'China and Central Asia', in J.K. Fairbank, ed., *The Chinese World Order*. Cambridge, 1974, p. 207; Immanuel C.Y. Hsu, *The Ili Crisis: A Study of Sino-Russian Diplomacy, 1871–1881*. Oxford, 1965, p. 5.
2 Morris Rossabi, *China and Inner Asia*. London, 1975, p. 145.

3 Ibid., p. 147.

4 Ibid.

5 L.I. Duman, 'The Qing Conquest of Jungariya and Eastern Turkestan', in *Manzhou Rule in China*. Moscow, 1983, p. 235.

6 *Ping ding Zungheer Foolue* (a description of the Pacification of Dzungars), 1772. Cited in Duman, 'Qing Conquest', p. 236.

7 Ibid.

8 After his final defeat in July 1757, Amursana sought refuge in Semi palatinsk, from where he was sent to live in Tobolsk where he died in September 1757.

9 *A History of the Mongolian People's Republic*. Moscow, 1954, pp. 161–2.

10 In a letter dated 17 July 1757 Deleg-gelong, a senior lama who crossed into Russia from Ili, wrote that the 'Qing troops were killing everybody on sight – men, women, the aged and children'. Cited in I.Y. Zlatkin, *A History of the Jungaar Khanate, 1635–1758*. Moscow, 1964, pp. 457–8 (in Russian).

11 A Jakinf, *A Description of Jungaar and Eastern Turkestan*. St. Petersburg, 1829, p. 126 (in Russian).

12 Shang Yue, ed., *Essays on the History of China*. Moscow, 1959, p. 549 (in Russian). According to a mid-nineteenth-century Chinese historian, Wei Yuan, about three-tenths of the population of Dzungaria were wiped out, with another four-tenths dying from epidemics, while two-tenths escaped to Russia. See his *Sheng wu Ji* (Records of the Wars of the Ruling Dynasty), 1841.

13 Cited in Rossabi, *China*, p. 148.

14 Fletcher, 'China and Central Asia', p. 238. The oasis-states of Turfan and Hami occupied an important transit zone on the main 'tribute' route from China to Central Asia. Besides, Hami used to supply large numbers of horses to China. See Ode Juten, 'Uighuristan'. *Acta Asiatica*, No. 34, 1978, pp. 22, 42.

15 Fletcher, 'China and Central Asia', p. 219. Rossabi, *China*, p. 148.

16 Duman, 'Qing Conquest', p. 240.

17 Ibid.

18 Ibid., p. 241.

19 *Chinting pingting Chun-ka-erh fang-ku-eh, Cheng Pein*. Cited in Fletcher, 'China and Central Asia', p. 219. The conquest of the whole of Xinjiang (including Dzungaria and Eastern Turkestan) was formally notified by the Qing general on 12 December 1759.

20 Rossabi, *China*, pp. 160–1. M. Mancall, 'The Qing Tribute System: An Interpretative Essay', in J.K. Fairbank, ed., *The Chinese World Order*. Cambridge, 1974, p. 72.

21 Rossabi, *China*, p. 161.

22 This office was created by the Qing emperor in 1762 AD. See Saguchi Toru, 'Kashgaria'. *Acta Asiatica*, No. 34, 1978, p. 63.

23 Ibid.

24 Ibid., p. 65.

25 J. Fletcher, 'Qing Inner Asia', in J.K. Fairbank, ed., *The Cambridge History of China*. London, 1978, Vol. 10, Part I, p. 79.

26 Ibid., p. 75.

27 Toru, 'Kashgaria', p. 64.

28 Fletcher, 'Qing Inner Asia', p. 37.

29 These government lands (*Kuan-ti*) were originally possessed by the Khojas and Moghul Khans. Some of this land was also confiscated from those fugitives and rebels who opposed the Qings. See Toru, 'Kashgaria', p. 69.

30 Fletcher, 'Qing Inner Asia', p. 59.

31 Ibid.

32 Ibid., pp. 59–60. Duman, 'Qing Conquest', p. 246.

33 Fletcher, 'Qing Inner Asia', p. 60.

34 Ibid., pp. 60–1.

35 Duman, 'Qing Conquest', pp. 244–5.
36 Ibid., pp. 246–7.
37 Ibid., p. 249. Fletcher, 'Qing Inner Asia', p. 65.
38 Duman, 'Qing Conquest', pp. 249–50.
39 For instance, in 1760 it was found that 300 *Taranchis* not only raised enough food for their families but also left a surplus enough to feed over 1,000 government troops for several months. Duman, 'Qing Conquest', pp. 245–6.
40 Toru, 'Kashgaria', p. 70.
41 Ibid., p. 71.
42 Fletcher, 'Qing Inner Asia', p. 65.
43 Paul B. Henze, 'The Great Game in Kashgaria'. *Central Asian Survey*, Vol. 8, No. 2, 1989, p. 63.
44 V.S. Kuznetsov, 'Tsiin Administration in Xinjiang in the First Half of the Nineteenth Century'. *Central Asian Review*, Vol. 10, No. 3, 1962, pp. 271–84. Soon after, the Qings extended similar concessions to traders from Bukhara, Kashmir and Badakshan, ostensibly to exhibit 'kind-heartedness' but actually to hide their fear of the Kokand Khanate from other Asiatic peoples. See Toru, 'Kashgaria', p. 72.
45 K. Warikoo, 'Chinese Turkestan during the Nineteenth Century: A Socio-Economic Study'. *Central Asian Survey*, Vol. 4, No. 3, 1985, p. 75.
46 Rossabi, *China*, p. 189.
47 Fletcher, 'China and Central Asia', p. 224.
48 Warikoo, 'Chinese Turkestan', p. 106.
49 Fletcher, 'Qing Inner Asia', p. 220.
50 Warikoo, 'Chinese Turkestan', p. 108.
51 Ibid.
52 Ibid.
53 Fletcher, 'Qing Inner Asia', p. 36.
54 Fletcher, 'China and Central Asia', p. 224.

5 Rethinking ethnicity in China

Qiu Yonghui

The Chinese have different views on ethnicity/nationality issues after the events of 14 March 2008 in Lhasa and the events of 5 July 2009 in Urumqi. The government officials, especially the officials in charge of minorities affairs, declared in the media that the violence and crimes that happened in Urumqi had no link to China's policies towards the minorities. In other words, there is no need for any change or rethinking of China's policies on national minorities. Wu Shimin, the Deputy Director General of the State Ethnic Affairs Commission, expressed such views.[1]

However, ordinary citizens have different and contradictory views. While the public did not care about the issue earlier, the 5 July events in Urumqi came as a big shock, making them realize the seriousness and urgency of the issue, as a number of people view it as the intention to separate Tibet and Xinjiang from China. Deeply worried over repeated social disorders in the towns and cities of Tibet and Xinjiang, as was witnessed in the 5 July event in Urumqi, Chinese academics have expressed their criticism and rethinking on the theory and policies regarding ethnicity/nationality over last 60 years. Professor Ma Rong of the Department of Sociology, Beijing University, pointed out that 'up to now, the issue of nationality has become a momentous matter for the central government and the whole society. It is the concern for the very core interests of our Chinese Nation'.[2]

This chapter does not attempt to review different aspects of the complex problem. It only seeks to evaluate generally the theoretical muddle, and more particularly, to examine the harmful results from any unsound policies concerning minorities in China. Its purpose is to contribute to the clarification of some aspects of this burning issue in China.

Challenge to the European concept of 'nation-state'

Nation, as a modern concept, has European origins. While some thinkers brought forward this concept, their followers designed the geographical and population borderline. Anthony D. Smith, Professor Emeritus of Nationalism and Ethnicity at the London School of Economics, considers a nation as 'a named population sharing an historic territory, common myths and historical memories, a mass public culture, a common economy and common legal rights and duties for its members'.[3] When speaking of nation-state, Anthony D. Smith observes, 'We may term a state a "nation-state" only if and when a single ethnic and cultural population inhabits the boundaries of a state, and the boundaries of that state are coextensive with the boundaries of that ethnic and cultural population.'[4]

Nationalist movements springing up first in Western Europe in the eighteenth century were aimed at putting forth the concept of nation and to create a series of 'nation-states'. Some scholars concluded that nationalism means that 'the human beings are divided into different nations by nature... the human beings could not reach a nice condition unless each nation has its own state and enjoys independence'.[5] Others consider nationalism as a theory regarding the political legitimacy which requires a political boundary for a particular race.[6] The nationalist movement in Europe in the eighteenth century got rid of traditional society, breaking away from the old social system establishing nation-states and a new social system based on the new political principles and thoughts.

From the eighteenth to the twentieth centuries, Western culture enjoyed a dominating position and, therefore, the concept of 'nation-state', based on the experiences of France and Germany, spread to other parts of Europe and to the rest of the world. Following this process, the world witnessed the partition of the Austro-Hungarian empire into Austria, Hungary, Czechoslovakia (which divided further into the Czech Republic and Slovakia at the end of the Cold War), Yugoslavia (which divided further into seven states including Serbia, Montenegro, Croatia, Bosnia, Slovenia, Macedonia and Kosovo). Almost during the same period of history, within the original territory of the Ottoman-Turkey empire, which once encompassed huge territory across Asia, Europe and Africa, more than 30 states including Turkey, Saudi Arabia, Syria, Lebanon, Iraq, Yemen, Egypt, Cyprus, etc. were created.

According to the logic of the 'nation-state' theory and based on the experiences in Europe and other areas, the normal pattern for semi-colonial China and colonial India to create their nationhood, even after the nationalist movements, can only be that of many nation-states composed of dozens of ethnicities/nationalities. There are at least three challenges faced by the 'nation-state' theory in China and India. First, both countries have been multi-ethnic, multi-cultural societies, with myriad religion, languages, creeds, rituals and customs. Second, being ancient civilizations and great cultures, the traditions of unity in diversity in both China and India have vitality and mightiness. Third, on the key issues of breaking away from the imperial and colonial order, and of founding independent countries, the main political forces in both the countries have a great deal of commonalities. As a result, China and India became the 'exception' from the European-styled nation-states. In fact, these two civilizations not only survived but started their own nation-building process, which can be termed as the state-nation building process.

The record of success in India and China is in contrast to those of other multi-cultural, multi-ethnic and multi-religious societies – in the Balkans, Middle East, etc., which either split up, or faced intensive rivalry and violent conflict. However, since the founding of the Indian Republic and the People's Republic of China, the challenges faced by both the countries have been serious. A sense of nationhood could not rest on geography, religion or language, as so often seemed to be the case in Europe. In India's circumstances, it must be forged consciously out of commitment to political democracy which could unite Indians and transcend earlier divisions and loyalties.

After independence, the deep-seated linguistic-cultural diversity and differences within different states and regions in India had to be negotiated carefully during the early years of state formation. Attaining independence along with the partition of the country made some national leaders like Jawaharlal Nehru and Vallabhbhai Patel apprehensive about the reorganization process, which, in their view, posed the threat of fragmentation of the new state. Therefore, these leaders carefully planned to strengthen the ideology of the nation-building exercise in various parts of the country on the one hand, and at the same time disintegrated the political architecture of the colonial state. The story of the 'integration of states' in post-colonial India is also a story of the disintegration and reintegration of various states and regions into more uniform and administratively rationalized units of state power.

The states needed to be reconstructed and reconstituted in this long process of political consolidation and formation of the Indian nation. The Indian experience of state formation through an extensive exercise of redrawing the boundaries and territories reveals the processes of identity formation of regions, sub-regions and of various communities and groups. India's success is based on the principles of linguistic-cultural distinctiveness, economic viability and geographical unity along with the federal political and administrative rationality.[7] Today, India is continuing on its path towards overcoming ethnic, regional and religious identities and strengthening the national identity as Indians in modern India.

Due to its different political system and cultural pattern, China has long been considered as an imbalanced exception. China is a big family comprising 56 ethnic groups and therefore certainly not a nation-state in the sense of political science as defined by the Europeans. Can the Chinese comprising 56 ethnic groups be called a state-nation? What are the characteristics of the state of China as a state-nation? What is China's political essence then? Even today, the intellectuals in the United States, Europe and China are trying to apply the nation-state/state-nation theory to explain and understand China.

Rethinking theory and policy of nationality in China

In contrast to the successful experience in India, the theory of nation, ethnicity/ nationality and state has put China into the paradox of a two-tier nationality – the Chinese as the national identity and 56 nationalities as ethnic identity. The practice of the policies on ethnic groups has troubled China and created crisis for social stability and national integration.

Theory error: a two-tier nationality

There was no such word as *Minzhu* (民族), the equivalence of the English word 'nation', in ancient Chinese books. The words that the ancient Chinese often used are *Zhu* (clan), *Min* (people), *Ren* (man), *Zhong* (genus), *Bu* (part), *Minzhong* (folk), *Mingqun* (folk groups), *Zhongren* (genus human), *Buren* (clan people) and *Zhulei* (species), etc.[8] From the very beginning of the usage of *Minzhu*, which came into being when a Chinese scholar translated the concept of nation innovated by the European political scientists and jurists, the Chinese scholars realized that the concept might mix up with race and the body politic of the state, and then create confusion among the people. However, in the context of 'save our motherland', Chinese thinkers and the elite generally intended to construct the modern state by taking into account the Western 'advanced pattern' and didn't visualize carefully the confusions and problems caused by the new terms.

The word *Zhonghua Minzhu* (meaning the Chinese nation) is a new name and a creation of the modern nationalist movement in the nineteenth century. The revolutionaries believed that the process of turning old China into a modern state has to be an inclusive process of including the Hans, Manchurians, Mongolians, Huis, Tibetans, Miaos and all other ethnic groups. In this process, 'the subjects of Qing Dynasty' become the citizens of a new republic. The Chinese nation as a name for all the people living and multiplying in China is obviously different from the European concept of singular nation. It reflected the understanding of Chinese intellectuals 'for the pluralism which emerged from the very nature of the country, consolidated by China's geography and affirmed by its history, especially during the period of hard, self-conscious struggle for independence and liberation'.[9]

The potential problem lies in the tendency of 'learning from the West' in all aspects of China, including learning the concept and ideas of the modern nation-state. The more lamentable and woeful influence came from the nationality theory of the Communist Party of the Soviet Union. After the founding of the Communist Party of China, its leaders followed and copied the ideas of 'Policy of Nationalities', expressed their support for 'self-determination' by nationalities such as Mongolians, Huis, Tibetans, etc. At the end of the anti-Japanese War, the Communist Party adjusted its policy towards the ethnic groups and named it as 'regional autonomy'. Unfortunately, they copied the ideas and methodology of the former Soviet Union again in the year 1950, to undertake the mission 'to identify the nationalities' in an extremely pluralist country with thousands of ethnic groups. With the result, Chinese intellectuals, consciously or unconsciously, created the paradox of a two-tier nationality – the Chinese as the national identity and 56 nationalities as ethnic identity.

Eric J. Hobsbawm, a left-wing historian, examined the Soviet theory of nationalities in depth and pointed out that it was exactly due to the misuse of nation as a concept, that the Soviet Union automatically created a split for herself. Multinational countries created by the communist parties after the Second World War dissolved along with this very split.[10] This may explain, in theoretical terms, what China faces today.

Practice mess: politicization of ethnic issues

Compared with the relative success in India, China has been for a long time on the way towards politicization of ethnic issues and hence has committed grave mistakes. First of all, along with the recognition of 56 nationalities, the population/settled boundary of different ethnic groups became clear and focused. Furthermore, the official requirements to select 'nationality' for the offspring of the mixed nationalities ridiculously drew a permanent boundary for dividing the ethnic groups of the Chinese.

Second, unlike the reorganization of the linguistic states in India, the Chinese government set up autonomous regions/districts/counties for various ethnic groups, thus drawing the regional loci and even strengthening the consciousness of specific territory for different ethnic groups. Unlike the continuous reorganization of the states and creation of smaller states in India, the Chinese government has not created any new provinces and autonomous regions. In fact, in the region which was once predominantly populated by Uyghurs, this group is now a minority in its own 'autonomous region'.

Third, as is the case with the reservation policy for Scheduled Castes, Scheduled Tribes and Other Backward Classes (OBCs) in India, the beneficiaries of reservation in China are ethnic groups excepting for Hans. But the content of reservation is comparatively much wider, covering issues from family planning to additional marks for the examinees and interviewees from the minorities, from bilingual education to cadre nomination, even the quota of the representatives in the Congress. All these measures are aimed at upgrading the minorities, which result in consolidating 'the national/ethnic consciousness'.

The cooperation and support among people of all ethnic groups is an important advantage for strengthening the national unity and promoting common development and prosperity of all ethnic groups. Unfortunately, the mistakes mentioned above result in intensifying the second tier of nationality and the national identity of the Chinese has been rendered ineffective and hollow.

The unpleasant consequence of the state policies to deal with the ethnic issues has become evident in the new situation. Since the reform and opening up to the outside world in the 1980, the spring tide of the market economy has struck the traditional linkage of heart and sensation among ethnic groups so that the 'national/ethnic consciousness' in some regions has become deep and extreme. This tendency has shown up in the following manner:

1   Some people among some nationalities/ethnic groups do not welcome people of other nationalities/ethnic groups to migrate to 'autonomous' areas. This partly explains why, after the 1980s, major immigration was no longer government-sponsored. Many Hans who want to take advantage of the market economy do so simply as 'drifters', and quite a few are unable to stay very long.

2   Those who do not encourage their sons and daughters to study their mother tongue, do so to take advantage of opportunities for education abroad or in

the metropolitan areas. On the other hand, these same people strongly oppose their poor compatriots learning Chinese and English, in the name of protecting the language.

3   Some regions are keen to cultivate and expand the 'economy of own nationality'.

4   Strengthening the 'national consciousness' and 'national cohesion' among the members through rewriting and re-educating of religion, folklore and local history, has become a trend in these regions.

As a result, lots of changes have taken place. Take the example of the Hui Muslims. Chinese Islam among the Hui retains characteristics that set it apart. Hui Muslims have imbibed well that 'women hold up half the sky' (words of Mao) and women's imams and women-only mosques have been playing a unique role in China. But orthodoxy amongst Chinese Muslims is on the rise as ever-increasing numbers of Huis perform the Hajj and youngsters return from their studies abroad in Muslim countries. As a Han official in Ningxia complained recently, 'Earlier the Hui were just like us except they didn't eat pork. Now they think they are very special. They think of themselves as foreigners.'

Ethnic mobilizations and state-nation building

The future of China and India, as societies and as civilizations, is durable although some changes in their content are inevitable. It is unfortunate that both China and India have been the victims of the Western theory of nation-state and continue to be so.

In both China and India, ethnic mobilization remains one of the hottest issues. And yet, ethnicity has been more of a paradox than an enigma. China and India, in turn, are and will be the most populated countries in the world. Of China's 56 ethnic groups, about 95 per cent of its population calls itself ethnic Han so that the other 55 ethnic groups are all the minorities and, among them, the Tibetans and the Uyghurs together make up only about 1 per cent of the total population of China. In India's case, the numerical preponderance of Hindus led the smaller religious groups to be ambiguously termed as minorities. However, rather than getting relegated to the footnote of history, the resilience of ethnicity has become a paradigm of everyday life in both countries.

Scholars both in China and India observe that ethnicity and ethnic consciousness are, however, a universal phenomenon. There is hardly any country, from the economically most advanced to the most backward, where such ethno-nationalist mobilizations have not taken place with a political agenda of separatism whose objective is to carve out an exclusive territorial and political space, excluding the 'Other' who has historically been part of the same territorial and political space, and has shared the same or similar ethnic identity. This phenomenon of invention and reinvention of identities is widespread in Assam and the northeastern states of India, and in Xinjiang as well. While the enriching process has made anything ethnic – food, dress, ornaments, etc. – fashionable and therefore unaffordable for the ethnic people, the real danger is that there is a growth and expansion of exclusive consciousness and factionalism. Therefore, when an element of fabrication enters this process of construction and invention, one has to question the very authenticity of such rigid identity assertions.

Every group of people possess specific identity markers. The family, the home, the kinship group, gender, religion, language, race, even the physical space that the people occupy – any and each one of these could be and indeed is a coordinate of the people's identity. It should be also noted that the boundaries of an ethnic group can be quite recognizable even when not all of its characteristics appear at the same time. And the trick is that these identity markers can be added endlessly so that any ethnic group can be further divided ad infinitum. In the former Yugoslavia Republic, people can be divided into Muslims and non-Muslims by religion. Among the Muslims, divisions at first were Serbians, Croatians and Bosnians, to which the Slovenians and Kosovars have been added. In Manipur, Nagas can at least be divided into three groups, Ze-mei, Liang-mei and Rong-mei. In the vast areas of Xinjiang, the diversity among Uyghurs is obvious in terms of language, religion, race and costumes, etc. In the events of 5 July 2009 in Urumqi, more than 40 Uyghurs died because the mobs from the southern part of Xinjiang also attacked the Uyghurs living in northern Xinjiang and some Uyghur women who didn't put on a hood (*burqa*) or who wore short-sleeves or pants also became targets. The phenomenon of mob fury in order to 'punish the traitors of Uyghurs' is a matter of deep concern.

China realizes that the key factor for the strategic effectiveness and China's ultimate success in frustrating the designs of 'extremists, separatists and terrorists' in Xinjiang rests on its recognition and response to the political nature of the threat. While China focuses on targeting an ever-growing pool of insurgents and terrorists, a more rapid economic modernization process is on the way and hopefully it will do something good on the ground to stop Al-Qaeda's attempts to train fighters and fund a local affiliate. Generally speaking, ethnic processes were viewed as ethnic practices articulating the new reality of seeking new identities as power groups. But they are probably to be viewed as secessionist practices in the political sense and in the background of war against terror. The scholars need to study ethnicity as a social reality under the shadow of the anti-terror campaign led by the United States after 9/11 and the perceptions of many countries.

Notes

1 Wu Shimin, 'The July 5 Event in Urumqi had no Linkage with China's Policies towards the Minorities', http://news.xinhuanet.com/politics/2009–07/21/content_11743400.htm.
2 Ma Rong, 'The Sticking Point and the Way Out for Ethnic Problem in Contemporary China', http://hi.baidu.com/%C9%FA%C9%FA%B2%BB%CF%A21999/blog/item/bb8930167611cf00c93d6d2d.html.
3 Anthony D. Smith, *Nationalism: Theory, Ideology, History*, Cambridge, Polity Press, 1991, p. 11.
4 Less than 10 per cent of existing states meet these criteria. Anthony D. Smith, *Nations and Nationalism in a Global Era*, Cambridge, Polity Press, 1995, p. 86.

5 E. Kedourie, *Religion and Politics*, 2002, pp. 7–8.
6 Ernest Gellner, *Nations and Nationalism*, Oxford, Basil Blackwell, 1983, pp. 1–2.
7 Asha Sarangi, 'Reorganisation, Then and Now', *Frontline*, Vol. 26, Issue 26, 19 December 2009–1 January 2010. See www.flonnet.com/fl2626/stories/20100101262 602100.htm.
8 *China Encyclopedia* (Volume Ethnicity), China Encyclopedia Publication, 1986, p. 302.
9 See Fiexiaotong, *The Pluralist United Patten of Chinese Nation*, Central University for Minorities Press, 1989.
10 Eric J. Hobsbawm, *Nation and Nationalism since 1780*, Cambridge: Cambridge University Press, 1992.

6 China's ethnic tangle with special reference to Xinjiang

K.R. Sharma

Relations among nationalities are a source of social tension in most of the multi-ethnic societies and only a few have handled the problem well. The record of many former communist countries such as Soviet Union, Poland, Yugoslavia, Czechoslovakia and several others in resolving the ethnic contradictions has been disappointing. There were many tangible reasons for the collapse of the communist world, among these, the crucial one was the patently wrong handling of the ethnic question. The quest of minorities for equality and dignity seems to be universal.

The Chinese nation has a relatively high degree of cohesion. Over 90 per cent of China's population consists of the Han and about 10 per cent make up the ethnic minorities. Translated in absolute numbers there are about 130–5 million minority people in China. Of these 55 minorities (in China the identification card and passport imprint every citizen's ethnicity) the most prominent are Chuangs (Koreans), Mongols, Tibetans, Huis (Muslims), Uyghurs, Kazakhs, Kyrgyz, Dai's, Bai's, Yi, Kawas, Manchus and several others. In the 1950s, when China's new government decided to have a headcount of minorities and ethnicities, around 200 ethnic groups applied for the status. After a thorough demographic survey, the state decided to accord official minority status to only 55. Out of China's 30-plus provinces, minority nationalities are scattered over 15 provinces. Of these 15 provinces, several such as Tibet, Inner Mongolia, Yunnan, Gansu, Guangxi and Xinjiang are heavily peopled by ethnic minorities. In Sichuan, Tsinghai and Ningxia there are concentrated populations of minorities.

More to the point, these 130–5 million minority people have a significance beyond their numbers. An ethnographic map of China would demonstrate the fact that the areas inhabited by these minority people are of great strategic importance for China. Borders with Korea, Laos, Vietnam, Myanmar, Mongolia, Muslim Central Asian Republics and India are all boundaries over which China has had diplomatic/military skirmishes and even confrontations. In the language of geo-politics, diplomacy and the legalities of the minority nationalities, Beijing's regime is a crucial variable in maintaining China's integrity. On her part, China has to keep these 'frontier' people in good humour. If satisfied and ethnically contented, they are the strategic reserves for China. In this regard, the

Uyghurs of Xinjiang are the 'Islamic' face of China. In terms of territory, these 55 ethnic minorities occupy almost 56–7 per cent of the land area of the country, though the largest chunk contains deserts, mountains and forests and only a small percentage of land is fit for agricultural cultivation. These minority areas are extremely rich in resources like oil, gas, metals, coal, timber, etc. Ethnic minorities can be defined as groups held together by ties of common descent, language, religious faith and cultural distinctiveness, feeling themselves to be different and distinct from the majority of a given political entity. It is this exclusive (inscriptive) sense of 'togetherness' which gives them personality and identity of their own. Also, it is this sense of 'belonging' which gives them the feeling of 'us' and 'them'.

Ethnicity has two major dimensions of self-identity. The majuscule part of this identity is primordial unlike the minuscule dimension which is situational or contextual. One more small theoretical confusion needs to be thrashed out. Is the primordial sense of ethnicity fixed, immutable and changeless? In other words, with the increasing march of modernization – industrialization, urbanization and globalization – the situational/contextual aspect of ethnicity are changing quite perceptibly but are the primordial ethnos too undergoing modifications and transformations?

Overview of the last 60 years

The methods, processes and the context of tackling the ethnic tangle have been widely researched and commented upon by sociologists, anthropologists and political scientists in the last one hundred years or so. Humanity has evaluated two broad models to tackle the problem, namely, integration and assimilation. The integration model is based on the matrix of persecution and incentive while the assimilation model is based on force and it reflects a sense of racial superiority and arrogance. Approached through an integration model, the ethnic/religious minorities, while retaining their autonomous character of ethnos, shift their loyalties and activities to the centre. In this case, the centre is the nation-state. In turn, the centre not only 'tolerates' their diversity and identity but even gives them recognition and respect. Democracy demands not only 'toleration' of cultural, religious and linguistic diversities but finds ways and means to celebrate them. These two – not only different but diametrically opposed – approaches have been expressed synoptically in the expressions 'salad bowl' and 'melting pot' by several eminent scholars.

In the last six decades or so, the policies and the practices of the party state have undergone several twists and turns. First, a small comment on the pre-1949 policy matrix. A young and an idealist Mao – literally in the theoretical footsteps of Marx, Lenin and Stalin – declared that all the minority nationalities (after liberation) shall be granted the 'right of self-determination'. Even this did not entice and motivate the minority nationalities (more so living on the borders and frontiers of China) to join Mao's revolution. The overwhelming number of China's minorities kept aloof and away from the communist revolution and no wonder, then, the Chinese communist revolution was almost an entirely Han affair, remaining confined to what is loosely called 'Inner China'. After coming to power, Mao and the party realized that self-determination for minorities was neither viable nor desirable. Accordingly, the self-determination paradigm was immediately replaced by 'autonomy' syndrome.

Beginning in 1949 (1 October 1949, when the People's Republic of China was declared), four distinct policies can be discerned towards ethnic minorities. From 1949 to 1957, it was a policy of integration towards minorities. Flexibility, caution and pragmatism were the watchwords. The minority areas were given substantial degree of autonomy. Special autonomous areas were carved out. Linguistic, cultural and religious differentiations were tolerated and even encouraged. This was the golden period not only for the minorities but for the whole of China. In 1957–8 this policy was suddenly reversed. With the onset of People's Communes, the Great Leap Forward and the General Line (three so-called Red Banners of Mao), the party and the state adopted a tough posture towards ethnic minorities. In 1957 (in conversation with an African delegation) Mao, under the impact of his theory of 'paramount revolution', announced that the 'nationality question is basically a class question'. If it is a class question, as Mao believed, then the dynamics of class struggle have to be applied. In Mao's eyes, 'Han Chauvinism' was not the devil. The devil was the ethnocentrism of the minorities. The religious and cultural distinctiveness (diversities) of the minorities were frowned upon. The study of Chinese language (Mandarin) was made obligatory in minority area. Large-scale Han migration was undertaken into minority areas.

The third and the tragic phase began with the Cultural Revolution (the Socialist Great Proletarian Cultural Revolution). This extreme radical phase began in 1966 and continued until the death of Mao in 1976. This period was based on forcible and violent assimilation of minority nationalities. Suppression, control, dominance and ruthless absorption became the salient characteristics of this phase. Mao's Cultural Revolution was a tragedy for all of China, but for the minority areas it was a tragedy of unprecedented magnitude. One may recall that the Chinese Communist Party in 1981 in certain Resolutions on the Questions of History, called Mao and his Cultural Revolution a period of 'feudal fascist dictatorship'.

The present phase is the ongoing phase in the sequence which started with Huyao Bang and Deng Xiaoping in command. Theoretically, this is a relaxed and liberal phase.

The exact nature of the problem in Xinjiang

The Uyghurs constitute the dominant ethnic minority in China. The exact population of Uyghurs in Xinjiang and the total migrated population of Hans in Xinjiang is also a matter of dispute. There is a feeling of plasticity about these figures. It is estimated that the total population of Xinjiang is around 22 million of which ten million are Han Chinese and ten million are Kazakhs, Kyrgyzs,

Uzbeks, Tatars, Mongols and Huis. Of these ten million non-Hans, almost all believe in Islam. First, a comment on Xinjiang's total population and its break-up. Donald Harowitz has coined the phrase 'census wars', arguing that 'winning the census' is important. As he puts it, 'numbers are an indicator of whose country it is'.

A few basic facts about Xinjiang and about the Uyghurs in Xinjiang, though highly contentious, must be stated here. With the coming of Islam, Arabic started enriching (even replacing) Uyghur script. Lexicographically the word Uyghur partly originated from the name of a tribe (of Turkic origin) and partly emanated from the speech (language). It subsequently acquired a political, geographic and cultural (not religious) identity. Surprisingly, then, for almost 500 years (1500–1920s) the word Uyghur was missing from the vocabulary. It was after the October Revolution that, at the suggestion of the Soviets, it was decided to restore the expression 'Uyghur'.

According to the Chinese historians – written and re-written Chinese official Uyghur histories – Xinjiang had been an integral part of China since the Han Dynasty. It was a tributary relationship of course. According to Uyghur histories, for most of the time (during Uyghur existence) Uyghurs remained independent of China. This means two things. For the best part of the time, Uyghurs were ruled by non-Chinese and, second, Uyghurs have a record of their fights and struggles against China. All Uyghurs believe strongly that their ancestors were the indigenous people of what is called the present Xinjiang (they prefer to call it Eastern Turkestan). This is also an undisputable fact that the Ching (Manchus) empire conquered, some say reconquered, this territory and gave it the present name Xinjiang which means 'new territory'. Moreover, the fact that almost 99 per cent of Uyghurs are peopled only in Xinjiang gives credence to the argument that Uyghurs are the indigenous people of Xinjiang. Thus Xinjiang was not claimed by China until the eighteenth century and was not a province of China (not incorporated in China's administrative structure) until the nineteenth century.

Again, the Yakub Beg rebellion that established the 13-year Kashgar Emirate (1864–77) crystallized Uyghur resistance to Chinese rule. The latest rebellion, which came quite close to success, was in 1931–4 in Hami and then in 1944–9 in the Ili region. Xinjiang (like the frontier areas of Inner Mongolia and Tibet) was peopled by races/ethnic groups which had strong traditions of independence from China. Many of them were engaged, every now and then, in a relationship of warfare with China. If China had an upper hand, she asserted and reasserted her right over those territories. The Chinese rule was always indirect and through local chieftains. Whenever the Chinese empire was weak, these frontier people (Xinjiang included) attempted independence. What have been the achievements of Chinese state in Xinjiang in the last 60 years or so? The Chinese state has succeeded in re-establishing its rule in Xinjiang. The province has been fully integrated into China. In 1957 the province was declared 'Xinjiang Uyghur Autonomous Region' and granted a substantial degree of autonomy. As stated above, the period from 1949 to 1957 was the golden period for the local populace of Xinjiang. Their language, social customs, myths and in fact the distinctive identity marks of the ethnic minorities were respected.

At the beginning of the last decade of the twentieth century ('Go West') the development of Xinjiang got a boost. It is a well known fact that Xinjiang is one of the 'resource rich' provinces of China. It is extremely rich in mineral resources like oil, gas, coal, copper, timber and several other rare and industrial raw materials. Before the 1990s Xinjiang was extremely backward in transport and communications. No more. The last two decades have witnessed a massive investment (approx. US$300 billion) in infrastructure development. The network of airlines, railways and roads created by the state speaks volumes about the commitment of China to develop Xinjiang economically. It has again became a gateway to Central Asia, West Asia, Europe (recall the Silk Route) as a result of this development. The province is no longer one of China's poorest. Xinjiang's GDP has appreciably gone up. As a result, per capita GDP in the province has also gone up. Between the Hans and Uyghurs, the income levels of the Hans are higher. Even among Uyghurs and other minority people, the rural per capita income is much lower than their town and city counterparts. Even the FDI which has come to Xinjiang in the last 20 years is impressive. The expanded cities and the emergence of new townships (along the new rail lines and gas pipelines) are the visible evidence of this new affluence and development. The literacy rate, educational levels and job opportunities have all multiplied several fold.

In spite of this material progress, levels of restlessness, disaffection, disquiet and turmoil have increased greatly in the last 30 years or so. Without going into the details of these clashes and confrontations between the Uyghurs and the Chinese state, it is enough to mention that in the last three decades thousands of people have been killed and several hundred have been executed. Most of the killed and executed have been Uyghurs. What are the reasons for this 'ongoing confrontation' between the Uyghurs and the Chinese state? Instead of going into the details of these causes, we will mention them only synoptically.

1   China's understanding of her ethnic minorities (especially Tibetans, Mongols and Uyghurs) and her public discourse about them is inherently faulty and skewed. To call those ethnic minorities 'primitive', 'exotic, 'living fossils', 'backward' and 'uncivilized' smacks of a colonial attitude (in this case internal colonialism).

2   Marx and Engels' understanding of ethnicities was partly brilliant and partly faulty. Marx was accurate when he said that since ethnics pre-date family, classes and state they wouldn't wither away before the withering away of private property, classes and state. Their acceptance of US anthropologist Morgan's argument on modes of production determining the levels of civilization was inadequate and one-sided. Ethnicity is not a false consciousness. In fact a Marxist solution to the ethnic problem has failed.

3   Several policy measures of Chinese state and party have resulted in alienating the Uyghurs. These 'negative' measures include the heavy influx of Han Chinese into Xinjiang, which has produced a Han majority and a Uyghur

minority in Xinjiang; imposing Mandarin on the Uyghurs in the schools, colleges and the universities; producing a social divide in Xinjiang reflected in separate restaurants, segregated travel, even separate schools and residential blocks and, finally, the taboo (to which both Hans and Uyghurs have contributed) of Han–Uyghur marriages and social intercourse.

Two epoch-making events (both occurring outside Xinjiang and China) have heavily impacted upon the ethnic tangle in Xinjiang. The disintegration of the Soviet Union (and several communist countries) in the 1990s and the emergence of the 15 independent states of the CIS emboldened the Uyghurs in Xinjiang. It is interesting to note that the emergence of five Central Asian Republics of Tajikistan, Turkmenistan, Kazakhstan, Kyrgyzstan and Uzbekistan has given a new hope to the ethnic minorities of China, particularly Uyghurs, that they 'can also do it'. This is not to argue that China would also go the Soviet way. The three 'hurt' and 'aggrieved' ethnic minorities of China – Tibetans, Mongols and Uyghurs – cannot cause China's callapse. It only points out the fact that China has serious fault-lines and the minority ethnic fault-line is also one of the fault-lines of China. One Uyghur intellectual told me that when the Soviet Union disintegrated, she disintegrated exactly along her historical, linguistic, ethnic and religious fault-lines. He was not very much off the mark.

The second event is the event of 9/11 in the United States. With the emergence of 'political' Islam, the war on terror has become a global phenomenon. It has become easier for many states – China included – to argue and propagate that Islam is unavoidably rebellious. In other words, Muslims as minorities are 'inherently problematic'. The Uyghurs in Xinjiang know and acknowledge that their struggle has become much more difficult.

Are the Uyghurs secessionists? Do they want a separate Uyghurstan? Do they really aspire to be separatists? These are difficult questions to give a yes or no answer to. My perception and understanding of the Uyghur problem is on the following lines. The opinion of Uyghur elites could be divided into three categories. One small category consists of those who could be termed as 'separatists' and secessionists. They harbour the hopes of Uyghurstan, if not immediately, then in the near or even the distant future. Their number could be counted on fingers. They are more active in Istanbul, Germany, Europe and the United States. There are several separatist organizations (of which some have been banned and declared terrorist outfits). The elites representing this stream can be called religious leaders based on political Islam. It is more of a cyber phenomenon with a limited following. There is another small groups of Uyghur elites (emulating Kazakhs, Uzbeks) who offer themselves as candidates for integration (even assimilation) and believe in full cooperation with Hans. In this process, they argue that Uyghurs should aim for better terms of bargain. Both the groups, the separatists and the collaborators, are two small extremes. The huge middle – as of today – are for the genuine autonomy for Xinjiang. This huge middle are keen to shift their 'loyalties' and 'activities' to the centre provided the Chinese state assures them not to 'Hanize' and 'nationalize'. All they demand is that they should be treated not as 'subjects' but citizens.

7 China's policy in Xinjiang, 1948–78

Debasish Chaudhuri

Whereas the influence of the Han literati of the early nineteenth century like Gong Zizhen and Wei Yuan suggested the possibility of transforming the landscape and replacing Xinjiang people with massive Han immigration,[1] Han bureaucrats and intellectuals of the late nineteenth century and early twentieth century in Qing court, republican revolutionaries, Guomindang (GMD) leaders and ideologues as well as the first generation of Chinese communists all perceived Xinjiang and other minority areas as potential outlets to ease demographic pressure in Han-dominated parts of China. Transfer of population from other parts of China was considered to be a convenient means to integrate the region and its people with rest of the country. The policies of the central government in the People's Republic of China (PRC) before the reform period were designed to integrate the region mainly through revolutionary integrative politics. The long-term implications of these policies laid the basic foundation for greater economic integration of the region in the last three decades of the reform period and economic motivation finally became the mainstay of the central government's policies towards this region.

The policy of ethno-regional autonomy in Xinjiang was introduced following communist takeover for the purpose of achieving greater integration of this restive minority region. The two most important components of the ideology of integration in China are official socialist ideology and nationalism. In Leninist political set-up, integration meant political, social, economic, cultural and ideological integration. Integration of Xinjiang has been designed within the framework of vertical relations between central government and regional governments. According to James D. Seymour, "integration may be distinguished in terms of whether political activities of individuals and groups are interdependent (fully integrated), are merely compatible (slightly integrated), or lie elsewhere on this scale."[2] In order to integrate Xinjiang as a region and its minority ethnic groups within the Chinese state the central government formulated some basic policies specific to Xinjiang. In fact these polices help the centre to underplay autonomous rights provided to the minorities in the Chinese constitution and autonomy law.

Despite over 60 years of state-driven process of territorial, political and economic integration of Xinjiang Uyghur Autonomous Region (XUAR), ethnic minorities of the region have remained least socio-culturally integrated with the majority Han community in China. In order to clearly grasp the PRC's policies towards Xinjiang and their resultant effects, it is imperative to first introduce the frequent changes of policies since the Republican Revolution in 1911 to 1944 under rule of three warlords and GMD's coalition experiments between 1944 and 1949.

Xinjiang under the warlords, 1911–44

After the formal abolition of Qing rule in the region after the Republican Revolution, the actual power slipped into the hands of Yang Zengxin, an old style bureaucrat of the Qing administration at Urumqi, who tried to reverse the course of the revolution and maintain the old ways. Yang Zengxin immediately declared his allegiance to the Chinese republic and received formal approval as governor of the province by the president of the Republic Yuan Shikai.[3] This was the beginning of warlord rule in Xinjiang.

From 1911 to 1944, Xinjiang was successively ruled by three Han warlords – Yang Zengxin (1911–28), Jin Shuren (1928–33) and Sheng Shicai (1934–44). A. Doak Barnett fittingly remarked that from 1911 to 1944 Xinjiang "was ruled by Chinese but not really by China."[4] However, the policy swings between extreme restrictions, indiscriminate repression and occasional relaxation formed a pattern that resembles frequent policy changes towards Xinjiang under the PRC in the second half of the twentieth century.

Yang Zengxin was aware that the central government was not in a position to exert its influence in the distant province, but he never indulged the idea of making Xinjiang a separate country. He knew very well that the authority and international standing of the central government in China was important for the protection of the province from any Russian invasion.[5] He was also afraid of revolutionary ideas penetrating into Xinjiang from Russia. Yang preferred to cooperate with the British in an attempt to counter the growth of Soviet power in the north of Xinjiang. But his attitude towards the Soviet Union changed after the signing of the Sino-Soviet agreement of 1924. The main achievement of Yang's career was that he cautiously guarded the province from any kind of change. Swedish explorer Dr. Sven Hedin described Yang as "an epitome of old society, old culture, old ethics and old tradition of China."[6]

Yang Zengxin had a strong conviction that the Han drifters and politicians coming from China proper were the major cause of disturbance in Xinjiang. He jealously maintained the old ethnic policy of the Qianlong period. The ethnic people of feudal background and merchants got preferential treatment during his period. He used Islam and Lamaism of the Mongols as tools to pacify their society. The authority of religious leaders of all ethnic groups was respected throughout his tenure. During this period the Muslim youths were encouraged to pursue religious study. He introduced a land tax, which gradually became a major source of provincial revenue, but he was extremely cautious not to push the Muslim peasantry into an open revolt. This ethnic policy helped Yang

Zengxin to maintain a relatively peaceful atmosphere in the province. Some scholars believe that Yang's benign policy towards Muslims helped him to contain the growth of Muslim Turkic nationalism in Xinjiang; otherwise, it could have separated from China like Mongolia.[7]

After the assassination of Yang Zengxin in 1928, Jin Shuren, then commissioner for civil affairs, managed to usurp power and later the GMD government of Nanjing appointed him as the provincial chairman and commander-in-chief. He also belonged to the imperial bureaucratic tradition. However, as an administrator he was far inferior to his predecessor. From the very beginning he suffered from a deep sense of insecurity and tried to improve the standard of armed forces, especially the secret police. During Jin's rule, the religious life of the Muslims of the region was restricted and they were forbidden to go to Mecca for the Hajj pilgrimage.[8] Censorship became more rigorous during this period. The level of corruption and exploitation by the officials and the chairman himself was so high that within one year the provincial administration lost all credibility and efficiency. The economic situation of the province also became bleaker from the early 1930s onwards. The Xinjiang government under his rule was especially infamous for its attitude towards Muslims.[9]

Already there were enough reasons for popular discontent. In addition to that the Muslims of the region were particularly unhappy because some policies of Jin's administration were designed especially against them. The economic burden of the peasants became heavier during this period. The new immigrants gradually deprived the local Muslim farmers of their source of water and took a major share of the pastureland and livestock of the nomadic tribes. The provincial government introduced a tax on butchering of all animals along with the already heavy land tax levied on the people. To control the nomadic tribes the administration made futile attempts to impose Han officials on them. In the face of forced collectivization and suppression of nomadism among the Kazakh and Kyrgyz communities in former Soviet Central Asia, a large number of nomads fled to Xinjiang from that region. The Jin administration drove many of these Kyrgyz nomads out of Xinjiang in a joint military operation with the assistance of the Soviet government. On another occasion Jin Shuren also offended the Mongols by killing a respected Lamaist leader. In this manner an inefficient ruler alienated all ethnic and religious groups of Xinjiang.[10]

During the rule of Jin Shuren, Xinjiang experienced several anti-Chinese uprisings and ethno-national movements by the Turkic Muslim population. The Eastern Turkestan movement also started for the first time during this period. It was amidst this political upheaval that the next warlord, Sheng Shicai, replaced Jin Shuren and became the ruler of Xinjiang.

Rapid expansion of the Chinese modern armies from the late nineteenth century onwards created bright opportunities for talented youth of China in the military profession. Sheng by temperament and training belonged to that generation of warlords. He successively played the role of a reformer, a revolutionary and a nationalist during his tenure in Xinjiang. He gave a revolutionary colour to the April 12, 1928 coup that brought an end to Jin's inefficient rule.[11] During the first phase of his rule the political situation in the province was so complicated that Sheng Shicai decided to bank on Soviet military strength to quell his enemies.[12]

Throughout his tenure Sheng carried out severe anti-religious propaganda and purges against the Muslims. After becoming a member of the Communist Party of the Soviet Union (CPSU), Sheng became more enthusiastic in carrying out anti-Muslim purges. Sheng's promise of equality of nationality proved to be an empty slogan.[13] By 1936 Russians were involved in every sphere of socio-economic life from oil surveying to education to religious matters. In north Xinjiang, Russian became the main foreign language in the school curriculum, young people were encouraged to go to the former Soviet Union for higher education, atheistic propaganda became common, mosques were converted into social clubs and theaters, and religious leaders were persecuted. The Soviet Union also got a golden opportunity to reinforce its military strength in Xinjiang on the pretext of protecting the region from Japanese invasion and thus increased its political influence in Xinjiang.[14]

It appears that Sheng wanted to counter the growing Soviet pressure by allowing Chinese communists to play a certain role in the provincial politics. In March 1937, about 400 men of the Left Detachment of the West Column entered Xinjiang under the leadership of Li Xiannian. On May 7, 1937 they reached Urumqi with the help of Chen Yun and Teng Daiyuan. This unit of the Red Army later became known as the Xinjiang Military Contingent. In October 1937, the Eighth Route Army sent its representative to Xinjiang and after negotiations with Sheng it opened a branch in Xinjiang with Teng Daiyuan as its representative. Chen Yun, Deng Fa and Chen Tanqiu successively acted as party representatives in Xinjiang from 1937 to 1942. During this period the Communist Party of China (CPC) leaders like Mao Zemin who had skill and experience in administrative work came to Xinjiang and worked in different departments of Sheng's government. The Chinese communists often performed their political activities in disguise and in fact they were extremely careful in spreading ideological propaganda in the Muslim-populated Xinjiang. As early as in 1934 Sheng Shicai established an Anti-Imperialist Society and when the Chinese communists were allowed to take charge of the organization, they utilized the opportunity to propagate the CPC's ideology in the form of an anti-Japanese campaign.[15]

Like his Soviet mentors, Sheng Shicai also carried out a reign of terror among the Kazakh[16] population in northern Xinjiang. Sheng considered the Kazakhs as an obstacle to the peaceful development and construction of Xinjiang as well as to his continued friendship with the former USSR.[17] In the early years of Sheng's rule some educated Kazakh leaders like Sharif Khan initiated progressive movements in education. During this time some people also tried to introduce techniques of advanced modes of production in agriculture in the pastureland of north Xinjiang. The land reclamation work was also started by the military garrison in the region.[18] In the course of the movements against the rich herd-owners excesses were done that forced many Kazakhs to flee to northern parts of the Altai mountains. There were many Kazakh refugees who fled to Xinjiang in the last years of the Tsarist regime and during the forced collectivization in Central Asia under the Soviet government. Soon anti-Soviet and anti-Sheng feelings spread among the Kazakh nomads in northern Xinjiang. By 1936 the network of Sheng's secret police also spread throughout the Kazakh-dominated region.[19] From 1937 onwards, Sheng began a pacification campaign against the Kazakhs under the belief that they were helping the Japanese in the province and this led to the arrest of several elderly Kazakh leaders and respected intellectuals of the community. In the early 1940s Sheng allowed Soviet geologists and miners to carry out survey operations in the province that also caused resentment among the Kazakhs.[20] Throughout Sheng's tenure there occurred several small uprisings in northern Xinjiang.

In April 1941, when the Soviet Union signed a non-aggression pact with Japan, Sheng took a strong anti-Japanese stand that made him acceptable both to the Chinese communists and nationalists.[21] To meet the need of war in Europe, the Soviet Union increased exploitation of oil and other minerals from Xinjiang that caused Sheng's further disillusionment with his big neighbour.[22] The series of defeats of the Soviet Red Army at the hands of the Nazis finally helped Sheng to decide to sever relations with the former Soviet Union. America's participation in the war after the Japanese attacks on Pearl Harbor in December 1941 made Chiang Kai-shek more confident about Japan's imminent defeat. He forgave Sheng for his past misdeeds in exchange for his allegiance to the GMD government. Talks between Sheng and the GMD began in March 1942 and by October 1942 Xinjiang reverted to the orbit of Nationalist China. Sheng then carried out a purge of pro-Soviet progressive elements and Chinese communists.[23]

In the last years of Sheng's rule and in the beginning of the GMD control in the province, a series of incidents occurred that finally led to widespread rebellion in the province. The Soviet authorities, immediately after the Soviet withdrawal from the province, closed the border with Xinjiang and thereby completely disrupted Xinjiang's trade with the former Soviet Union, which had always been a major source of the province's economy. After the establishment of Nationalist control, the provincial government introduced the inflation ridden Chinese currency that further damaged the economic situation of the province. Economic corruption also increased rapidly during this time. The provincial government not only took no measures to reduce the economic burden of the people, but it continued to extract taxes from the poor people of Xinjiang. With widespread unrest in the north the provincial machinery became more and more repressive. Anti-Sheng and anti-Chinese feelings spread among every section of the Xinjiang population.[24] In the midst of an unpredictable situation in Xinjiang, the Nationalist government in Chongqing removed Sheng Shicai and assigned General Zhu Shaoliang to take charge of the province as acting Chairman.

From the beginning, the central and provincial GMD leaders were sure about the Soviet involvement in the East Turkestan Republic (ETR) movement. The new chairman, Wu Zhongxin, of the GMD in the province took charge in October 1944. With a view of winning support of the anti-Soviet faction of the ETR, he reinstated some ethnic leaders, who had been languishing in Urumqi jail since Sheng's time, back to their native places. However, his appeasement policy did not yield the desired result at the height of revolt.[25] Considering the gravity of the situation the Chongqing government signed the Treaty of Friendship and Alliance with the Soviet Union in August 1945. But when the ETR army air-raided the Nationalist army in Wusu that forced them to retreat within the range of the provincial capital, Chiang Kai-shek consulted the US ambassador and then summoned the Soviet ambassador to express his protest against Soviet assistance to the ETR forces. Finally Chiang Kai-shek sent General Zhang Zhizhong to Xinjiang to deal with the issue. Before leaving Chongqing General Zhang asked for suggestions and sought cooperation from three exiled Uyghur leaders, Masud Sabri, Muhammad Emin Bugra and Isa Yusuf Alptekin.[26] During this time Hami leader Yulbar Khan, who was in exile in Nanjing, re-entered Xinjiang. Following Zhang's arrival in Xinjiang in September 1945 an era of coalition started in the province. The coalition experiments in the province were based on the principles of united front and General Zhang made utmost efforts to bring all political factions within the fold of the coalition.

Communist takeover of Xinjiang

Zhang's attempts to introduce reforms in various aspects of the socio-political life of the province met with little success, mostly because of the uneasy coalition of various political forces. According to his understanding the prolonged conciliatory measures were necessary to heal the trauma inflicted upon the ethnic population of the province for more than three decades under the rule of Han warlords. In the face of large-scale Uyghur protests and communal riots between Uyghurs and other ethnic groups, Zhang's relations with Ahmadjan Qasimi, the leader of the ETR movement at Ili, also deteriorated. Besides, the strong pressure from the clique of the GMD further harmed Zhang's well-intended reform plans and finally he was removed from the province in May 1947. Song Xilian, the commander of 100,000-strong Xinjiang garrison and member of another strong clique of the GMD, openly supported the erstwhile ETR ally Kazakh leader Osman Batur with arms that also became a thorny issue between the GMD and the Ili group.[27] Apparently to win the support of the Uyghur population of the province, Masud Sabri, originally from Ili, was appointed chairman of the province.

Despite their reputation as Uyghur nationalists, the Ili leaders all along despised the three former representatives of Xinjiang in the central government because of their anti-Soviet views. But the local Muslim population, especially those from southern Xinjiang, had strong hatred for Masud, because of his close association with the CCP clique, which was ultimately considered the main criteria for his appointment.[28] In protest against Masud's appointment, riots broke out in Kashghar, Turfan, Shanshan and Toksun oases. The Nationalist army readily suppressed these riots and General Song of Xinjiang garrison announced that there were agents of Ili groups among the rioters. The nexus between Osman and Song had already embittered relations between the GMD and the Ili group. Ahmedjan Qasimi denied the allegation of the Ili group's involvement in the riots in southern Xinjiang and shortly thereafter the Ili group left Urumqi on August 26, 1947. This incident not only caused the collapse of the coalition government, but also led to a complete division of the Uyghur society along two different political lines: the Uyghur elite of south Xinjiang supported the GMD faction in Urumqi, whereas tradition-bound Uyghur peasantry tilted towards the progressive leaders of Ili.[29]

The Soviet Union once again started negotiations with the GMD government through Zhang Zhizhong, in which Burhan Shahidi, the former vice-chairman of the coalition government, took a major part as a negotiator. The political situation in Xinjiang continued to worsen. All-round failure of Masud's rule made it imperative to remove him from the chairmanship of the province. The GMD government, worried over the persistent victories of the CPC in the civil war, showed a conciliatory gesture to the Soviet Union by placing Burhan Shahidi in charge of Xinjiang in December 1948.[30] At the same time General Tao Zhiyue, a moderate GMD military officer, was also sent to Xinjiang in place of Song. With this moderate team in Xinjiang, Zhang continued negotiations with the Soviet Union on the question of Xinjiang until May 1949.

By this time the CPC achieved political victory over the GMD by defeating them in other parts of China. The high morale and excellent propaganda machinery of the communists created a nationwide euphoria. The politically conscious Muslim population of Xinjiang was divided into various political lines, such as the pan-Turkic nationalists, Islamists, pro-Soviet progressives, pro-Chinese nationalists, nomadic Kazakhs, and liberal and conservative GMD members occupied the political arena of Xinjiang until the arrival of the Chinese communists. A peace agreement was negotiated between the GMD led delegates headed by Zhang Zhizhong, head of coalition government Burhan Shahidi and the CPC leaders. The sudden death of a group of pro-Soviet young communist leaders of the East Turkestan movement led by Ahmadjan Qasimi in a plane crash on their way to Beijing for a meeting with the central CPC leaders facilitated the process of transfer of power from the GMD to the CPC.[31]

Most of the pro-GMD nationalist Uyghur leaders could not accept Burhan's submission to the CPC. Leaders like Isa Yusuf Alptekin and Muhammad Emin Bugra managed to escape the ensuing purge of Uyghur leaders and fled to Turkey via India. Hami leader Yulbars Khan continued fighting against the PLA for a few months after the establishment of the communist rule in the region and finally he too left for Taiwan. The Kazakh leader Osman Batur, long forsaken by the Soviet Union and the Mongolian People's Republic, and who fought to the end, was finally captured and hanged in April 1951.[32] This is how the so-called "peaceful" liberation of Xinjiang ended.

CPC on self-determination

An important feature of China is that the minorities, who constitute 8 percent of China's population, occupy more than 60 percent of the territory, a large chunk of which was incorporated within Chinese territory by the Qing dynasty. Dai

Jitao, as a top policy advisor on the frontier question of the Nanjing central government argued that it was pointless to save the country (*jiuguo*) while losing nearly 60 percent of its territory. There had been a conviction among many Chinese that the success or failure of China's struggle against foreign imperialism depended on its ability to protect the frontier regions.[33] The demographic pressure in the Han-dominated areas and unequal distribution of territorial share between the Hans and minorities have been a major concern for many Chinese intellectuals in the modern period. It was often suggested that the colonization of Manchuria, Mongolia, Xinjiang and Tibet and the assimilation of the peoples of these regions would not only provide room for increased population and a market for growing trade, but would also ensure territorial integrity.[34] This type of mentality is based on traditional wisdom of the Han Chinese, which has a strong chauvinistic underpinning. For many educated people in the republican period colonization of the minority regions was a "progressive policy."[35]

The question of territory also took precedence in Mao Zedong's writings on national minorities though he belonged to a different ideological tradition. In both his works, *On the Ten Major Relationships* and *Correct Handling of Contradiction among the People*, he stated that a large share of national territory belonged to numerically small national minorities. In his typical style of writing he posed the question "But who has more land?" It seems that because the national minorities possess vast territory and rich resources, he wanted to justify the importance of maintaining good relations between the Han community and minorities. The two essays were written a few years after the liberation, but specific portions dealing with nationality are very useful for understanding how Chinese communists perceive the national question. In both the texts Mao criticized Han chauvinism and discrimination of minorities.[36]

The issue of land is a very fundamental question in any debate on ethnicity and nationalism. There is a strong historico-cultural essence in the concept of unification in China, but need for unification of China as a physical entity was felt in the modern period when international legal concepts like sovereignty (*guojia zhuquan*), territorial integrity (*lingtu wanzheng*) and national boundary (*guojie*) entered into China. In the process of defining state boundaries, the peripheral existence (*bianjiang shuxing*) of the national minorities became prominent.[37] In the period of transition from the imperial to the modern phase of its history state sovereignty in China was under tremendous threat. China managed to retain a monarchial regime despite serious challenge by a number of imperial forces in the modern period, but in the semi-colonial set-up the Qing rulers were compelled to sign unequal treaties and pay indemnities, give legal privileges for outsiders, accept a free trade regime imposed by the outside powers, and allow imperial powers to interfere in its internal affairs.[38] One-sided application of international law by the imperial forces inculcated a deep sense of injustice, or fear of injustice, that consolidated modern Chinese national identity.[39]

The most important feature of modern China is that the physical limit of its "geo-body"[40] was formed under the rule of the non-Han Qing dynasty and greater parts of its territory belong to non-Han peoples. Besides, during the time of war between the nomadic powers of Inner Asia and Chinese imperial authority, the periphery as a natural space or peripheral peoples as ethno-national entity were not structurally disadvantaged under the Qing rule.[41] The situation started changing as Han immigrants began to settle in the borderlands of the Qing territory. With the fall of the Qing empire the centrifugal forces erupted in Mongolia, Tibet and Xinjiang. The Han-dominated central authority in the republican period found it difficult to legitimize sovereign claim over the imperial frontier of the Qing, protect the land, resources and its non-Han peoples from foreign aggression and transform the vast natural habitat of the minority peoples as an inseparable part of the country.[42]

The Chinese communist leadership became concerned about the peripheral peoples for ideological as well as strategic reasons. At the second national congress the CPC leadership formally adopted Lenin's theory about nationalities and colonies. It was during this time that the CPC decided to pursue "nationalist revolution" and work with the GMD to achieve this goal.[43] Mao not only thought in terms of class but also in terms of nation. He invented a rich revolutionary tradition in the Chinese antiquity and glorified the Han people for their role in peasant uprisings and struggle for dynastic changes.[44] Fusion of oppressed class and advanced nation imbued with revolutionary thinking created a huge mass ready to be mobilized for the revolutionary cause. Inspired by strong nationalist feelings during the Japanese invasion the Han peasant population supported the communist-led anti-Japanese war and subsequent revolutionary war against the GMD.[45] Mark Selden refuted the assumption that wartime Chinese nationalism led to convergence of interests of the Han and minority peoples.[46] But it seems that there was enough scope of reconcilement between the Han and minority nationalities.[47] The reason why convergence between the interests of the two did not take place lies in how the Chinese communists manipulated the issue of national self-determination and imposed a revolutionary regime on the minority peoples.

In the beginning the CPC's policy towards the nationalities was guided by the Soviet representatives and they accepted the principle of right to self-determination of nationalities as a criterion of the United Front. In the second national conference of the CPC in 1922 the party leadership fully acknowledged the right to self-determination of nationalities (*minzuzijue*) and rejected the principle of federalism in the provinces of China proper (*zhongguo benbu*). It was observed in the conference that the separatist warlord regimes were the main obstacle for the implementation of self-determination and autonomy in Mongolia. It was emphatically stated that the Chinese people should oppose separatist self-rule in the provinces and forceful unification (*wuli tongyi*). The conference proposed that Mongolia, Tibet and Huijiang (historically Muslim-dominated South Xinjiang was known by this name) should be allowed to act independently (*zizhu*) and advocated promotion of a Chinese federal republic (*zhonghua lianbang gongheguo*) comprising China proper and the three democratic autonomous federal states (*minzhu zizhibang*) of Mongolia, Tibet and Huijiang.[48] In 1923 and 1924 the GMD also recognized the right to self-determination in its party manifesto. The political development of Outer Mongolia in the 1920s made both the parties aware of the dangers of granting self-determination to the minorities.[49] Chiang Kai-shek refused to mention anything about self-determination when he succeeded to the GMD's leadership following Sun Yat-sen's death in 1925 and his position was reflected in the successive constitutions of the nationalist party.[50]

For the Soviet Union, building a socialist state in Outer Mongolia was another success story of Leninist revolutionary strategy that encouraged backward countries to arrive at communism by skipping the capitalist stage of development.[51] The CPC did not like Soviet involvement in the Mongolian affairs. Situation in Outer Mongolia became more complicated after the Japanese occupation of Manchuria and Inner Mongolia in 1931. The Inner Mongolian communist leader Ulanfu accepted the line of the Chinese communists that the main target of social revolution was not separation from the Chinese rule.[52] The Chinese communists came in direct contact with the non-Han peoples during the Long March and anti-Japanese war. On the basis of the new experiences the CPC formulated its ideological foundation on the national question and adjusted its stand on the issue of national self-determination.[53] The Chinese communists, who were struggling hard to save the country from foreign invasion and national strife, realized that the problem relating to the nationalities in the vast frontier region of the country was basically a question of territorial sovereignty and domestic security.

However, the CPC kept on promising self-determination to the minorities. In the sixth national congress in 1928 the CPC reiterated its earlier position. In the first national congress of Jiangxi Soviet in 1931 a resolution on national minorities was passed which clearly stated the position of the party and the Soviet government on the national question. This is the first time that the party opposed all forms of exploitation and advocated thoroughgoing liberation (*chedi jiefang*) of national minorities. The congress solemnly declared: "Chinese Soviet Republic absolutely recognize right to self-determinations of these national minorities without any precondition." The resolution stated that the laboring masses of the non-Han population of certain regions like Mongolia, Tibet, Xinjiang, Yunnan and Guizhou who constitute majority of the population in their respective areas would decide their own affairs. The congress called for a joint struggle of the laboring masses of the national minorities and workers and peasants of China against imperialists, warlords, landlords, bureaucrats and capitalists. In 1934 Mao Zedong maintained the earlier stance on national self-determination in the second national congress of the Soviet. Following are some important points of the party's position on the national question that were discussed in the two congresses:[54]

1   National question is a component of Chinese revolution and liberation of national minorities is inseparable from the liberation of Chinese people. The national minorities will achieve complete liberation only by overthrowing imperialists, GMD reactionary rulers and the landlords, hereditary rulers, Lamas, aristocrat class and profiteers of their respective community.

2   In order to ensure right to self-determination of national minorities and put autonomous rights into practice, the party and Soviet will train minority cadres so that they can manage works of autonomous organs.

3   In order to assist national minorities to catch up with the advanced nationalities, the party and government will take care of development of productive forces of backward nationality areas and improve their culture.

4   Minority languages will be given due respect and conditions for developing minority language education will be created in the schools situated in the minority regions.

5   Absolute separation of politics and religion will be observed, and freedom in the religious practice will be guaranteed.

In the 1935 Zunyi Conference Mao Zedong first reversed his position on the question of right to self-determination of minorities. Distinction was made between self-determination (*zijue*) and self-rule or autonomy (*zizhi*). Mao felt that recognition of the right of self-determination in socialist countries was not necessary. He argued that the national minorities should be mobilized in the struggle against imperialism.[55] After the Zunyi Conference, the term *zijue* had been occasionally used only to gain support from the minority people in the anti-Japanese war. In October 1938 Mao emphasized that national minorities only possessed the right to manage their own affairs and constitute a unified state with the Han nationality. On the nineteenth anniversary of the death of Sun Yat-sen in March 1944, Zhou Enlai again raised the issue of self-determination, but after the end of anti-Japanese war the party took a clearly different position. From now onwards, the party leadership not only opposed secession of minority regions, but also considered that the Soviet style federal structure was not suitable for China's national condition.[56] However, until 1949 the CPC maintained that federal arrangements would be used to resolve the problem of national minorities and local autonomy would be implemented in dealing with differences between centre and local. Finally in September 1949 the central leadership formulated national regional autonomy (*minzu quyu zizhi zhidu*) for the minority areas in the common program of the party.[57]

Policy of autonomy for minority nationalities in Xinjiang

The first phase of socialist construction in China started when the ideals of New Democracy still remained a valid official line to provide a flexible instrument for defining and re-defining strategies. The Common Programme, based on the principles of New Democracy and the spirit of the United Front, remained as the main guidelines for economic and social construction until 1954, which emphasized gradualism and long-term objectives of economic development. During this period the regions of China experienced transition from the PLA control to civilian authority. The duration and process of this transition was certainly different from region to region. As the regional governments gradually became functional in administrative affairs, the role of the military was reduced to security and garrison functions. Following the consolidation of the CPC's hold at the center, a process of decentralization was started during this period.[58] The policy guidelines for minorities and criteria for sanctioning regional autonomy to minorities were enumerated in the fiftieth and fifty-first articles of the sixth chapter of the Common Program. It clearly stated the principle of equality in dealing problems related to all non-Han nationalities living within the borders of the PRC. The central government promised to implement the policy of unity and mutual assistance, oppose imperialism, fight against the common enemy of all nationalities as well as big nation chauvinism (*daminzuzhuyi*) and national parochialism (*xiaaiminzuzhuyi*), and prohibit inter-ethnic discrimination, exploitation and separatist behavior.[59]

In the 1954 constitution the policy of national autonomy was first mentioned and it ensured that the state would show concern for special characteristics in the development of different nationalities and their needs. It mentioned the need to fight against imperialism, dominant-nation chauvinism and local nationalism.[60] But the 1954 constitution did not sufficiently guarantee practical implementation of regional autonomy, protection of the rights of dispersed minorities and economic rights for all nationalities.[61]

Ethno-regional autonomy in China is in fact an amalgamation of regional autonomy and ethnic autonomy. The Inner Mongolian Autonomous Region is the first of this kind of administrative division, which was established as early as in 1947, and in October 1955, the Standing Committee of the National People's Congress approved regional autonomous status for Xinjiang, modeled after the Inner Mongolia Autonomous Region. Following the Soviet practice, each autonomous area was named after the minority group whose population was largest in the area. Applying the same formula central government created ethnic autonomous areas at prefecture, county, township and village level.[62] On the basis of this criterion Xinjiang was made an autonomous region of the Uyghur minority.[63]

Though autonomous regions in China are endorsed to different minorities, but any particular autonomous region neither belonged to nor is supposed to be constituted of a single minority ethnic group. There were originally 13 different ethnic groups in Xinjiang, but as a result of population transfer from other parts of China the number has increased in the last 60 years. However, the purpose of describing Xinjiang as a multi-ethnic region of 47 ethnic groups in the official documents is to undermine the Uyghur claim over the region. It also helps the state to legalize other minority groups' share of autonomy in the region. Therefore, the ethno-regional autonomous system is still considered as the best ideological weapon to fight against the aspiration of national minorities for self-determination.

Nationalities of an autonomous region enjoy some rights and preferential treatment within the unitary centralized state in which party plays a greater role than other state organs. Since the main body of the CPC's central and regional leadership always comprised of the majority Han Chinese, the minority nationalities were naturally deprived of even the limited rights provided by the autonomy law.[64] Various departments of the Nationalities Affairs Commission (NAC) of the State Council deal minority issues from the national level. The NAC is composed of minority delegates of the National People's Congress (NPC), and they do not have real power other than taking part in discussion and approving the decisions taken by other organs of the central administration. The NAC has branches at different autonomous regions and other lower level autonomous areas. The religious associations, cultural departments and nationality educational institutions also function under the NAC.[65]

The autonomous regions are provided with the following special rights over other administrative divisions:[66]

1   The chairman of an autonomous region should be a member of the main ethnic group of the region and there must be appropriate representation of all ethnic groups of the region in the Regional People's Congress (RPC).
2   The RPCs have power to formulate separate laws subjected to the approval of the NPC.
3   The organs of self-government of the ethnic autonomous regions can independently administer educational, scientific, cultural, public health and physical cultural affairs. Minorities can also choose their own path of economic development under the guidance of the state plan.
4   The state and the party encourage greater involvement of the minority nationalities in the regional administration.
5   The people of the autonomous regions enjoy greater liberty in using local languages.

According to Mingxin Pei, the autonomy provided by these laws is not adequate and this system "just allows a slightly higher degree of decentralization of power to minority-inhabited areas than Chinese-inhabited areas."[67]

Policy of gradual integration

The central leadership of the CPC and the first generation leaders of Xinjiang took some concrete measures in building confidence among the Muslims of the province. Not only that all separatist elements were ruthlessly suppressed and any form of local nationalism was severely criticized, the party also sought to eradicate anti-Han and anti-communist feelings. By creating various mass organizations the party took the initiative to feel the pulse of the people and slowly penetrate into different layers of the society. In the early 1950s the Han cadres of the province were told to respect local customs and give importance to their Muslim counterparts. The central party leadership also launched campaigns against Han chauvinism prevalent among the Han cadres.[68]

It appears that the Muslims of China received special considerations during the early 1950s. In 1952 a Chinese version of the Quran was published by the Commercial Press, Shanghai. In the preface of the translated edition some selected passages from the holy book were cited to show that Islam and communism were not inharmonious. In May 1953 the Chinese Islamic Association was established and

Burhan Shahidi, the first governor of Xinjiang, was chosen chairman of the only legally approved association of the Chinese Muslims.[69] The earlier religious organizations in Xinjiang were replaced by the newly established Chinese Islamic Association. Slow and steady measures were taken to confiscate Waqf property, and people's courts gradually replaced the judicial authority of Islam. Burhan personally condemned that some "counterrevolutionaries" had infiltrated Islam in order to hinder the process of "revolutionary unity."[70]

It seems that the party faced problems in communicating its actual policy of land reform to the cadres and peasants of the region in the early stages of its implementation. For this reason excesses were committed in many places, which caused tension and led to ethnic conflict. Maybe because of these initial problems, the region experienced slower progress in land reform. In early 1955, Wang Enmao admitted that the socialist transformation movement was lagging behind expectations in the region. Apparently collectivization was not stressed until 1957. The Kazakh-populated pastoral region in Xinjiang was mostly left outside the land reform. Though government reports usually described productive relations among the pastoral peoples in oversimplified terms of relations between herdsmen and herd-owners, it appears that in the early 1950s the age-old collective mode of production of the pastoral Kazakh people was taken into consideration. Only after Mao's directive of July 1955 the pace of collectivization and reforms in the pastoral areas of Xinjiang was stepped up.[71]

Revolutionary integration of Xinjiang

Heavy Soviet influence in the region was one of the greatest hindrances against the PRC's effort to integrate the Muslim-inhabited western frontier. The Soviet influence in social and cultural life, especially in the northwest of Xinjiang, was so profound that it posed serious challenge to the Chinese authority to establish political control over this part of the region. By 1956 both the countries became involved in bitter ideological disputes that resulted in the complete withdrawal of Soviet economic aid and assistance to the PRC, also marking the rapid reduction of Soviet influence in Xinjiang. From this time on the internal political system became more and more complicated due to various movements that cast a far-reaching impact on the life of minorities of Xinjiang.

During the Hundred Flowers Movement and anti-Rightist Movement the main debates in Xinjiang took place on the issues of Han chauvinism and local nationalism. In the beginning of the anti-Rightist Movement the Han population of the region was attacked for criticizing the party beyond the limits set by the authorities, for superiority feelings among the Han cadres, and for "counterrevolutionary" activities. In the later stage of the movement when the national minorities of the region started criticizing the PRC's rule in Xinjiang, the local authorities initiated severe attacks against several high ranking minority cadres and party members for their strong sentiments of local nationalism and anti-PRC feeling.[72] In 1958 China began the Great Leap Forward (GLF) for creating a new model of socialist construction different from the Soviet path, marking a complete shift from the policy of developmental integration and gradualism to revolutionary integration of nationalities with the broad mass of the Han Chinese.

The rapid collectivization and establishment of communes in urban, rural and pastoral areas were the main thrust during the GLF, which also encompassed several aspects of the life of minorities. Rural communes were established in most of the minority areas. The Chinese leadership stopped criticizing Han chauvanism and the superiority of the Han nationality in certain stages of historical development was recognized. The exemption from the national marriage law was withdrawn. The teaching of Han languages was now emphasized.[73] Establishment of communes began in the agricultural areas of the region in the autumn of 1958. Within six months around 93 percent of the agrarian population and 70 percent of pastoral herdsmen were brought under the commune system. A large number of agricultural laborers were engaged in labor-intensive capital production. It seems that the regional leadership soon recognized the difficulties of the minority nationalities in accepting universal collectivization and slowed down the process. The northern Xinjiang pastoral area was more affected than the grain-producing Tarim basin in the south.[74]

From the anti-Rightist Movement down to mid-1971, extensive revision was made in the earlier nationality policy. The distinctive features of the national minorities and their territories were completely overlooked during the first half of the Cultural Revolution. From 1968 to mid-1971, there was a clear absence of minority issues in the official documents. The national question was in fact treated as a class problem (*minzu wenti shizhi shi jieji wenti*). During this time special national characteristics and favorable nationality policies were attacked as counter-revolutionary and anti-class struggle. In the period of the Cultural Revolution attack against the minorities became more intense.[75] In some places regional national autonomy was abolished during the period of ten years of Cultural Revolution. The principle of regional national autonomy was even removed from the 1975 constitution, only to be restored in the 1978 revised constitution.[76]

The regional party chief of Xinjiang, Wang Enmao, made earnest efforts to contain the upsurge of the Cultural Revolution in the initial stage, but by September 1966, the first tide of the Cultural Revolution reached there with full force. During the Cultural Revolution, hundreds of mosques were destroyed and all kinds of Islamic practices were severely attacked.[77] In 1968, three violent border clashes with the Soviet Union took place near the city of Tacheng, and in May and June 1969, clashes occurred again in the same place. This international threat to the security of the western border forced the central leadership to curtail the Cultural Revolution in Xinjiang in 1969.[78]

Demographic policy

The strategic considerations impelled the leaders of the early period of communist rule to formulate special policies conducive to the local conditions of the region. Some of the policies were based on China's age-old wisdom of handling its western region. The control of population distribution since 1949 has been a major component of the population policy in China. Since 1949, the CPC has been encouraging Han settlement in sparsely populated Xinjiang from China proper, a policy practiced by the Qing government after 1884 as well as by some incompetent leaders during the Nationalist period. The policy of population transfer serves the following purposes: populating the border region, reducing minority problems through physical separation, diluting the ethno-religious and linguistic content of the population, and creating a Han working force and militia in this remote province.

According to the inter-census data from 1953 to 1982, Xinjiang ranked only second to Heilongjiang province in terms of rate of population increase.[79] In 1945, the minority population of the region was 93.8 percent of the total population, which decreased to 59.7 percent in 1982, whereas the Han population increased to 40.3 percent. The huge increase of population occurred mainly because of population influx in the region.

The period 1949 to 1953 witnessed government-mobilized migration, when a huge number of PLA contingents, political cadres, engineers, doctors, college students and skilled workers migrated to Xinjiang. Maximum population entered into the region between 1953 and 1960. In the year of the GLF the Han population increased by 62.27 percent from the previous year. There was a steady influx of Han migration in the 1960s and 1970s. During the three years of famine more than a million people migrated to Xinjiang. From 1961 to 1966, approximately 127,000 educated young people from the big cities of eastern China entered Xinjiang, 97,000 from Shanghai alone.[80] Similar trends prevailed throughout the Cultural Revolution.

A large number of the immigrant population settled in the newly reclaimed areas in north Xinjiang, which has effectively increased the food grain production in the north. However, the growing population pressure has also created various environmental disorders in this water-scarce region. Ninety-five percent of the population is concentrated in the oases of the region, which covers only 3.5 percent of the region's landmass. With only 11 persons per sq. km, the region ranks twenty-fourth in China, but the population density in the oases areas is more than 207 persons per sq. km, which, in terms of actually inhabited area, is nearly equal to that of the coastal regions.[81] Until 1949, over 70 percent of Xinjiang's population lived in the south, and only 25 percent of the population lived in the north. Due to population influx and development in the north, by 1980 its population exceeded that of the south.[82] The Han concentration in three big cities, Urumqi, Karamai and Shihezi, as well as in Changji, Bortala, Tacheng, Hami and Bayangol prefectures, far exceeds the minority population. The increase of the Han population is also responsible for the rapid urbanization in the region.

As a result of a huge influx of Han immigrants the population of Xinjiang swelled to ten million by 1973, with the Han Chinese constituting 35 percent of the total.[83] The minority nationalities first started blaming the huge Han immigration for their hardships when southern Xinjiang was facing acute shortage of food grains in the early half of the 1970s.[84] A severe economic crisis persisted in this part of Xinjiang until the early years of the reforms. Like Xinjiang, Tibet was also facing a serious threat due to huge Han immigration under the PRC rule. In the reform period, especially after Hu Yaobang's visit to the region in 1980, a programme was initiated to reduce the number of Hans in the Tibet Autonomous Region (TAR). The minority nationalities of Xinjiang also raised the issue of the transfer of Han population out of the region. However, the central authorities did not take steps in that direction, causing widespread discontent among the minorities.

Despite strong protests against the large-scale Han immigration in the early reform period, no effort was taken to check the flow of new settlers into this region from other parts of China. The reforms in rural policies allowed surplus rural labor to leave their native places for better opportunities. For many Hans coming from rural areas, Xinjiang was a place that would bring future prosperity. It was estimated that a large number of Hans settled temporarily in Xinjiang during the first half of the 1980s – on an average, 200,000 immigrants per year.[85] The local Muslim perception of Han settlement in their region was that of a deceitful Chinese trick to colonize the original homeland of the Eastern Turkic population.

Although the one-child policy was rigorously applied on the Han population after 1978, the minority nationals of China were exempted from the strict family planning policy in the beginning. Many Hans do not welcome this preferential policy. There has been anxiety among the Hans that if this continued, the minority population would eventually exceed the Han population.[86] The central government had fixed its population target at 1.2 billion by the end of the twentieth century, in which Xinjiang's quota was 17 million. To achieve this projected population growth, the regional authorities of Xinjiang introduced family planning policies amongst the non-Han population of the region from late 1985 onwards.

Xinjiang Production and Construction Corps (XPCC)

The population policy in Xinjiang is inseparable from Xinjiang Production and Construction Corp (XPCC, *Xinjiang shengchan jianshe bingtuan*) or *bingtuan* for short, which is predominantly a Han organization. It is a militia-cum-production organization established in 1954 when Xinjiang Military District (XMD), originally a part of the North Western Military Region, was abolished. In the following year the XMD was recreated under the name of Xinjiang Military Region (XMR) and brought directly under the control of the central military organs in Beijing. The public security and border defense troops, support troops, military districts in northern and southern Xinjiang, and the XPCC were the major components of the XMR. Of all these organizations the XPCC was not a regular armed force.

The concept of such militia-production organization has its origin in the Han period and the Qing reintroduced this type of military organization. As early as

Februry 1952 Mao Zedong issued an order on *bingtuan* formation.[87] In 1950, Wang Zhen took the initiative in constituting a big labor force comprising of demobilized PLA men, former GMD soldiers of Xinjiang garrison, and the unorganized Han immigrants, which later developed into the XPCC. By the end of 1952, about 270,000 PLA soldiers and officers were transferred to the XPCC to work on land reclamation and to establish the manufacturing and mining industries. The XPCC was officially established in 1954 when it had over 200,000 members. In the late 1960s there were eight XPCC units in northern Xinjiang and four in the south with a total strength of 500,000 men. The XPCC was a soft armed organized labor force which served the following purposes: strengthening long-term and sustainable national defense; supplying military labor for exploration and development of national resources in the border regions; bolstering border defense militarily and politically; solving the problems of unemployment for retired and demobilized soldiers; engaging educated youth to avert social problems; and generating new opportunities to utilize the manpower resources.[88]

Since the first-generation leaders of Xinjiang were more concerned about the defense and economy of the region, the regional military, except for a few years during the Cultural Revolution, was not deeply involved in political and ideological matters. The XPCC continued to play the dual role of maintaining regional security and creating a niche for incoming Han immigrants.

Ethnic unrest in the early reform period

The minority nationalities, the Han immigrants, and the PLA and XPCC were the main players in the social and political affairs of Xinjiang and in the early years of reforms these three social groups were pitted against each other. In 1975, possibly because of the economic crisis, the XPCC was abolished, but the disbanded corps members were not allowed to leave the region.[89] The XPCC used to provide security to the Han immigrants and in absence of this militia force the Han settlers became anxious about their life and property in the face of growing resentment among the minority population. Many Han youths from Shanghai and urban centres, who were earlier rusticated to this region, were also eager to leave for their native places. It was reported that in the face of pressure from the Han immigrants, the Xinjiang authorities issued exit permits to some Han youths from Shanghai, which were later rejected by the Shanghai city government. The frustrated youths carried out militant demonstrations in Aksu in April 1980.[90]

In this chaotic situation Han–minority relations deteriorated and caused ethnic unrest in Aksu and surrounding areas. Many authors have written about the riot in the region in April 1980, when Han settlers were beaten up, their homes looted, and a factory run by the Hans damaged.[91] During McMillen's visit to Xinjiang in March 1982, the local cadres admitted that there had been disturbances in the region for the previous three years, particularly in the Aksu region. His request for permission to visit was rejected by the local authority, citing logistic reasons, which clearly indicates the gravity of the situation in that region during those days.[92]

In October 1980 a military truck ran over and killed a Uyghur pedestrian in Kashgar. Though the local government sentenced the PLA truck driver to death, the local public security refused to execute the government order under the pressure of the PLA unit involved in this case. The concerned PLA unit rescued the person from jail, and threatened the local authorities with armed action if necessary. This caused tension in the region. The Uyghur demonstrators attacked the Han settlers and a PLA base in Kashgar in June 1981. Only after the execution of the death sentence of the truck driver was the situation brought under control.[93] There are other instances of the PLA's involvement in local affairs in the early reform period. It seems that the remnants of various cliques during the Cultural Revolution were still active among the troops of the Urumqi Military Region, who were dissatisfied with Deng's liberal policies.[94] The involvement of troops to quell local disturbances in southern Xinjiang caused greater casualties.

Among central and regional leaders there were people who did not appreciate Deng's liberal policies and they viewed the unrest in southern Xinjiang as an obvious outcome of the liberal policies.[95] Regional security remained a major concern in Xinjiang in the reform period, creating tension in certain areas along the Sino-Soviet border. Before the military invasion of Vietnam in 1979, the State Central Military Commission, being watchful of Soviet retaliation along the western border of China, ordered the evacuation of population of three prefectures of northern Xinjiang, which created a chaotic situation and further deteriorated inter-ethnic relations in this part of Xinjiang.[96] Sino-Soviet clash in the Tersadi area of Tacheng county and the Soviet invasion of Afghanistan in December 1979 worsened the overall security scenario of the region.[97] Though there was no threat of war between the two countries, the possibility of low scale border clashes persisted until the mid-1980s.

No initiative was taken to change the hierarchical order within Han-dominated local party organizations and minorities remained underrepresented in the decision-making process in the regional politics. The relations between the Han and minority cadres also deteriorated over the years. In August 1981, the Uyghur members of the Provincial Committee practically revolted against the majority Han members. On account of deteriorating Han–minority relations, Deng Xiaoping, then vice-chairman, visited Xinjiang from August 10 to 18, 1981.[98] It is reported that Deng faced an "unsteady" situation during his inspection tour in which the Uyghur dissidents openly called for self-rule. Deng ordered immediate reorganization of the regional leadership.[99] To meet the challenge of this critical situation, the central government sent Wang Enmao, an old hand of Xinjiang affairs, to take charge as the region's first secretary in the month of October 1981.

During his pre-Cultural Revolution years, Wang Enmao had stressed the importance of economic development and accommodative policies in ethnic and religious matters. He basically followed these old methods in handling the situation in the region, which properly suited Deng's reform plans. He skillfully utilized his old acquaintances to reduce the inter-ethnic tension. The XPCC was formally reconstituted in June 1982. This ensured the security of the Han immigrants as well as production and construction work in the fields of agriculture and industry. The local government took the initiative to raise the morale of the PLA. Attempts were made to reorganize the military leadership and educate the soldiers to understand the importance of Han–minority relations for maintaining regional stability. The party also started fostering new generation religious personnel under its direct supervision.[100] Though most of the basic problems remained unresolved, within one year Wang managed to restore law and order in the region, which helped to improve the economic condition of the people.

Wang Enmao served as a regional party head for another three years. After his visit to Xinjiang in August 1985, Hu Yaobang, general secretary of the CPC Central Committee, expressed his gratification to see a scene of nationality solidarity and prosperous development in both northern and southern Xinjiang.[101] Wang's apparent success during his second tenure, however, cannot explain the outburst of student protest within two months of his retirement from the post of the first party secretary. It should be mentioned here that McMillen made a correct assessment of the overall situation of Xinjiang in 1984, when he suggested that some of the various difficulties in Xinjiang went beyond mere 'contradictions among the people' and their resolution would be a long-term and complicated process.[102]

Conclusion

A wide range of issues, from the question of territorial sovereignty over Xinjiang to the problematic definition of the Chinese nation (*Zhonghua minzu*), are involved with the minority problems in China. The foreign policy as well as security and military matters are also the major components of Chinese policies towards Uyghur and Kazakh people of Xinjiang. For these reasons the minority policy in China is considered as ideologically sensitive and strategically vital, and the policy-making process is under party control and exclusively confined to the hands of regional and central Han cadres. The introduction of family planning policy among minorities in the subsequent years of the reform period and the policy of population transfer to Xinjiang from other parts of China have become sources of resentment among ethnic minorities. The well-being of the minority people, who are by definition weak economically, is perceived and claimed to be a foremost duty for the Chinese party state. Despite continuous assertion of removing the hurdles left by history and uplifting the ethnic minorities to the higher stage of development in the minority policy, certain policies in the reform period have created huge economic inequality as well as racial differences in the region, resulting in a deep sense of deprivation among the Uyghur population in the region.

Notes

1 James A. Millward, *Beyond the Pass – Economy, Ethnicity, and Empire in Qing Central Asia, 1759–1864*. Stanford, Stanford University Press, 1998, pp. 15–18, 245–52.
2 James D. Seymour, *China: The Politics of Revolutionary Reintegration*. New York, Thomas Y. Crowell Company, 1976, p. 183.

3   Aitchen K. Wu, *Turkistan Tumult*. Reprinted, Hong Kong, Oxford University Press, 1984, first published by Methuen, 1940, pp. 37–45.

4   A. Doak Barnett, *China on the Eve of Communist Takeover*. New York and London, Praeger, 1963, p. 244.

5   C.P. Skrine and Pamela Nightingale, *Macartney at Kashgar: New Light on British Chinese Russian Activities in Sinkiang 1890–1918*. London, Methuen, 1973, p. 214.

6   Bai Zhensheng and Liyuan Xinyi, eds, *Xinjiang xiandai zhengzhi shehui shilüe* (Political and Social History of Xinjiang in the Modern Period). Beijing, CASS Publication, 1992, pp. 98–9.

7   Ibid., pp. 119–22. Also see Peng Wulin, "Lun Yang Zengxin de minzu zongjiao zhengce" (On Ethnic and Religious Policy of Yang Zengxin), in He Yan and Zhang Shan, eds, *Zhongguo minzu lishi yu wenhua* (Chinese Minority History and Culture). Beijing, Central Nationality Institute Press, 1988, pp. 146–57.

8   Bai Zhensheng and Xinyi, *Xinjiang*, pp. 174–6.

9   Andrew D.W. Forbes, *Warlords and Muslims in Chinese Central Asia: A Political History of Republican Sinkiang, 1911–1944*. Cambridge, Cambridge University Press, 1986, pp. 38–42.

10 Ibid., pp. 70–1.

11 Bai Zhensheng and Xinyi, *Xinjiang*, p. 221.

12 Forbes, *Warlords*, pp. 120–1. Burhan Shahidi, the first chairman of Xinjiang under the PRC, rule wrote in his memoirs that Soviet influence in Xinjiang during the mid-1930s was similar to its dominant presence in political, military and socio-economic matters in Guangzhou in 1925. See Burhan Shahidi, *Xinjiang wushi nian* (50 Years in Xinjiang). Beijing, Zhongguo wenshi Press, 1994, p. 233.

13 Forbes, *Warlords*, pp. 153–5 and Bai Zhensheng and Xinyi, *Xinjiang*, pp. 319–22.

14 Forbes, *Warlords*, pp. 137–45. Throughout the anti-Japanese War the Soviet Union remained neutral and maintained full diplomatic relations with Japan. It seems the GMD was also happy to see the Soviet policy of not discriminating between the communists and the GMD in supplying aid in the cause of Chinese struggle against Japanese invasion. On April 13, 1941 the Soviet government signed a Neutrality Pact with Japan. In this pact, Japan recognized the so-called Republic of Outer Mongolia in exchange for Soviet Russia's recognition of so-called Manchukuo. This was not only detrimental to China's territorial sovereignty but also violated the Sino-Soviet Agreement of 1924 and the Sino-Soviet Non-aggression Pact of 1937. See Chiang Kai-shek, *Soviet Russia in China*. New York, Farrar, Straus and Cudahy, 1957, p. 96.

15 *Xinjiang jianshi* (Brief History of Xinjiang). Institute of Historical Research, Xinjiang Academy of Social Sciences, ed., Urumqi, Xinjiang People's Press, 1980, Vol. 3, pp. 256–88.

16 The Kazakh people, a nomadic Turkic Muslim group mostly concentrated in the three districts of Ili, Tarbagatai and Altai, was the second largest nationality in the province, comprising more than 53 percent of the population in northern Xinjiang at that time.

17 Linda Benson and Ingvar Svanberg, "The Kazaks in Xinjiang," in Linda Benson and Ingvar Svanberg, eds, *The Kazaks of China: Essays on an Ethnic Minority*. Stockholm, Uppsala, 1988, p. 52.

18 Bai Zhensheng and Xinyi, *Xinjiang*, 1992, pp. 347–8.

19 *Xinjiang Hasakezu qianxishi* (A History of Migration of Xinjiang Kazakh People). Urumqi, Xinjiang University Press, 1993, p. 75.

20 Bai Zhensheng and Xinyi, *Xinjiang*, pp. 346–58.

21 Henry G. Schwarz, "Comment: Sinkiang and the Soviet Union." *China Quarterly*, No. 18, April–June 1964, p. 212.

22 Forbes, *Warlords*, pp. 148–9.

23 Ibid., pp. 159–60.

24 Ibid., pp. 165–7.
25 Linda Benson, *The Ili Rebellion: The Moslem Challenge to Chinese Authority in Xinjiang, 1944–49*. Armonk, M.E. Sharpe, 1990, pp. 49–50.
26 Ibid., p. 52.
27 Ibid., pp. 115–19 and Forbes, *Warlords*, pp. 208–9.
28 Benson, *Ili Rebellion*, pp. 119–20.
29 Forbes, *Warlords*, pp. 211–12.
30 Ibid., p. 219. Also see Benson, *Ili Rebellion*, p. 171. Burhan, born in a Tatar family in Soviet Central Asia, migrated to Xinjiang at an early age and served in various administrative posts from Yang Zengxin's time to Zhang's government, barring seven years' imprisonment (1937–44) when he was accused of "Trotskyism." By the time of his appointment as provincial chairman, he had already proved his ability to survive in the turbulence of Xinjiang politics.
31 Burhan gave a detailed description of the communist takeover of Xinjiang in his autobiography. On August 16, 1949 Ahmadjan Qasimi wrote a letter to Burhan prior to his departure from Yining. On August 28 Burhan received a telegram from Moscow that informed him of the death of Ahmadjan and three other prominent leaders of the Eastern Turkestan movement in a plane crash on August 22. See Burhan Shahidi, *Xinjiang wushi nian* (Fifty Years of Xinjiang). Beijing, Zhongguo wenshi chubanshe, 1994, pp. 372–3. The Uyghur people still have apprehensions about the mysterious death of Ahmadjan and some other outstanding leaders of the Ili movement.
32 Linda Benson, "Osman Batur: The Kazak's Golden Legend," in Linda Benson and Ingver Svanberg, eds, *The Kazaks of China: Essay on an Ethnic Minority*. Stockholm, Uppsala, 1988, pp. 150–63. The communist attitude towards Batur was extremely cruel. Even in 1988, during his second visit to Xinjiang, Doak A. Barnett got the impression that the Kazakhs were the most poverty-stricken people in Xinjiang. He suspected that the deplorable condition of these people was the outcome of "deliberate Han political discrimination against the Kazakhs" because of the firm resistance of their leader, Osman Batur, against the communist takeover. See A. Doak Barnett, *China's Far West: Four Decades of Change*. Boulder, Westview Press, 1993, p. 359.
33 James Leibold, "Competing Narrative of Racial Unity in Republican China – From the Yellow Emperor to Peking Man." *Modern China*, Vol. 32, No. 2, April 2006, p. 187.
34 In 1922 the migration of ten million people to the northwestern regions within the next 25 years was proposed by a student in his postgraduate dissertation. The entry of a huge number of Han population was supposed to enhance the process of assimilation with the natives and increase dependency on the "mother country." However, it was proposed that the central government should stop sending criminals, fugitives and vagabonds to the minority regions, which was an age-old imperial practice. See Eu-Yang Kwang, "The Political Reconstruction of China" (M.A. dissertation in St. John's University, Shanghai). *St. John's University Studies*, No. 1, 1922, pp. 179–84. Prasenjit Duara cites number of articles published in the journal *Xinyaxiya* in the 1930s, where the authors aired assimilationist views. See his "Imperial Nationalism and the Frontier," in *Sovereignty and Authenticity – Manchukuo and the East Asian Modern*. Lanham, Rowman & Littlefield, 2003, pp. 191–2, 205–6.
35 During a trip from Japan to Taiwan in 1911, Liang Qichao felt that the "Japanese technique of colonization" was useful for China to make plans for Xinjiang and Manchuria.
36 Mao Tsetung, *Selected Works*. Peking, Foreign Language Press, 1977, Vol. V, pp. 295–6, 406.
37 Zhang Zhirong, *Zhongguo bianjiang yu minzu wenti – dangdai zhongguo de tiaozhan ji qilishi youlai* (China's Border Regions and Ethnic Problem – Historic Origin of Challenges of Contemporary China). Beijing, Peking University Press, 2005, p. 13.

38 Mao Zedong described imperialist penetration in China in "The Chinese Revolution and the Chinese Communist Party," December 1939, in *Selected Works*. Peking, Foreign Language Press, 1975, Vol. II, pp. 310–12.

39 Dong Wang, *China's Unequal Treaties: Narrating National History*. Lanham, Lexington Books, 2005, p. 128.

40 In a recent work Thongchai Winichakul suggested that the formation of territory through the demarcation of unmarked boundaries and politico-geographical representation of maps need to be considered as important elements for defining nationhood. The term "geo-body" describes one of the concrete features of nation being that defines the concept of historical continuity of territorial integrity and sovereignty. See Thongchai Winichakul, "Maps and the Formation of the Geo-Body of Siam," in Stein Tønnesson and Hans Antlöv, eds, *Asian Forms of the Nation*. Richmond, Curzon Press, 1996, pp. 67–70.

41 The Qing occupation "rarely interfered in the affairs of ordinary people, but, by its presence, held indigenous hierarchies in their position of power and preserved, even rigidified, local institutions." See Joseph Fletcher, "Ch'ing Inner Asia c. 1800," in John King Fairbank, ed., *The Cambridge History of China*. Cambridge: Cambridge University Press, Vol. 10, Pt. I, p. 105.

42 Prasenjit Duara discusses the process of producing frontiers as an inalienable part of Chinese national self within ethnological discourse. See Duara, "Imperial Nationalism," pp. 188–201.

43 Zhou Siyuan, "The Chinese Communists' Inquiry into the Social Role of Intellectuals before the May 30th Movement in 1925," *Social Sciences in China*, Winter 2005, pp. 75, 80–1.

44 Mao Zedong, "The Chinese Revolution and the Chinese Communist Party," December 1939, *Selected Works*, Vol. II, pp. 306–7.

45 In *Peasant Nationalism and Communist Power*, Chalmers Johnson argued that war-induced peasant nationalism was the decisive factor in communist victory in China.

46 Mark Selden, *China in Revolution: The Yenan Way Revisited*. Armonk, M.E. Sharpe, 1995, p. 234.

47 In "The Inland Crossroads of Asia," Owen Lattimore commented in 1944 that the young and more progressive groups among the Turkish-speaking minorities of Xinjiang, Mongols and Tibetans would "tend to gravitate towards China" if progressive policy towards minorities had been continued and developed. See his *Studies in Frontier History: Collected Papers 1928–1958*. London, Oxford University Press, 1962, p. 132.

48 Zhou Xiyin, *Hongjun changzheng shiqi dang de minzu zhengce* (Party's Nationality Policy during the Long March of the Red Army). Chengdu, Sichuan Nationality Press, 1985, p. 13.

49 The Soviet army entered Outer Mongolia in July 1921 and under their direct support Mongolia declared independence. The Soviets acknowledged Chinese sovereignty over Mongolia in the Sino-Soviet Agreement signed on May 31, 1924, but they did not fulfill their promise of troops withdrawal. In June 1924 the People's Republic of Mongolia was established. See Peng Wulin, chief ed., *Zhongguo jindai minzu guanxi shi* (History of Ethnic Relations of Modern China). Beijing, Central Nationalities University Press, 1999, p. 264. The situation in Outer Mongolia became more complicated after the Japanese occupation of Manchuria and Inner Mongolia in 1931.

50 Walker Connor, *The National Question in Marxist-Leninist Theory and Strategy*. New Jersey: Princeton University Press, 1984, pp. 67–8.

51 Thomas T. Hammond, "The Communist Takeover of Outer Mongolia: Model for Eastern Europe," in Thomas T. Hammond, ed., *The Anatomy of Communist Takeovers*. New Haven and London, Yale University Press, 1975 (Yale University publication), pp. 108–9.

52 Sechin Jagchid, "The Failure of a Self-Determination Movement: The Inner Mongolian Case," in William O. McCagg, Jr. and Brian D. Silver, eds, *Soviet Asian Ethnic Frontier*. New York, Pergamon Press, 1979, p. 234.
53

It is at Yanan that the CPC achieved its identity in its more practical policy towards minority ethnic groups, especially the ethnic autonomous system, identical with neither its former proclamation nor the Soviet Republic's. But the culturally foreign Leninist strategy and Stalinist conception of *minzu* remained intact, as reflected in the CPC's later discourse, although the discrepancy between theory and practice has always been discernable.

See Zhang Haiyang, "Wrestling with the Connotation of Chinese 'Minzu'." *Economic and Political Weekly*, 26 July 1996, p. PE-77.
54 Zhou Xiyin, *Hongjun changzheng shiqi dang de minzu zhengce*, pp. 13–16.
55 Dawa Norbu, "Chinese Communist Views on National Self-Determination, 1922–1956: Origins of China's National Minorities Policy." *International Studies*, Vol. 25, No. 4, 1988, pp. 322–3.
56 Ma Rong, *Minzu shehuixue – shehuixue de minzu guanxi yanjiu* (Sociology of Ethnicity: A Sociological Study of Ethnic Relations). Beijing, Peking University Press, 2004, p. 166.
57 Yu Xilai, "Zhongguo difang zizhilun" (Theory of Chinese Local Autonomy). *Strategy and Management*, No. 4, 2002, pp. 13–14.
58 Frederick C. Teiwes, "Establishment and Consolidation of the New Regime," in Roderick MacFarquhar, ed., *Cambridge History of China*. Cambridge: Cambridge University Press, Vol. 14, Pt. I, pp. 79–83.
59 Xu Xing, "Zhou Enlai yu xinzhongguo de minzu zhengce" (Zhou Enlai and Nationality Policy in New China). *Ethno-National Studies*, No. 2, 2005, pp. 1, 4.
60 *Constitution of the People's Republic of China*, adopted on September 20, 1954. Peking, Foreign Language Press, 1954, p. 5.
61 Thomas Heberer, *China and its National Minorities: Autonomy or Assimilation*. Armonk, M.E. Sharpe, 1989, p. 41.
62 Along with five ethnic autonomous regions there are at present 30 prefecture level, 120 county level and 1,256 village and township level ethnic autonomous areas throughout the country. See Table 1-1 Administrative Divisions of Ethnic Minority Autonomous Areas, in *Chinese Ethnic Statistical Yearbook 2004*. Beijing, Minzu chubanshe, 2004, p. 234.
63 The Uyghurs accepted state-imposed identity in exchange for an autonomous region in their name. This helped them to consolidate contemporary Uyghur identity cutting across the region. See Dru C. Gladney, *Muslim Chinese: Ethnic Nationalism in the People's Republic*. Cambridge, MA, Harvard University Press, 1991, p. 301.
64 Heberer, *China*, pp. 52–3.
65 June Teufel, "Ethnic Minorities and National Integration," in *China's Political System: Modernization and Tradition*. London, Macmillan, 1993, 1996 (second edition), p. 285.
66 *Constitution of the People's Republic of China*. Fourth edition. Beijing, Foreign Language Press, 1999, pp. 51–4.
67 Mingxin Pei, "From Nominal Autonomy to Genuine Self-Administration: A Strategy for Improving Minority Rights in China," in Wollfgang Danspeckgruber and Arthur Watts, eds, *Self-Determination and Self-Administration*. Boulder and London, Lynne Rienner Publishers, 1997, pp. 290–1.
68 Donald H. McMillen, *Chinese Communist Power and Policy in Xinjiang, 1949–1977*. Boulder, Westview Press, 1979, pp. 113–16.
69 Richard C. Bush, Jr., *The Religion in Communist China*. Nashville and New York, Abingdon, 1970, pp. 271–3.
70 McMillen, *Chinese Communist Power*, pp. 113–16.

71 Ibid., pp. 136–7, 154.
72 Among the repressed minority leaders were Ziya Samedi, a prominent Uyghur writer and the head of the Cultural Department and chairman of the Union of the Writers of the XUAR at that time, Ibrahim Turdy, a poet who headed the Internal Affairs Department of the region, Abduraim Saidi, mayor of Urumqi, Abduraim Aisa, head of the Ili district, and Kajykumar Shabdanov, a Kazakh writer. See T.R. Rakhimov, "Great-Hanist Chauvinism instead of the Leninist Teaching on the Nation Question," in M.I. Sladkovsky, ed., *Leninism and Modern China's Problems*. Moscow, Progress Publishers, 1972, p. 113.
73 Henry G. Schwarz, "The Treatment of Minorities," in Michel Oksenberg, ed., *China's Development Experience*. New York, Praeger, 1973, p. 203.
74 McMillen, *Chinese Communist Power*, pp. 138–43.
75 Jin Binggao and Chen Ye, "Lun Deng Xiaoping minzu lilun de zhuyao shijian" (On Deng Xiaoping's Theories of Nationlities), Part I, in Lei Zhenyang, chief ed., *Minzuxue renleixue luntan* (Forum of Ethnology and Anthropology), Vol. I. Beijing, Minzu chubanshe, 2006, p. 212.
76 Mou Benli, "Minzu quyu zizhi zhidu de bijiao yanjiu" (Comparative Study of National Regional Autonomous System). *Ethno-National Studies*, No. 5, 2001, pp. 1–2.
77 Bush, *Religion*, pp. 293–5.
78 Benson and Svanberg, "The Kazaks," p. 71.
79 Yuan Qing-li, "Population Changes in the Xinjiang Uighur Autonomous Region (1949–1984)." *Central Asian Survey*, Vol. 9, No. 1, 1990, pp. 50, 57.
80 Zhang Yi and He Bingyu, "Xinjiang bingtuan renkou qianyi yu Xinjiang shehui fazhan" (Bingtuan of Xinjinag, Population Migration and Social Development of the Region). *Journal of Xinjiang University* (Social Science), Vol. 27, No. 4, December 1999, p. 31.
81 "Renkou guimo yu fenbu" (Size of Population and Distribution), www.tianshannet. com.ce/GB/Channel/11/50/200112/12/13843.html (accessed on January 21, 2004).
82 Yuan Qing-li, "Population Changes," p. 65.
83 McMillen, *Chinese Communist Power*, p. 10.
84 June Teufel Dreyer, "The PLA and Regionalism in Xinjiang." *The Pacific Review*, Vol. 7, No. 1, 1994, p. 45.
85 Yuan Qing-li, "Population Changes," p. 64.
86 Heberer, *China*, pp. 84–5.
87 James D. Seymour and Rechard Anderson, *New Ghosts Old Ghosts: Prisons and Labour Reform Camps in China*, Armonk, M.E. Sharpe, 1998, fn. B, p. 45.
88 Donald H. McMillen, "Xinjiang and the Production and Construction Corps: A Han Organisation in a Non-Han Region." *The Australian Journal of Chinese Affairs*, No. 6, 1981, pp. 65–75. Also see Wu Chao, "A Study of the Chinese Communist Buildup of 'Production and Construction Crops' along the Sino-Soviet Frontier." *Issues & Studies*, Vol. 6, No. 2, November 1969, pp. 59–61.
89 Dreyer, "The PLA," p. 45.
90 Ibid., p. 88.
91 K. Warikoo, "Ethnic Religious Resurgence in Xinjiang." *Eurasian Studies*, Vol. 2, No. 4, Winter 1995/6, p. 34.
92 Donald H. McMillen, "Xinjiang and Wang Enmao: New Direction in Power, Policy and Integration." *China Quarterly*, No. 99, 1984, pp. 574–5 and n. 19.
93 Dreyer, "The PLA," p. 47.
94 McMillen, "Xinjiang," p. 578.
95 From 1979 on, senior economist Chen Yun had sensed the danger inherent in too much liberalization: "The masses want to raise the lid of the pot. Once the lid is off, we run the risk of losing power." See Pierre-Antoine Donnet, *Tibet: Survival in Question*. London and New Jersey, Zed Books, 1990 (reprinted, Delhi, Oxford University Press, 1994), p. 94.

96 Dreyer, "The PLA," p. 46.
97 Donald H. McMillen, "The Urumqi Military Region: Defence and Security in China's West." *Asian Survey*, Vol. 22, No. 8, August 1982, p. 727.
98 McMillen, "Xinjiang," p. 581.
99 Ibid.
100 Ibid., pp. 581–90.
101 *Xinhua* in Chinese, 0305 gmt, August 17, 1985, SWB/FE/8034/B2/1 (August 20, 1985).
102 McMillen, "Xinjiang," p. 592.

8 Kazakh diaspora in Xinjiang

History and perspectives of ethnic migration in Kazakhstan

Natalia Ablazhey

Russia as an empire was engaged in the process of constant growth encompassing new territories and ethnic groups into its orbit. In the eighteenth and nineteenth centuries Russia was intensively moving in Central Asian and Far Eastern directions that made the Russian Empire and China close neighbours. As a result huge territories of Central Asia and Kazakhstan were no longer just a buffer zone. Successful colonization of Kazakhstan and Central Asia by the Russian Empire during the nineteenth century accelerated the process of acceptance of the Russian citizenship by ethnic Kazakhs. It is worth mentioning that some Kazakhs accepted Russian citizenship in the eighteenth century. Territories with compact residence of Kazakh population were rapidly integrated into Russia and China during the first half of nineteenth century. When Russia returned the Ili region to China, the issue seemed to be finally resolved, and territories with Kazakh population were incorporated into new mega-regions: the Steppe province in Russia, and the new province of Xinjiang in China. In both countries, the administrative and territorial division only partially met ethnic specifics that led to growing contradictions and conflicts in future.

The division of Kazakh ethnos between Russia and China followed demarcation of the state borders in the second half of the nineteenth century. As an outcome of these transformations, the territory of residence of Kazakhs became much broader as compared with national state frontiers. Russian–Chinese borders were fixed mostly in accordance with the geographical approach, which divided the Kazakhs living in the trans-border territory. Some 137,000 Kazakhs stayed in the Chinese province of Xinjiang on the territory of three districts (Ili, Tarbagatai and Altai). Despite the fact that an agreement was achieved in 1914 on citizenship depending on the date of migration, the issue of citizenship of the Kazakh population was not finally settled either by Russia or by China. As a result of intensive migration processes and the population inflow from Russian Turkestan to the western regions of China, a large Kazakh diaspora appeared in the above-mentioned three districts and reached about 225,000 people by the year 1911.[1]

The issue of migration of Kazakhs has always been acute for both countries. The process of colonization and migration from European Russia to peripheral territories of the country sharpened land and ethnic issues on the outskirts of Russia populated by the titular ethnic groups. Russian colonial policy stimulated emigration of Kazakhs to China. Kazakhs lost some 20 per cent of their lands in the region as a result of Stolypin agrarian reform in Russia that resulted in serious tensions between the native people and Russians represented mostly by Cossacks. During the period of 1897–1916, some 1.5 million people migrated from European Russia to Kazakhstan. For the first 15 years of the twentieth century some 300,000 Kazakhs migrated to China and Inner Mongolia that meant diminishing of the Kazakh population of the Russian Empire by 10 per cent.[2]

The new wave of ethnic migrations from Russia to China refers to the period of the First World War and is connected with the national liberation movement of 1916. In the years of the First World War total military mobilization was extended to all indigenous population. There was, however, a compromise version of mobilization connected with engagement of labour for military purposes that de facto meant mass requisition of cattle. It resulted in mass ethnic unrest across the territory of the Russian Empire. In 1916, ethnic uprising began in Kazakhstan and Central Asia. Although migration of Kazakhs to Xinjiang was an outcome of Russian colonization policy and ethnic tensions in Russian Turkestan, Chinese authorities considered it as a factor stimulating Russian influence in the region. For this reason, China insisted on the repatriation of migrants. The estimation of migration in the year 1916 that resulted in an ethnic unrest, made by the Kazakh researchers, equals over 300,000 migrants.[3] After this migrant inflow in the year 1916, an additional 270,000 Kazakhs resided on the frontier territory of Xinjiang.[4] It was only after the Provisional Government took power in Russia in February 1917, that Russia–Xinjiang negotiations took place that concluded with the signing of a treaty on amnesty to rank and file refugees and their return to the motherland. The repatriation campaign lasted from the spring of 1917 to autumn of 1918. According to available data, more than 160,000 people returned to Kazakhstan by May 1917.[5]

Mass migration took place during the years of the civil war in Russia. However, the Chinese authorities, fearful of any punitive Russian expeditions, insisted on the repatriation of refugees back to Russia. Although migration of Kazakhs to Xinjiang was a result of Russian migration policy and ethnic tension in Russian Turkestan, the Chinese administration considered it as a factor of strengthening of the Russian influence in the region. As such China insisted on the repatriation of Kazakhs, which was initiated by the Provisional Government and continued by the Soviet regime. As for the return migration, it has been taking place the beginning of 1920s, when about 30 per cent of ethnic migrants returned to their home country in the framework of implementation of the Ili agreement of 1920.

The famine that took place at the start of the 1930s caused the migration of over 350,000 people from Kazakhstan to China and neighbouring countries.[6] Intensive emigration from these regions continued in 1920s. However, a repressive campaign against wealthy peasants (so-called Kulaks) and forced collectivization that started in Soviet Russia at the end of 1920s until the beginning of 1930s, led to mass unrest which stimulated the migration process. Mass migration of Kazakhs to neighbouring territories started again in the spring of 1930 and reached a peak at the end of the 1930s until the first half of 1931 when all the territory of republic suffered from famine and starvation. Those who moved out of the country can be treated simultaneously as refugees and ethnic migrants. Migration of indigenous people is seen as border land migration with some character of forced migration which affected a substantial part of the population. Representatives of traditional society with its clan structure participated in the migration movement, thus making it specific. The authorities of Kazakhstan tried to use preventive measures against the migration and insisted on return of refugees back to the country but return migration remained at the level of only a few per cent. It was caused by the humanitarian catastrophe which was not only due to just poor harvests but also the agrarian policy connected with the forced collectivization.

In Soviet Kazakhstan general losses because of starvation were assessed at the level of 40 per cent of the native population. At the end of the 1980s until the beginning of the 1990s, some Kazakhstan experts made a preliminary evaluation of the decline in the Kazakh population due to hunger, and estimated it to be around 200,000 people.[7] According to Russian historian and demographer A.V. Vishnevsky, the hunger at the beginning of 1930s caused a sort of forced or semi-forced 'push' of ethnic minorities out of their country.[8] The emigration of Kazakhs to China in the beginning of 1930s was one of the massive waves of migration in the history of the Kazakh people. Starvation became the most important 'pressing' factor in the emigration of Kazakhs.

Thus, Russia, and later on the USSR remained the source of migration for about half a century, feeding the growth of the Kazakh population in Xinjiang. It is worth mentioning that researchers from Kazakhstan consider the Kazakh population of China both as diaspora, as irredenta, politically sharpening the issue of the status of the Kazakh population in Xinjiang. The issue of ethnicity is considered as a determinant of the migration processes. It is necessary to point out that the migration of Kazakhs should be considered as mass migration, ethnic in its character, not only because migrants of just one nationality participated in the migration process but also because it was determined by the factors connected with the preservation of this ethnos mainly, or with some important parts of this ethnic group. Thus, the ethnic factors determined, first, mass emigration of Kazakhs from the USSR to China, and, second, a return migration (remigration) from China to Kazakhstan.

The Kazakh population in Xinjiang in the first half of the twentieth century can only be roughly estimated. Only in the middle of the 1940s, after the census in Xinjiang, is exact data available – there were 438,500 Kazakhs (11 per cent of the total population of the province) including 383,400 (or over 50 per cent) in the trans-border regions.[9] Although Kazakhs actively participated in the national movement, political instability in the period of the Eastern Turkestan Republic did not substantially impact the population as the Kazakh population reached 53 per cent in their settlement area.

Intensive migration movement on the Soviet–Xinjiang border took place in the 1940s. The growth of migration to Kazakhstan was a result of uprising among titular population of the province, the growth of separatism in the region, proclamation and liquidation of the Republic of Eastern Turkestan. In many respects return migration was determined by the relations with the USSR. Mass migration was registered in the period 1944–7 and was caused by the political instability in the region. Soviet Kazakhstan was eager to accept refugees from Xinjiang. In the second half of 1940s, its government many times advised Moscow about their special concern regarding the situation on the north of Xinjiang and insisted on broadening of ideological and cultural work among the Kazakh population.

Soviet policy on the 'national question' was followed by the Chinese authorities setting up ethnic administrative units at different levels in multi-ethnic Xinjiang. The way 'the Kazakh issue' was solved in the early 1950s in Xinjiang, that was included into the People's Republic of China (PRC) as an autonomous region in 1949, is connected with the liquidation of separatist tendencies and military opposition. According to the first All-China Census of 1953 the number of Kazakhs reached 504,500 people.[10] Three autonomous districts were formed in the regions of compact Kazakh population settlements. In November 1954, Ili-Kazakh Autonomous territory was organized. Establishment of national autonomy radically changed the situation for Kazakhs in China. Along with the other five big ethnic groups representing national minorities, Kazakhs received a 'status of the state level'.

Later, during the period of campaign against local nationalism, the leaders of the Kazakh autonomy movement were incriminated, for their participation in the 'three districts revolution' (the Ili uprising), and for their efforts to prevent mass migration of the Han population to the autonomous region and intentions to consolidate the Kazakh population within the borders of the autonomous territory. This was interpreted as an attempt to establish an independent Kazakh state. This idea got a new impetus towards the end of 1980s and early 1990s when the Kazakh elite raised the issue of reconsidering of status of the Ili-Kazakh autonomous territory. The idea of having an ethnically pure Kazakh state has always been attractive for the Kazakh national elite.

Diminishing of the Soviet influence in Xinjiang in the second half of 1940s was partially compensated by the mass Sovietization of the White Russian emigrants and ethnic migrants. In the second half of 1940s, the number of Soviet colony in Xinjiang increased to 150,000 people which included 110,000 ethnic Kazakhs. Chinese authorities considered some 30 per cent of Kazakhs who resided in Xinjiang as emigrants. Moscow always demonstrated a special interest in the situation in the north of Xinjiang. The government of Soviet Kazakhstan insisted on expanding ideological and cultural work among the Kazakh population as, in its opinion, 30 per cent of the population of the Chinese trans-border territory were migrants from the Soviet Union. During the period from the 1950s until the early 1960s, there was high migration activity of the Kazakh population.

'The Thaw' in the USSR–China relations led to normalization and development of bilateral cooperation. However, the Chinese government considered the

Russian-speaking population permanently residing on the territory of China as a heritage of Russian colonial policy and insisted on its return to the USSR. In 1954 the former USSR and PRC began a large-scale programme of repatriation that was caused by the shortage of labour resources in the agrarian sector of the Soviet economy. It entailed further mass Sovietization. In the middle of the 1950s, the USSR liberalized its migration policy in order to attract labour force from abroad, including China. Emigration from China was undertaken in the framework of the Virgin Lands campaign, and migrants were planned to be used in the agrarian sector of the Soviet economy. According to the decision on mass repatriation adopted by the PRC State Council, mass emigration was supposed to take place mostly from the northwest territory of China. As far as Xinjiang is concerned, mostly Russian-speaking people were considered as potential emigrants from this area. The government of Xinjiang Autonomous Region of China from the very beginning was cautious regarding the possibility of repatriation of all Soviet and pro-Soviet population, thus favouring the emigration of Russians and Tatars, at the same time, objecting to repatriation of Kazakhs and Uyghurs. It is necessary to mention that the rise in emigration intentions of the Kazakh population was caused by the wide range of political and socio-economic reasons like the repressive campaign against Kazakhs who participated in the national uprising, beginning of mass migration of the Han-Chinese population to Xinjiang, discriminatory policy towards national minorities, and beginning of socialist transformation in Chinese agriculture.

Step-by-step repatriation received more evident ethnic character, and the share of Kazakhs was permanently growing. Such a mass repatriation to the former USSR necessitated a decision over the issue of citizenship of migrants in the trans-border territory. In 1955, the first year of repatriation, China announced that all descendants of earlier immigrated Kazakhs and Uyghurs who were born on the territory of China were to be considered as citizens of China. In 1957, when migration activity and migration intentions which could not be implemented in the course of the repatriation programme were high, the Soviets made an unprecedented proposal. They proposed to introduce a practice of double citizenship for the inhabitants of the trans-border regions or consider a possibility of selection of citizenship. However, Chinese authorities refrained from signing a convention on double citizenship.

Repatriation from China to the former USSR in the second half of the 1950s until the beginning of the 1960s was one of the most massive repatriation campaigns. The USSR became one of the world leaders in immigration. In 1954–5, some 115,000 people came to the USSR from China. They were settled exclusively in the rural areas on the territory of those republics where the Virgin Lands campaign took place. In 1954–5, more then 65,500 people migrated from China to the Kazakh Republic of the USSR. Of them, about 50 per cent were represented by Kazakhs and Uyghurs. Later on these were mainly representatives of titular nationality who immigrated to Kazakhstan. Immigrants concentrated, as a rule, in economically depressive regions and were planned to be used as a labour force for acceleration of economic growth. All targets set for the resettling of migrants from China to the Virgin Lands areas of the USSR were achieved. However, secondary migration became a fact right away, and the authorities could do nothing about it.

Some 57,300 people, including 40,000 Kazakhs and 9,500 Uyghurs, migrated from Xinjiang. For the next two years 15,000 left Xinjiang on the legal basis, most of them being Kazakhs and Uyghurs. Repatriation of 1958–9 could not radically decide the issue of Soviet colony in Xinjiang, although it led to its substantial diminishing, especially in the border regions. The issue of citizenship of people who resided in these border areas was not resolved. The situation became really acute as repatriation led to division of families that could become a reason for the next migration wave.

At the end of 1950s repatriation from Xinjiang began en masse again. It could cause an outflow of the Kazakh population from the border territories of Xinjiang. Having understood the growth of migration activity and high migration expectations of the Kazakh population, Chinese authorities demanded from the former USSR to stop repatriation from the region. The policy of the accelerated cooperation of individual peasants and 'communization' in the cattle breeding areas of Xinjiang entailed massive starvation there. In the year 1960, return of the Soviet specialists to the USSR and interruption of provision of economic assistance to China soured Sino-Soviet bilateral relations. The administration of Xinjiang undertook some measures to ban emigration of specialists representing the titular population of Xinjiang: it was interpreted as 'a leak of national cadres'. On the contrary, the Soviets liberalized immigration policy and accorded Soviet citizenship for those who came from Xinjiang.

Since the beginning of 1960s emigration from Xinjiang could not be properly controlled, which made relations between China and the USSR very tense. Alongside with the continuation of official repatriation, migration was step by step becoming a spontaneous process since the beginning of 1960s. In the spring of 1962 the Soviet Union de facto unilaterally opened its border that evoked very strong reaction from the Chinese authorities: it banned emigration of the representatives of ethnic minorities of Xinjiang from China. In the spring of 1962 only about 72,000 illegal migrants crossed the border (most of them were Kazakhs). Of them some 30 per cent did not have citizenship at all, and the rest had temporary Soviet documents. Chinese authorities insisted on the deportation of these migrants but the Soviet Union did not plan to return them back to the west of China. Integration of refugees into the Soviet society was delegated to the administration of Kazakhstan. Over 200,000 people, mostly Kazakhs and Uyghurs, insisted on getting the Soviet citizenship and repatriation to the USSR, mainly to Kazakhstan. Mass protests with the slogans of immigration to the Soviet Union took place in Xinjiang at the end of May 1962, which were suppressed by employing weapons against the Kazakhs. These events became famous as the 'Ili incident' of 29 May 1962, which was referred to many time in all the Soviet–China negotiations in the 1960s. Repatriation was resumed in the autumn of 1962 after mutual agreement, and more than 26,000 people arrived in Soviet Kazakhstan in an organized order. In 1962–3, according to the official statistics, Kazakhstan received 119,000 repatriated people.[11]

In the period of confrontation between the former USSR and PRC economic and humanitarian cooperation stopped and the repatriation movement ceased to exist. In the beginning of the 1960s when relations between the USSR and the PRC became very tense, the Chinese side put forward territorial claims to the Soviet Union on Kazakh and Kyrgyz territories. In August 1969, the border row led to a military clash. In the period of Soviet–Chinese confrontation the border regime looked like an 'iron curtain': contacts were just minimal and there were no possibilities for migration and other informal practices of interaction between the population of the border territories.

Normalization of Soviet–Chinese relations in the second half of 1980s, transformation of political system in the former USSR and changes in the economic policy in both countries positively impacted the liberalization of the border regime in many respects. It entailed a revival of the migration of Kazakh population in the border areas which had a long history. After the collapse of former USSR, Kazakhstan expanded cooperation with China that contributed to intensive migration exchange. Opening of the border stimulated contacts among 'the divided' ethnos. The establishment of an independent national state where the Kazakh population belonged to the ethnic majority stimulated the growth of ethnic consciousness and sharpened the problem of repatriation. Radical transformations in economic and political spheres, growth of ethnic identity, development of national and cultural dialogue, inter-ethnic tensions and surplus of labour resources in some countries where Kazakhs resided, led to new intensive ethnic migration flows directed towards Kazakhstan. Repatriation of Kazakhs in 1990s was in fact their remigration, their return to the historical motherland. Once again the issue of the migration movement became acute and it required balanced action from the side of the recipient society.

The repatriation programme had long-lasting consequences for the former USSR and for China. In particular it led to an increase in the Kazakh population because of the migration of ethnic Kazakhs from abroad and partially compensated for the mass migration of Russian-speaking population to this territory. For the period of 1954–62, more than two million people had come to Kazkahstan in the framework of the Virgin Lands campaign. Due to mass migration of the Russian-speaking population, the number of ethnic Kazakhs had declined to about 30 per cent. The inflow of the Russian-speaking population had negatively impacted the functioning of the Kazakh ethnos. The process of re-emigration contributed to the growth of the Kazakh population, preservation of the Kazakh language and their ethnic identity.

Respective legislative and regulatory basis, mechanisms of naturalisation, labour use and cultural adaptation of immigrant ethnic Kazakhs were elaborated in the former USSR. The state provided material support to migrants for ten years. Chinese authorities could use repatriation from Xinjiang for changing the ethnic structure of its population and accelerate integration of Xinjiang into the PRC. Due to repatriation from Xinjiang, Chinese authorities managed to change the ethnic structure of the population and facilitate the integration of Xinjiang in the PRC.

Establishment of the independent Republic of Kazakhstan after the collapse of the former USSR indicated a policy of repatriation of ethnic Kazakhs to the 'motherland' that was a part of the 'state revival' policy. Kazakhstan proclaimed its ethnic migration policy, implementing the programme of repatriation of ethnic Kazakhs at the state level since 1991. It was in the year 1998 that the issue of repatriation of ethnic Kazakhs to their historical motherland became the official programme of the Kazakhstan government. Now this issue is seen as one of the major priorities of Kazakhstan's migration policy. The country is pursuing a policy of repatriation of ethnic Kazakhs who left its territory, as well as their descendants who reside in other countries. The transfer of ethnic terminology into Kazakhstan legislation and regulation practice is evidence of the ethnic character of immigration. Kazakhstan practically refused the terminology used in the international laws with regard to ethnic migrants and introduced specific ethnic category *oralman* which in translation from the Kazakh language means 'returning to the motherland'.

This programme is aimed at:

1   providing for an inflow of the native population in order to compensate for mass outflow of the Russian population from the republic, and
2   implementing the ethnic consolidation policy.

The status and privileges of ethnic immigrants are fixed in the legislation. The current migration to Kazakhstan is mostly legal. There are some quotas for all countries with substantial Kazakh diaspora and immigration quotas directly depend on the economic situation. The annual quota for immigration has been diminishing since the beginning of 1990s from 10,000 families in 1993 to 500 families in 1999.

There has been growth in the emigration intentions of the Kazakh population in Xinjiang and a softer policy of the central Chinese authorities in this respect since the mid-1990s. In our opinion up to recent time mass migration from China has been hampered by the Kazakhstan authorities since they are afraid of growth of separatism and radical Islamism. The higher living standards in the PRC compared to Kazakhstan also impacted the situation. One agrees with the opinion of the Kazakhstan expert K.L. Syroezhkin that the tendencies of diminishing possibilities for national and cultural development of the Kazakh diaspora in China would substantially influence the intentions of emigration among the Kazakhs of Xinjiang.[12]

However, everything changed in the beginning of the 2000s. The annual quota for immigration in 2001–8 was 15,000 families; in 2009 it increased to 20,000 families. The national project *Narly Kosh* was started in 2008. It is focused on the planned settlement of ethnic repatriated Kazakhs, mainly in the rural areas of northern, eastern and central regions of Kazakhstan. This migration policy stipulated the mass inflow of ethnic Kazakhs to Kazakhstan. According to official estimates for the last two decades up to one million ethnic Kazakhs emigrated to Kazakhstan in total. For the years 1989–2005 more than 717,000 people emigrated to Kazakhstan, including 410,000 immigrants during the period of 2003–5 only, 60 per cent of immigrants being from the CIS countries. The share of ethnic Kazakhs among all immigrants has been permanently growing for all these years and is above 70 per cent at the moment. Implementation of the programme of return of native population to their motherland led to the growth of ethnic Kazakhs in the overall share of population by 5 per cent. If in the 1990s most of the Kazakh immigrants arrived from Mongolia, since the beginning of 2000s the share of China has been increasing, and it rose from 3 per cent to 13 per cent for the whole period. Although just over 14,000 people immigrated to Kazakhstan from China for 15 years, including 12,500 Kazakhs, the number of *oralman* is growing year to year. For the years 2003–5, there were about 10,000 of them.[13]

Currently there are about 1.5 million ethnic Kazakhs residing in China, equal to 7.5 per cent of the population of Xinjiang. According to the opinion of demographers from Kazkahstan, the representatives of Kazakh diaspora from China and Uzbekistan would constitute the potential immigrants to Kazakhstan in the coming years. It may be stated that though all Kazakhs represent the same ethnic group, they had different historical experiences. In Kazakhstan, Kazakh ethnos developed under the strong impact of Russian culture. In China, it was under the Chinese cultural influence. This factor determined the difference in mentality in the past and will determine it in the future.

Notes

1 G.M. Mendikulova, *Istoricheskie Sudby Kazakhskoy Diaspory: Proiskhozhdenie I Razvitie* (Historical Fates of Kazakh Diaspora: Origin and Development). Almaty, Gylym, 1997, p. 83.
2 Ibid.
3 *Istoria Kazakhskoy SSR* (History of the Kazakh Soviet Socialist Republic). 2 vols. Alma-Ata, Nauka, 1957, Vol. 1, p. 578.
4 K.L. Syroezhkin, *Kazakhi v KNR: Ocherki Sotsialno-Economicheskogo I Kulturnogo Razvitiia* (Kazakhs in CPR: Essays of Socio-Economic and Cultural Development). Almaty, 1994, p. 87.
5 Mendikulova, *Istoricheskie Sudby Kazakhskoy Diaspory*, p. 88; V.A. Moiseev, *Rossia I Kitay v Tsentralnoy Azii Vtoraia Polovina 19 veka – 1917* (Russia and China in Central Asia in the Second Half of the Nineteenth Century – 1917). Barnaul, 2003, p. 309.
6 See for more details, N.N. Ablazhey, 'Emigratsionnye Posledstvia Kollektivizatsii I Goloda V Nachale 1930kh Godov Na Vostoke SSR (Emigratis Kazakhov)' (Emigration Consequences of Collectivization and Starvation in the Beginning of 1930s on the East of the USSR: Emigration of Kazakhs), in V. Lamin and O. Shelegina (eds), *Adaptatsionnye Mekhanizmy I Praktiki V Traditsionnykh I Transformiruushikhsia Obshchestvakh: Opyt Osvoeniia Aziatskoy Rossi*. Novosibirsk, Sibirskoe Nauchnoe Izdatelstvo, 2008, pp. 100–2.
7 Zh.B. Abylkholzhin, M.K. Kozybaev and M.B. Tatimov, 'Kazakhstanskaia Tragediia' (The Kazkahstan Tragedy), *Voprosy Istorii* (Moscow: No. 7); M.Kh. Asylbekov, 'Vneshniia Migratsiia I Ee Vliianie Na Strukturu Naseleniia Kazakhstana V 20 Veke' (External Migration and its Impact on the Composition of the Kazkahstan Population in the 20th Century), in M.K. Kozybaev (ed.), *Uroki Otechestvennoy Istorii I Vozrozhdenie Kazakhskogo Obshchestva*. Almaty, Kazakhstan, 1999.

8 A.G. Vishnevsky, *Serp I Rubl: Konservativnaia Modernizatsiia v SSSR* (Sickle and Rouble: Conservative Modernization in the USSR). Moscow, Obedinennoe Gumanitarnoe Izdatelstvo, 1998, p. 262.

9 Data for the year 1944 is taken from: She Lingyun, 'Yi jingji jianshe jiu Xinjiang yongjiu heping' (Economic Set Up of Xinjiang as an Instrument of Preservation of Peace), *Tianshan Yuegan*, 1, 15 October 1947, pp. 9–15. Data is provided in: L. Benson and I. Svanberg (eds), *Istoria Kazakhstana v Zapanykh Istochnikakh 12-go – 20-go Vekov* (History of Kazakhstan in Western Sources of 12th – 20th Centuries). Almaty, 2005, Vol. 3, Part 1.

10 Official results of the Xinjiang Census since 1954 were originally introduced into research discourse in the USSR by S.I. Bruk. See S.I. Bruk, 'Etnichesliy Sostav I Razmeshchenie Naseleniia V Sintsian-Uygurskom Avtonomnom Rayone Kitayskoy Narodnoy Respubliki' (Ethnic Composition and Distribution of Population Over the Territory of XUAR). *Sovetskaia Etnograhiia*, Moscow, 1956, No. 2.

11 The number of migrants is calculated on the basis of Archives of the President of the Republic of Kazakhstan, F. 708, Op. 36, D. 1508, L. 23; Archives of the Russian Federation External Policy, F. 100. Op. 47. P. 383. D. 42. L. 12.

12 K. Syroezhkin, 'Kazakhi Kitaia: Problemy Repatriatsii' (Kazakhs of China: The Problem of Repatriation), *Kontinent*, 2000, No. 16, available at www.continent.kz/2000/16/22.html.

13 Statistical data is provided by A.N. Alekseenko, 'Rol Immigratsii V Formorovanii Demograhicheskoy Politiki Respubliki Kazakhstan' (The Role of Immigration in Forming of Demographic Policy of the Republic of Kazkahstan), in A.N.Alekseenko (ed.), *Etnodemograficheskie Processy V Kazakhstane I Sopredemnykh Territoriyakh*. Ust-Kamenogorsk, Ust-Kamenogorskiy Pechatnyi Dvor, 2008, pp. 25–6, 29–30.

9 Economic cooperation between Xinjiang and Central Asian Republics

Kh. Umarov

Introduction

For the past 22 years China has played the leading part in the socio-economic and political development of the Central Asian Republics (CARs) after their independence, by providing consumer goods and political support. China's support compensated the losses which were incurred by the Central Asian countries as a result of breaking down of economic ties between various regions of the former Soviet Union. Whereas the process of acceleration of economic development is going on in these republics, the rehabilitation stage of economic development is coming to its end. The main feature of this stage has been the mass delivery of consumer goods to Central Asia from China, whereas Central Asia has been delivering raw materials to China. The Central Asian countries realize the necessity to change this situation. As such, the structure of goods' exchange maintains the backward economic structure of one of the partners (CARs). There are various options of changing the situation of existing commercial–economic relations between China and the CARs.

Now the CARs have begun the development of a new economic model, which can be characterized as investment. It means that only new investments, mainly direct foreign ones, are able to ensure further economic development and ensure realization of structural change in the market relations in Central Asia. In all the CARs the resources of rehabilitation models have exhausted. The available resources are unable to compete both in external and in the internal markets. Only China can ensure mass delivery of machinery and new technologies suited to Central Asia. The CARs need equipment and machines which are able to replace imported ones. Nowadays, in all CARs, the strategy of developing exports is being worked out. The import replacement strategy has vital significance for CARs. Without working out and realization of such a strategy, home-made goods will be ousted from the market and export development strategy can lose its internal base. It will not lead to the achievement of its main goal, i.e. raising the capability of goods manufactured in the CARs to compete in the external markets.

The main features of the investment model of economic development in the CARs are as follows:

1   growth of direct foreign investments;
2   gradual end to regional disintegration process and development of inter-governmental investment in the market;
3   growing competition between the main geopolitical forces of the modern world for influence in the region, and creation of advantageous position in the relations with neighbouring countries, especially China and Russia which have leading supremacy in regional blocks.

In the trade and economic relations between China and the CARs, the economic structure of Xinjiang occupies the most advantageous geographical position vis-à-vis the CARs. Xinjiang has several important advantages for creating firm, stable and large-scale economic ties with the CARs.

First, some organizations can successfully work here, which on the one hand are capable to secure orders from the private and state owned sectors of CARs for consumer goods, machinery and technological equipment, and on the other hand can determine the main suppliers of such goods in Central Asia and southern regions of China, for executing such orders.

Second, there are favourable opportunities for organizing technical services of those Central Asian enterprises, which are equipped with modern Chinese production facilities.

Third, Xinjiang itself can be converted into the largest manufacturing base of machinery and equipments, which can be delivered to the CARs.

Fourth, Xinjiang already possesses potential opportunities for participating in the development of physical infrastructure in Central Asia, which is being built with the support of other countries, international and regional economic organizations.

A capital of more than US$250 billion is required for the CARs. Only in two small countries – Kyrgyzstan and Tajikistan – investment of US$950 million is needed to change the outdated tractor parks. As such, in the technical re-equipment of the Central Asian economy, China can play the lead role as it has hard competitive advantages, such as:

1   comparatively low price of technical equipment, machinery and building machinery;
2   convenient geographical location of China, and Xinjiang particularly in rela-tion to the CARs with the nearly complete absence of transit transportation;
3   high adaptability of Chinese machinery and technological equipment to spe-cific socio-economic, demographic and natural climatic condition of the CARs.

Lately, a tendency of expanding the process of regional cooperation and trans-formation of disintegration process into integration has been noticed. The coun-tries rich with hydro-carbon resources – Turkmenistan and Kazakhstan – are intending to invest in other countries of the region. President of Kazakhstan Nur-sultan Nazarbaev's proposal to restore the Central Asian economic community, is being supported in all countries of the region. There has appeared a hope of formation of common customs space, with gradual transformation to common economic space and creation of conditions for free delivery of goods, capital and work force.

China can play a very active part in the realization of plans of economic cooperation in CARs, which can be ensured by remarkable structural changes in the economy of Xinjiang. Participation of Chinese firms in development of three directions of regional cooperation in the CARs – hydropower, transport and food supply – is especially important. It is necessary that Xinjiang and western regions of China determine relatively two standards of regional integration for Central Asia – one standard covering the CARs and the other standard for Greater Central Asia, which includes Xinjiang, Mongolia, Altai Territory of Russian Federation, Afghanistan and North-Western bordering provinces of Pakistan, besides the five CARs. Such integration processes are going on. Five bridges to Afghanistan on the Panj river have been built thereby ensuring increase in goods exchange between Tajikistan and Afghanistan many times throughout the year. These bridges have brought Xinjiang closer to the northern regions of Afghanistan.

All these three directions of integration in Central Asia have great significance for Xinjiang. Construction of railway and automobile roads from China to the CARs and their inclusion in the regional network of roads implies the growth of integration of Central Asian and Xinjiang's economy. Construction of pipelines and electric-transmission line has also great significance.

The participation of China in solving the food problem in the CARs is important. The most important part of cooperation can be in the restoration of seed-growing, pedigree cattle and industrial poultry farming, which would increase the productivity of agricultural crops, cattle farming and volume of food, thereby sharply reducing the dependence of the CARs on the foreign market for food supply.

However, there arises a question about the processes of inevitable integration of the economy of Xinjiang with the economy of the CARs. Though this process is inevitable in theory, it remains unresolved in practice. During the past 22 years the rate of economic cooperation between the CARs and China has been many times more than the corresponding rate amongst the CARs themselves. The horizons of integration in the eastern direction (China, Xinjiang) look much clearer, in comparison with northern, southern and south-western directions.

In this plan, much work is done by the CAREC (Central-Asian Regional Economic Cooperation) constituting eight countries. In the framework of this organization a complex plan of action was approved at the fifth ministerial conference on 20 October 2006 in Urumqi. The Urumqi Declaration of CAREC noted the strategic structure of the plan of actions supported by four pillars of activities:

1   pillar of regional infrastructural networks (transport corridors, energy markets and trade infrastructural projects);
2   pillar of knowledge and harnessing of potential (investigation projects, trainings and dialogues on regional cooperation issues);

3   pillar of trade, investment and business development (integration structures for improving investment climate, improvement of ties of commercial enterprises with regional and world markets);
4   pillar of regional public support (settlement of transport problem, management of hydropower resources, prevention of natural calamities, infectious diseases and so on).

Economic ties between the CARs and China are manifested by the delivery of a large volume of consumer goods to the CARs. Delivery of such low-priced Chinese food products, clothing and footwear, goods for children, household electronic goods into the internal market has played a great humanitarian role. Such supplies saved the population from the threat of starvation and inflation besides preventing the worsening of the socio-economic situation, due to the break-up of economic ties with Russia and other post-Soviet countries.

Development of trade relations between China and the CARs

During the period after independence, economic ties between China and the CARs started developing at a high rate. These include trade in goods and services, scientific-technical cooperation, transport and telecommunication ties. With a long common border, potentially low transport expenditure, detailed information about quality of exported goods, positive response of the population to the imported goods, existence of centuries of confidence between peoples on both sides of the border, and trade in the framework of the 'Great Silk Road', friendly relations between China and the CARs create a favourable background for large-scale trade and economic cooperation.

Especially favourable is the trade in goods. In the CARs, Chinese goods are marked by their low cost, practicality and adaptability to the local conditions. Proximity of the border, favourable transport arrangements and low labour costs on both sides of the border facilitate this mutual trade in comparison with trade both among the CARs and China with other regions of the world.

Large prospects in the scale and effectiveness of trade between CARs and China are related to the development of the economy of Xinjiang. Due to the centralized capital investment of China made during the past 22 years, Xinjiang has witnessed fast socio-economic development, which in turn led to the creation of effective and large-scale trade with the CARs, Russia, Middle and Near East. Economic prosperity of Xinjiang can serve as an independent factor of accelerating the rate of trade between China and Central Asia.

Soon after gaining their independence, trade between the CARs and China grew. However, a very high rate of trade between the two regions has been noted during the last few years. During the period 1999–2007, the general volume of registered trade between the CARs and China grew from US$0.7 billion to US$16 billion, or by 22.8 times. During this period, the share of China's external trade grew from 3.4 per cent to 14 per cent.[1]

China is a favourable and powerful accelerator of trade and economic relations with the CARs. There exist very few formal and non-formal barriers in trade between the CARs and China, compare to those with other regions of the world and also between the Central Asian countries. The high rate of development in trade and economic relations between China and the CARs can be seen in Table 9.1.[2]

This data shows that there is high rate of trade between China and some Central Asian countries. During the period of 1992–2007 the volume of trade between China and CAR grew 38 times, between Kazakhstan and China 32.2 times, between Uzbekistan and China 12 times. During the period 1997–2007, trade exchange between China and Turkmenistan grew 13 times, between Tajikistan and China 15 times. The leading place in trade between China and the CARs is occupied by Kazakhstan. In 1992, the share of Kazakhstan in trade between China and the CARs was 88.4 per cent, in 1995 80 per cent, in 2000 79.2 per cent, in 2001 84.8 per cent, in 2002 88.6 per cent, in 2003 86.4 per cent, in 2004 85.1 per cent, in 2005 83 per cent, in 2006 81.4 per cent, and in 2007 72.2 per cent.[3] This data shows a definite linkage between specific volume of trade with China among the CARs and the economic reforms. One can judge accordingly the comparative data of trade of Uzbekistan and Kyrgyzstan with China. In 2007, Uzbekistan's trade with China was 10 per cent of the general volume of trade between China and the CARs. Kyrgyzstan, whose population is seven times less in comparison with Uzbekistan, and its territory is two times less, had the share of 6.1 per cent in the general volume of trade between the CARs and China. It is because in Kazakhstan and Kyrgyzstan the level of liberalization of external economic relations is higher as compared to Uzbekistan which employs protectionist methods.

The volume and rate of export and import of CARs with China has been developing in different ways, as per the data given in Table 9.2.

This shows an extremely motley and dissimilar situation in the export from the CARs to China. This situation is characterized by the following factors:

1   Until the year 2001, the volume of export from the whole of Central Asian macro-region to China was insignificant. Large-scale delivery of goods to China started only in 2002.
2   Until 2004 individual Central Asian countries didn't use opportunities to increase their exports to China, and essentially remained the consumers of Chinese goods and services. State organs of these countries (Kyrgyzstan, Uzbekistan, Tajikistan, Turkmenistan, etc.) didn't take any serious steps in the direction of balancing their trade with China.
3   Whereas Tajikistan and Turkmenistan did not export goods and services to China until the 2000s, Uzbekistan had a low volume of export as compared to its actual export potential.

As regards the CARs, their import is greatly different from that of export which can be seen in Table 9.3.

Table 9.1 Trade between CARs and China[a] (in million US dollars)

Year	China–Kazakhstan	China–Kyrgyzstan	China–Uzbekistan	China–Turkmenistan	China–Tajikistan	China–CARs total trade
1992	373	44	–	–	–	417
1993	428	72	–	–	–	500
1994	219	66	–	–	–	285
1995	392	30	–	–	–	422
1996	495	43	136	–	–	674
1997	489	64	127	–	–	680
1998	448	60	–	–	–	508
1999	556	62	80	29	–	727
2000	825	80	–	37	–	942
2001	1,253	71	107	–	–	1,431
2002	2,478	97	132	91	–	2,798
2003	2,856	96	216	122	15	3,305
2004	3,694	125	370	117	32	4,338
2005	6,762	422	628	105	229	8,146
2006	8,784	757	817	125	313	10,796
2007	12,385	984	1,608	377	684	16,038

Note

a The given Agency of the Republic Kazakhstan on statistics.

Table 9.2 Export of CARs to China[a] (in million US dollars)

Year	Kazakhstan	Kyrgyzstan	Uzbekistan	Turkmenistan	Tajikistan	Total export of CARs to China
1992	128	18	–	–	–	146
1993	239	29	–	–	–	268
1994	89	36	–	–	–	125
1995	197	4	–	–	–	201
1996	229	16	64	–	–	309
1997	242	22	57	–	–	321
1998	198	16	–	–	–	214
1999	273	25	17	7	–	322
2000	370	34	–	11	–	415
2001	511	26	22	–	–	559
2002	985	42	18	3	–	1,048
2003	1,310	23	52	19	0	1,404
2004	1,634	29	103	17	3	1,786
2005	2,782	84	238	16	44	3,164
2006	3,654	158	352	18	72	4,254
2007	5,380	182	741	63	101	6,467

Note

a B. Paramonov, A. Strokov and O. Stolpovsky, *Rossiyei Kitay v Centralnoy Azii: Politica, economica, bezopasnost* (Russia and China in Central Asia: Politics, Economics and Security) (in Russian). Bishkek, 2008, pp. 155, 160, 162, 164, 165, 166, 167, 169.

Table 9.3 Import of CARs from China[a] (in million US dollars)

Year	Kazakhstan	Kyrgyzstan	Uzbekistan	Turkmenistan	Tajikistan	Total import of CARs from China
1992	245	26	–	–	–	271
1993	189	43	–	–	–	232
1994	130	30	–	–	–	160
1995	195	26	–	–	–	221
1996	266	27	72	–	–	365
1997	247	42	70	–	–	359
1998	250	44	–	–	–	294
1999	283	37	63	22	–	405
2000	455	46	–	26	–	527
2001	742	45	85	–	–	872
2002	1,493	55	114	88	–	1,750
2003	1,546	73	164	103	15	1,901
2004	2,060	96	267	100	29	2,552
2005	3,980	338	390	89	185	4,982
2006	5,130	599	465	107	241	6,542
2007	7,005	802	867	314	583	9,571

Note

a B. Paramonov, A. Strokov and O. Stolpovsky, *Rossiyei Kitay v Centralnoy Azii: Politica, economica, bezopasnost* (Russia and China in Central Asia: Politics, Economics and Security) (in Russian). Bishkek, 2008, pp. 155–69.

First, the volume of imports of the CARs from China was not much up to the year 2000. The high growth of imports can be seen from early 2000 onwards. Second, in a number of countries (Uzbekistan, Turkmenistan, Tajikistan, etc.), there is no clear data about imports from China for several years. This, however, does not mean that there weren't any imports of Chinese goods by these countries, as such imports were mainly carried out through shuttle traders. The practice shows that such trade in a large degree is attended with corruption compared to other forms of organized trade. As such, it is difficult to have exact statistical data. Third, as regards the imports, the overwhelming share belongs to Kazakhstan. In 1992, the specific share of Kazakhstan in the general volume of imports of the CARs from China was 90.7 per cent, in 1995 88.2 per cent, in 2000 80.3 per cent, in 2005 79.9 per cent, in 2006 78.4 per cent, in 2007 73.2 per cent. Here one can see that the specific share of Kazakhstan's imports from China has decreased in the general volume of import of the CARs from China. Herewith such decrease is not enough, if we compare productive and consumer potential of other countries of Central Asia with Kazakhstan. Whereas Uzbekistan pursues a protectionist policy regarding the import of consumer goods from China, Turkmenistan is mainly oriented towards trade with Iran, Turkey and Europe rather than with China. However, the situation has been changing during the last few years. For example, during the period 2004–7, the volume of import of Kazakhstan from China grew 3.4 times, of Kyrgyzstan 8.4 times, of Uzbekistan 3.2 times, of Turkmenistan 3.1 times and of Tajikistan 20.1 times.

With the exception of Kazakhstan, the Central Asian countries suffer high levels of poverty, so the delivery of cheap Chinese goods plays a positive role in lowering the level of poverty. For the whole period after getting state independence, the balance of trade of the CARs with China has remained negative. This is seen from the data in Table 9.4.

One can see that with the exception of 1993, trade relations between the CARs and China have a negative trade balance for the CARs. Such a situation is applicable to every CAR, because export from these countries to China is mainly of raw materials. Export of machines, equipment and consumer goods is nearly impossible, first because of undeveloped export oriented sectors, and due to the low competitive capability of goods produced in the CARs. For increasing the export of ready-made products from the CARs to China, it requires great capital investments for the technical reconstruction of production capacities. Besides, there is no demand in China for delivery of food products and various technological equipments produced in the CARs.

There is a need to understand the conception of export orientation of the CARs in conformity with China. It is necessary to encourage the export of Central Asian energy equipment with value-added price, including electrical energy produced at large hydropower plants and also increasing the volume of services provided by Chinese firms in the territory of these countries. Besides, there is scope for the development of tourism and increasing the volume of transit cargos passing through the international transport corridors in this region.

Table 9.4 Correlation of export and import between CARs and China[a] (in million US dollars)

Year	Export to China	Import of CARs from China	Balance of Trade (+ and −)
1992	146	271	−125
1993	268	232	+36
1994	125	160	−35
1995	201	221	−20
1996	309	365	−56
1997	321	359	−38
1998	214	294	−80
1999	322	405	−83
2000	415	527	−112
2001	559	872	−313
2002	1,048	1,750	−702
2003	1,404	1,901	−497
2004	1,786	2,552	−766
2005	3,164	4,982	−1,818
2006	4,254	6,542	−2,288
2007	6,467	9,571	−3,104

Note
a Calculations are made on the basis of official statistical data of the CARs.

It may be pointed out that the statistics of trade relations between the CARs and China need perfection. Statistics provided by the Chinese side are more reliable than the statistics coming from Central Asian sources. For example, if one takes statistical data about trade balance given by separate Central Asian countries and China, it is shown differently. In the exchange of goods between Kazakhstan and China, positive trade balance is in favour of Kazakhstan (according to the data of Kazakhstan US$1209.1 million, and according to Chinese data US$74.4 million). But in the trade relations between other Central Asian countries and China, there is a negative balance in favour of China. In 2006 goods exchange between Kyrgyzstan and China, there was a negative trade balance in favour of China (according to the data of Kyrgyzstan US$44.3 million, according to the Chinese data US$244.2 million). Trade exchange between Tajikistan and China also has negative balance with the loss of Tajikistan (according to data from Tajikistan US$63.6 million, according to data from China US$31.6 million). Analogical situation is seen in the trade exchange between Uzbekistan and China, according to the data given by Uzbekistan (US$120.8 million).

Both the Chinese as well as Central Asian sides need to make the exchange of goods between corresponding sides completely free of corruption. For this purpose it is necessary to have more active coordination of customs, statistical and other organs of the CARs and China. In spite of highly dynamic trade and economic relations between the CARs and China, China is still behind Russia so far as its import from CARs is concerned. Table 9.5 testifies to this.

This data shows that in the geographical structure of export and import of CARs, China is yet to occupy the leading position. Among the five main trade

Table 9.5 Main trade partners of CARs in percentage (2006)[a]

	Uzbekistan		Kazakhstan		Kyrgyzstan		Turkmenistan	
Export	Country	Share (%)	Country	Share (%)	Country	Share (%)	Country	Share (%)
	Russia	18.1	Russia	19.4	Russia	25.2	Netherlands	40.0
	United Kingdom	7.4	Switzerland	11.5	UAE	20.1	Turkey	16.7
	Iran	6.9	Italy	10.3	Kazakhstan	15.1	Uzbekistan	10.2
	Kazakhstan	6.7	China	10.1	Switzerland	11.9	Switzerland	8.3
	Turkey	4.1	France	3.7	China	10.0	Latvia	3.4
	Total	43.2	Total	55.0	Total	82.3	Total	78.6
Import								
	Russia	33.2	Russia	32.33	Russia	29.9	Russia	20.7
	China	17.8	China	25.9	Kazakhstan	27.9	Kazakhstan	20.7
	South Korea	9.1	Ukraine	6.1	China	18.1	Uzbekistan	16.1
	USA	7.9	Germany	5.2	Uzbekistan	11.6	China	13.7
	Germany	5.5	USA	2.9	Germany	4.4	USA	2.8
	Total	73.5	Total	72.4	Total	91.9	Total	79.2

Note
a Calculations are made on the basis of official statistical data of the CARs.

partners of Uzbekistan with regard to its imports, China has second place. In both the exports and imports of Uzbekistan, the Russian Federation occupies the first place. Since, geographically speaking, China is rather close to Uzbekistan as it is with other Central Asian countries than Russia, there are wide opportunities for China to be the leading partner of Uzbekistan in its exports, by increasing its export of gas, ferrous metal and precious metals, cotton fibre, cotton and silk yarn, cargo airliners and military equipment to China. As regards its imports, if Uzbekistan removes its limits in the way of delivery of consumer goods, China will have a favourable potential opportunity to be the first in the list of leading partners of Uzbekistan. It assumes importance as the population of Uzbekistan faces large difficulties in consumer goods supplies particularly in clothing, footware, household items, etc. at the present time.

In the structure of export of Kazakhstan, China occupies the fourth position, but in its import structure, it has the second position. However, there are opportunities for China to occupy the first position in the structure of export and import of Republic of Kazakhstan. The long common border between the two countries, favourable road-transport conditions, ethnic affinity of the population of Kazakhstan and Xinjiang create a firm basis for the accomplishment of this task.

In the list of foreign trade partners of Kyrgyzstan, in its export China occupies the fifth position, in imports the third position. It looks absurd that in terms of geographical distance, the United Arab Emirates (UAE) occupies the second position for exports from Kyrgyzstan, whereas China has the fifth position. The transportation of cargos from Kyrgyzstan to the UAE has incredible difficulties. Most probably, the presence of the UAE as the leading partner of Kyrgyzstan is explained by the wide presence of Kyrgyzstan mafia in that country. Probably, in 10–15 years, Russia and Kazakhstan will remain at the top of the list of leading countries for import by Kyrgyzstan, by exporting fuel and lubricant materials, grains, power energy (during the winter period), and also machines and technological equipment to Kyrgyzstan.

China is not present in the list of leading trade partners in the exports from Tajikistan. Tajikistan has favourable opportunity to increase its export of aluminium, cotton fibre, cotton and silk yarn, and in future electric energy to China. Astonishingly, China is not the leading trade partner of Tajikistan's import and Azerbaijan and the United States are ahead of China according to the volume of import by this country. However, on the counters of retail trade, the share of goods of Chinese origin makes up more than 70 per cent of the general volume of imported goods. There are wide opportunities for China to occupy the leading position in imports from Tajikistan. It is necessary to diversify imports, simplify visa opportunities and day and night functioning of the Khorogh–Tashkurghan highway over the Kulma pass. China can deliver to Tajikistan technological equipment for small enterprises, aggregates for micro-mini hydropower plants, equipment for wind, biological, solar, geothermal energy aggregates.

Even a superficial glance at the data of Table 9.6 shows that geographical location has no bearing on the foreign trade ties of the CARs. It is hard to imagine that between 73.8 and 92.3 per cent of exports and between 64.5 and

Table 9.6 Share of neighbouring and non-neighbouring countries in foreign trade of CARs[a]

	Neighbouring country			Non-neighbouring country		
	Export (%)	Import (%)	Total trade (%)	Export (%)	Import (%)	Total trade (%)
Kazakhstan	26.2	50.5	35.5	73.8	49.5	64.5
Kyrgyzstan	24.5	26.3	25.6	75.5	73.7	74.4
Tajikistan	7.7	20.8	15.1	92.3	79.2	84.9
Uzbekistan	13.4	10.1	11.6	86.6	89.9	88.4

Note
a Calculations are made on the basis of official statistical data of the CARs.

88.4 per cent of all foreign trade turnover of the CARs is with the countries not having common borders with Central Asia. Here it is obvious that the CARs and China, as neighbouring countries, are still far from the realization of the full potential of trade relations between them.

Kazakhstan increased export of its goods to China in the period of 1999–2006 by 6.4 times. However, during the same period export of Kazakhstan's goods to the European countries increased 7.8 times, to South Korea 6.9 times, to Mongolia 8.3 times, and to Iran 7.9 times. As regards Kazakhstan's import, during these years import from China increased 11.1 times, from European countries 4.1 times, from South Korea 5.9 times, from India 3.3 times, from Russia 5.6 times, from Iran 2.5 times, from Turkey four times. As per this data China is the leading importer from Kazakhstan. Thus, export and import relations of Kazakhstan with China develop diametrically in opposite directions, and the trend has temporary character due to delivery of Kazakhstan oil to China.[4]

In the period 1999–2005, the volume of export of goods from Kyrgyzstan to China increased 1.9 times, to India 4.1 times, to Turkey 5.2 times, to the UAE 99.3 times, to Russia 3.1 times. At the same time the volume of import from China to this country increased 6.1 times, from Russia 3.4 times, from Turkey 3.9 times, from bordering countries of CIS 3.1 times. This data also shows contradictory trends. The sharp rise in the volume of import from the UAE against the modest rate of growth of import from China is surprising, though the same consumer goods could be delivered from China at a relatively cheaper price.[5]

During the period 1999–2005, exports of Tajikistan to China grew 3.1 times, to the European countries 4.4 times, to Afghanistan seven times, to Iran 6.6 times, and to Turkey 159.4 times. At the same time imports from China increased 44.1 times, from Afghanistan 52 times, from India 4.9 times, from the UAE six times, from Iran nine times, from Turkey 39.1 times, from Russia 4.4 times, and from Azerbaijan 5.6 times. The situation looks alarming, as the growth rate of imports from China outstrips the growth rate of exports to China by 9.9 times. This multiplies the imbalance of trade between the two countries, as the structure of Tajikistan's exports is dominated by raw materials.[6]

In the period 1999–2006, export of goods from Uzbekistan to China increased six times. At the same time export to the European countries increased by 30.1 per cent, to Japan 19.4 per cent, to South Korea 15.5 per cent, to Afghanistan 29.1 per cent, to India 15.1 per cent, to Iran 12.1 times, to Turkey 5.5 times, and to Russia 2.3 times. Import from China grew 9.0 times, from European countries 19 times, from Japan it declined 2.1 times, from Russia 3.6 times.[7]

The structure of goods export from Kazakhstan is dominated by mineral resources which include hydro-carbon raw materials (61.4 per cent) and non-precious metals (23.1 per cent). In the structure of exports of Kyrgyzstan mineral resources prevail at 16.1 per cent, precious metals and precious stones 38.2 per cent, and non-precious metals 6.1 per cent. As a whole, the share of raw materials in the structure of Kyrgyz exports reaches 61.1 per cent. In the structure of exports from Tajikistan, primary aluminium and cotton fibre prevail to the tune of 71.2 per cent and 14.5 per cent respectively. The share of raw materials in the structure of Tajik exports exceeds 85 per cent. The structure of exports of Uzbekistan differs greatly from the structure of exports of other CARs as it is not dominated by raw materials. Precious metals, ferrous and non-ferrous metals in the structure of export of Uzbekistan constitute 25.5 per cent. The share of mineral resources (including energy bearing resources) in the structure of Uzbek exports reaches 16.2 per cent.[8] Side by side with Turkmenistan, this country is a large producer and exporter of natural gas. Overall, the structure of exports of CARs has raw material character.

As far as the structure of import is concerned, one can see not only remarkable difference with the structure of exports but there is also great difference between the countries of the region. In the goods structure of imports of Kazakhstan machines, equipment (including electric ones) and mechanisms prevail (26.8 per cent). It is due to the ongoing large-scale process of technical reconstruction of the real sectors of economy in Kazakhstan. This process has been going on particularly since 2000s and China has taken remarkable part in this process, including the modernization of technological equipment. During the years 1999–2005, the volume of import of machines, equipment and various mechanisms increased 4.8 times. Share of land and air transport means remains essential. The volume of their import during these years grew 3.7 times. During the last seven years, more than 60 per cent of trucks and cars and other means of public transport have been imported. Import of mineral resources (including energy ones) amount to 14.7 per cent. As a whole, import of raw resources doesn't exceed 22 per cent. Import of textiles and textile goods, footware, machinery and other goods of personal use doesn't exceed 5 per cent.

In the goods structure import of Kyrgyzstan, mineral resources (including energy bearers) prevail at 29 per cent, chemical and pharmaceutical products, fertilizers, perfume and washing soap at 12 per cent, machinery, equipment (including electrical) at 11.4 per cent, land and air transport means, their parts (7.5 per cent), food products including alcohol and alcohol free drinks, tobacco and its substitutes (8.8 per cent). In comparison with Kazakhstan, the rate of technical reconstruction remains at a low level and the country imports oil products, natural gas, food and non-food products. Share of clothing, footware and other things of personal use makes up 5.1 per cent. China takes an active part in the technical re-equipment of the economy in Kyrgyzstan as well as in the delivery of food and non-food products.

In the goods structure of import of Tajikistan chemical and associated products prevail at 26.9 per cent, mineral resources including energy bearers (20.3 per cent), leather, natural fur, saddle makers' things (14 per cent). It is necessary to note that in the structure of import of Tajikistan share of natural gas, oil products, energy, aluminium and coke is remarkable. These are largely imported from Uzbekistan, Kazakhstan and Russia. However, delivery of these goods from Uzbekistan doesn't have a stable character because of political factors. Tajikistan possesses enough resources of unexplored natural gas, raw aluminium and hydropower resources. Their prospective exploitation is connected with the cooperation and support from China. The same is true of the exploitation of deposits of a number of ferrous metals (tungsten, pewter, lead, zinc, steel drill, nickel). There are wide opportunities for import of food and non-food items from China. In the structure of import of Tajikistan, the share of machines, equipment (including electric ones) is 0.6 per cent. It is the lowest indicator as compared to other Central Asian countries. This shows that nearly 90 per cent of the main productive funds have been physically and morally exhausted. Further continuation of such a situation is risky from the position of the country's national security.

In the structure of import of Uzbekistan a determining role is played by machines and equipment (including electricity) at 32.4 per cent. The share of these goods in the import of Uzbekistan occupies the first position in Central Asia. Share of land and air transport and their parts makes up 19.3 per cent. Uzbekistan occupies the first position in the region, which is due to its carrying out of technical reconstruction of leading fields of economy. The main industrial enterprises of Uzbekistan are nearly reconstituted. Each year Uzbekistan buys locomotives and railway cars on a large scale.

In the goods structure of Uzbekistan's import, share of food products including alcohol and alcohol free drinks, tobacco and its substitutes is 7.7 per cent. And unlike other CARs, the share of mineral resources (including energy bearers) in the import of Uzbekistan is not much. This country completely supplies its economy and population with oil products, natural gas, coal and electricity out of its own production, thus ensuring the economic security of Uzbekistan. The structure of import is more rationally represented as compared to Tajikistan and Kyrgyzstan. During the last few years Uzbekistan has taken a number of protectionist measures concerning import of goods which are directed to defend its own manufacturers. Instead of consumer goods, importance is given to the import of machinery and technology required for the production of consumer goods, processing of its own agricultural produce, development of agriculture and its own infrastructure. Chinese firms can assist not only Uzbekistan but other CARs as well in the reconstruction of folk art and handicrafts industry.

It may be noted that the Central Asian population positively views the expansion of trade relations with China. According to the public poll carried out by the World Bank, 41 per cent of the population of Central Asia think that the most important partner for Central Asia is the Russian Federation. Whereas 15 per cent of the population view China to be the most important partner, 9 per cent of respondents favour their relations with the United States, 6 per cent were in favour of Iran, 6 per cent in favour of Turkey, 4 per cent in favour of European countries, 4 per cent in favour of other countries of the former USSR, 3 per cent in favour of Japan and so on. The attitude of respondents (15 per cent) concerning China being the most important trade partner of Central Asia serves as a high mark.[9] Since the Central Asian market is rapidly developing and from this point of view it is also of interest for China. The data about dynamics of this market is represented in Table 9.7.

This data shows that in Kyrgyzstan and Tajikistan the volume of import has been systematically exceeding the volume of export. At the same time in Kazakhstan, Turkmenistan and Uzbekistan the opposite picture is observed. In all Central Asian countries (except in Tajikistan) recession stopped in 1996. However, the increase of foreign trade ties began later. Volume of export by Kazakhstan began increasing in 1999 and increase in import started in 2000. In Kyrgyzstan exports began increasing in the year 2003, and in the case of Turkmenistan and Uzbekistan exports started increasing from 1999 and 2003 respectively. Some countries – Kazakhstan, Turkmenistan and Uzbekistan – follow the policy of developing exports. In other countries – Tajikistan and Kyrgyzstan – the policy of export orientation is being worked out and the trade balance continues to remain negative in their case. Negative trade balance, and also negative balance of payment can be fraught with social and political tension in corresponding societies. Such a situation has already taken place in Kyrgyzstan, which resulted in open anti-government protests by the people following which President Akaev was forced to resign. The situation in Kyrgyzstan remains tense at the present time. The potential tense situation remains in Tajikistan as well. But for the enormous transfer of remittances by the Tajik migrants working abroad, the situation could go out of control in Tajikistan.

Thus, the dynamics of foreign trade ties and co-relation of export and import together with state debt begins to exert pressure in the CARs. It is necessary for China to rationalize its foreign trade ties with the CARs, which would serve not only the basic interests of the CARs, but also the economic, social and geopolitical interests of China. The enormous and rapidly growing economy of China can be a favourable background for the effective settlement of the serious problems of socio-economic development in the CARs. China is able to provide support to the CARs concerning their foreign trade ties in the following directions:

1   balancing of foreign trade;
2   gradual lowering of raw material character of the Central Asian exports;
3   providing effective export strategy;

Table 9.7 Export and import of goods in CARs in 1997–2005 (in million US dollars)[a]

Export	1997	1998	1999	2000	2001	2002	2003	2004	2005	In % from GDP 2004
Kazakhstan	6,497	5,404	5,872	8,812	8,639	9,709	12,927	20,096	31,431	45
Kyrgyzstan	604	514	454	505	476	486	582	719	955	36
Tajikistan	746	597	682	784	652	737	797	915	1,050	42
Turkmenistan	751	593	1,187	2,505	2,555	2,710	2,949	3,144	4,620	25
Uzbekistan	4,026	3,218	2,928	2,816	2,808	2,514	3,190	4,279	5,512	44

Import	1997	1998	1999	2000	2001	2002	2003	2004	2005	In % from GDP 2004
Kazakhstan	4,301	4,257	3,655	5,040	6,446	6,584	8,409	12,781	17,115	30
Kyrgyzstan	709	841	600	554	467	587	717	941	1,020	42
Tajikistan	750	711	663	675	688	721	881	1,375	1,721	61
Turkmenistan	1,228	1,007	1,478	1,788	2,210	1,819	1,964	2,596	3,201	24
Uzbekistan	4,186	3,125	2,841	2,697	2,815	2,426	2,663	3,392	4,095	38

Note
a *Sadriyestva Nezavisimikh Gosudarstv v 2006g* (Statistical Digest of the CIS, 2006). Moscow, State ejegodnik, 2006, p. 95 (in Russian).

4   strengthening the potential of internal market and consumer goods production in the CARs;
5   transfer of new technology to CARs and assistance to raise labour productivity.

One of these tasks is directed to provide economic independence to the CARs by gradual and structural change of imports with the aim of sharp acceleration of technical re-equipment of real sectors of economy. Such a task assumes predominance, as the delivery of consumer goods has not only sharply lowered the level of competition capability of a large number of enterprises, but has stopped most of them, resulting in unemployment and social and political tension in the CARs.

Xinjiang's role in China–Central Asia trade

Xinjiang occupies a determining place among the provinces of China in its trade with the Central Asian countries. Trade between Xinjiang and the CARs is growing at a high speed. Xinjiang has direct borders with Tajikistan, Kyrgyzstan and Kazakhstan. The government of China pays great attention to the development of productive forces of Western China and the strengthening of economic ties between Xinjiang and Central Asia. Rapid development of productive forces of Xinjiang and the growing orientation of its economy on trade and economic cooperation with the CARs has already yielded results. The data of Table 9.8 testifies to this.

As a whole, during a year, trade exchange between Xinjiang and the CARs increased by 55.4 per cent, the volume of export from Xinjiang to the CARs grew by 75.7 per cent, import from the CARs by 29.3 per cent. The difference between exports and imports for Xinjiang is high enough: in 2004 it was equal to US$443.3 million, in 2005 it grew to US$1.6 billion, i.e. more than 3.3 times.[10] According to Central Asian experts such a situation needs radical change in order to achieve the balanced development of export and import. Further continuation of such tendencies can worsen the trade management between the above-mentioned countries.

Among the CARs the determining position in trade with Xinjiang belongs to Kazakhstan. In 2005, the share of Kazakhstan in trade exchange between Xinjiang and the CARs made up 84 per cent, in export from Xinjiang to the CARs 79.4 per cent and in export from the CARs to Xinjiang 90.5 per cent. In spite of high growth rate of mutual trade, the share of Turkmenistan remains insignificant. In the general volume of trade exchange between Xinjiang and the CARs, the share of Turkmenistan is only 0.22 per cent, in the volume of export from Xinjiang 0.33 per cent, and in import from Xinjiang 0.04 per cent.[11]

Mutual trade between Uzbekistan and Xinjiang has great potential for development. In Uzbekistan, the population exceeds the population of Kazakhstan by about 45 per cent. However the volume of its trade with Xinjiang in comparison with the volume of trade of Kazakhstan with Xinjiang makes up only 2.8 per cent, in export from Xinjiang 1.4 per cent, and in import from Xinjiang 4.9 per

Table 9.8 Trade between Xinjiang and CARs (in million US dollars)[a]

	2004			2005			Change in 2005 in % over 2004		
	Trade turnover	Export to Xinjiang	Import from Xinjiang	Trade turnover	Export to Xinjiang	Import from Xinjiang	Trade turnover	Export to Xinjiang	Import from Xinjiang
Kazakhstan	3,286.1	1,781.7	1,504.4	5,015.6	3,042.0	1,973.6	52.6	70.7	31.2
Kyrgyzstan	762.1	357.7	104.4	746.9	645.9	101.0	61.6	80.6	-3.3
Tajikistan	30.9	22.6	8.3	99.3	90.2	9.1	3.2	4.0	9.6
Turkmenistan	3.6	2.4	1.2	13.5	12.6	0.9	3.7	5.3	-25.0
Uzbekistan	85.8	16.5	69.3	138.3	41.5	96.8	61.2	2.5	39.7
CARs as a whole	4,168.5	2,180.9	1,687.6	6,013.6	3,832.2	2,181.4	55.4	75.7	29.3

Note
a Xinjiang Statistical Yearbook, 2006. Urumqi, 2006, pp. 501–3.

cent. As such the opportunities in trade between Uzbekistan and Xinjiang are not utilized. Such opportunities of development of trade also exist with Tajikistan and Kyrgyzstan.

In the year 2005, the volume of export of Xinjiang to Kazakhstan was 60.4 per cent of export of the whole country. Coincidently export of Xinjiang to Kyrgyzstan made up 81.4 per cent, to Tajikistan 56.6 per cent and to Uzbekistan 22.2 per cent. In the year 2010, the volume of import of Xinjiang from Kazakhstan was 72.3 per cent of the general volume of import of China from Kazakhstan. Coincidently, import of Xinjiang from Kyrgyzstan was 66.5 per cent, from Tajikistan 55.4 per cent and from Uzbekistan 11.2 per cent of the corresponding general volume of import of Chinese. The low volume of Uzbekistan in export and import with Xinjiang shows that both in export and in import of this country the determining position is occupied by Eastern and Central regions of China. It shows that the structure of export of Uzbekistan to China and import from China essentially differs from the corresponding structure of other CARs.

China is interested in getting energy resources from Central Asia with the aim of satisfying the country's needs to maintain its high rate of economic growth. Central Asia is rich in natural gas, oil and hydro-energy resources. Industrial resources of gas in CARs are 6.5 trillion cubic m. (2.8 trillion cubic m. in Turkmenistan, 1.9 trillion cubic m. in Uzbekistan and 1.8 trillion cubic m. in Kazakhstan). Reserves of natural gas in Central Asia constitute 10 per cent of the volume of gas reserves in the CIS. Whereas in the Soviet period, Uzbekistan had its highest level of gas extraction, during the past few years, Turkmenistan has become a large gas exporter in the region. These countries control more than 2 per cent of the world market of natural gas. As regards the oil reserves, Kazakhstan occupies the leading position in Central Asia. Oil deposits containing 85.1 per cent of all oil resources of Central Asia are situated in Kazakhstan. Table 9.9 shows the deposits of primary sources of energy in Central Asia.

During the last few years oil extraction in Kazakhstan is being carried out at high speed. The Chinese market is likely to swallow a considerable part of oil exported from Kazakhstan through an oil pipeline from Atasu to Xinjiang. It is planned to deliver ten million tons of oil through this pipeline annually, reaching 20 million tons in the long term. China has completely invested in the modernization of Kenkiyak oil deposit and provided a soft loan for carrying out the primary phase of construction of the pipeline.

Uzbekistan and Turkmenistan as well as Russia can become huge exporters of natural gas to China. A more effective means of reaching this aim is through the expansion of gas re-export by using the gas pipeline network of Russia. Yet at the time of the visit of the Deputy Prime Minister of China to Turkmenistan in July 2005, China expressed its high interest in the long-term delivery of energy resources from Turkmenistan. Tajikistan possesses the largest potential of hydropower resources in the CARs. Tajikistan can deliver a large amount of hydropower energy to Xinjiang. In our opinion, the speed and structure of energy consumption in Xinjiang is already moving forward towards the delivery of highly effective energy bearers from Central Asia, as is shown by Table 9.10.

Table 9.9 Deposits of primary sources of energy in Central Asia[a]

Types of primary sources	Unit	Kazakhstan	Kyrgyzstan	Tajikistan	Turkmenistan	Uzbekistan	Total
Crude oil	MTOE	1,100	5.5	1.7	75	82	1,264
Natural gas	MTOE	1,500	5	5	2,252	1,476	5,238
Coal	MTOE	24,300	580	500	small	2,851	28,231
Total	MTOE	26,900	591	507	2,327	4,409	34,734
In percent	%	77.4	1.7	1.5	6.7	12.7	100
Hydropower potential	GWt in year	27,000	163,000	317,000	2,000	15,000	524,000
	MTOE/year	2.3	14	27.3	0.2	1.3	45.1
In percent	%	5.2	31	60.5	0.4	2.9	100

Notes

MTOE means million tons of the oil equivalent; GWt/h – gig watt/hour.

a UNDP, *Central Asia Human Development Report*. Bratislava, 2005 (in Russian), p. 107.

Table 9.10 Structure of energy consumption in Xinjiang (in %)[a]

	1985	1990	1995	2000	2005
Coal	72.0	69.6	66.2	63.6	56.1
Oil	19.3	22.5	23.8	23.3	26.2
Natural gas	5.2	3.5	5.6	8.6	13.7
Renewable energy	3.6	4.4	4.4	4.5	4.0

Note
a *Xinjiang Statistical Yearbook, 2006*. Urumqi, 2006, p. 479.

This data shows that the structure of energy consumption in Xinjiang isn't effective enough both in economic and ecological terms. It needs to be changed in favour of sharp increase in the volume of natural gas and renewable energy (hydropower, solar, wind, biogas, geothermal, etc.). For the period of 1991–2005, production of coal per capita grew from 1,358 to 1,962 kg or by 44.5 per cent, production of oil products from 490 up to 1,212 kg, and production of electricity from 510 kw/hour up to 1,545 kw/hour or by 3.03 times.[12] Thus the main part of electricity was produced in oil and thermal power stations. Clearly electricity produced at hydropower plants is not only clean but is much cheaper. As such, the participation of China in the construction of huge hydropower projects in mountainous regions of Kyrgyzstan and Tajikistan with the condition of delivery of a considerable part of the produced energy to Xinjiang is advisable.

In our opinion, the investment policy of China in Central Asia must be oriented towards the creation of favourable import-oriented conditions. Investment of China needs to promote growing realization of the export potential of the region, not only to CIS or to other regions, but also for export from the CARs to China. Especially important is the question of the investment policy of China in the CARs in order to achieve balanced trade between them. It is widely believed that long-term continuance of imbalanced foreign trade in favour of import by CARs from China would cause negative influence on the national security of these countries.

In this context, the present direction of Chinese investment in the CARs has begun to follow rational and corresponding interests of these governments. In Kazakhstan, China invests considerable resources in the development of the energy and banking sectors, on the creation of new and technical reconstruction of the enterprises of food industry and production of building materials, on automobiles and so on. In Uzbekistan, China invests in the exploitation of oil deposits in Ferghana valley, modernization of the electronic industry, development of networks for the processing of agricultural raw materials, for improving and widening the irrigation network. China has directed considerable resources to the development of the banking sector in Uzbekistan during the last few years. In Kyrgyzstan, China assists to convert this country into a trans-shipping point for Chinese exporters and importers with the aim of development of their relations with Kazakhstan, Tajikistan and Uzbekistan. China thus helps Kyrgyzstan in its attempts to become the trade centre of the region. Besides, China directs its investments to exploit the hydropower resources of the country, exploitation of iron ore, tungsten and lead. China is also financing the construction of an automobile highway from Xinjiang to the CARs through Kyrgyzstan to the tune of US$1.5 billion, which will accelerate trade between Kyrgyzstan and China.

In its relations with Tajikistan, China pays special attention to the development of energy infrastructure, construction and modernization of roads of national importance and the development of the communication network. Lately, an agreement about the participation of Chinese firms in the construction of Zerafshan hydropower station was signed. Completion of the automobile road – Khorogh–Kulma–Tashkurghan – provides the opportunity to increase trade between Tajikistan and Xinjiang. Total Chinese investments in Tajikistan, according to the concluded contracts, have reached US$1,050 billion.

In economic ties between China and the CARs (in particular Xinjiang and the CARs) tourism remains nearly untouched, though both Xinjiang and the CARs possess enormous opportunities to develop this sector. Tourism can be converted into one of the profitable resources of mutual relations during the next 10–15 years. At present, export of tourist services from Xinjiang to the CARs is confined to shuttle tourism. In essence, it is shuttle trade. Small and medium private traders from the CARs arrive in Xinjiang (mainly Urumqi), make purchases and go back. Tourists from Kazakhstan, Kyrgyzstan and Tajikistan are involved in this shuttle trade. Thanks to this category of tourists, nearly all consumer goods of Chinese production are delivered to the above-mentioned countries. Uzbekistan and Turkmenistan are not involved in this shuttle tourism. Uzbekistan encourages the import of machines and equipment and restricts the import of consumer goods, but in Turkmenistan, particularly during the years of rule of Turkmenbashi, shuttle trade was oriented towards Iran and Turkey with whom this country has common borders. As far as Uzbekistan is concerned, it is necessary to develop the tourism trade here by organizing modern business-tours not only to Xinjiang but to other regions of China. For this, it is necessary to improve ties between tourist firms of Xinjiang and China with the corresponding tour-operators and businessmen of Uzbekistan. It is likely that shuttle-trade tourism will be gradually reduced in future as big private and cooperative companies will play larger role in mutual trade ties between the CARs and China. There are favourable conditions to develop wide scale non-commercial form of tourism from CARs to Xinjiang. However, the issues of existing hotels, restaurants, camping sites, automobile roads, buses, taxi parks, passenger trains, arts and crafts, concert organizations, folklore groups and so on, need to be settled.

Kazakhstan adopted the state programme on the 'Revival of historical centres of the Silk Road, maintaining and acceptable development of cultural heritage, creation of infrastructure of tourism'. In the framework of this programme, reconstruction and restoration of historical centres and architectural monuments, reconstruction and construction of automobile roads, development of folk arts and crafts and so on are being carried out. It is necessary to adopt such a programme in other countries of Central Asia. Ancient and medieval cities and settlements, monuments of history and culture of nomad civilization, religious and cultural centres on both branches of the Great Silk Road-North (steppe) and South (oases) passing through the territory of the CARs and through the territory of Xinjiang, need to be made part of regular Xinjiang international tourist fairs in Urumqi and Kashgar. Historical places in Kulja, Turfan, Hami, Kashgar, Yarkand, Khotan, etc. can be turned into pilgrimage, craftsmanship and cultural-ethnographic complexes.

There are wide opportunities for the realization of a number of other tourist projects, such as medical-sanitation. In Central Asia, such a traditional system of medicine, as Chinese, Tibetan, Mongol, Uyghur, etc. are very popular. Hundreds of thousands of people go to Xinjiang and other provinces of China annually for consultation with medical specialists of these medical systems. Besides, a stream of patients from the CARs rush to Urumqi for complicated surgery, because such services are cheaper here than in Europe, Israel and even in Russia. It is necessary to create favourable opportunities for tourists to drive along interesting routes in their cars to Xinjiang to see historical, natural monuments, and take rest at medical-sanitation establishments. The Chinese part of the Pamirs and north-eastern slopes of the Tienshan are very beautiful and suitable for mountain tourism and mountaineering. Tashkurghan can become a large base for wide scale development of these varieties of tourism. Modern road infrastructure existing in the Pamirs can attract a stream of tourists not only from the CARs but also from Russia and Europe.

Constraints in trade relations between China and the CARs

In spite of the rapid growth of trade relations between China and the CARs, especially between Xinjiang and the CARs, there are constraints connected with transport, transit, customs clearance of cargos, etc. Customs procedures in all Central Asian countries remain complicated and take a long time. Both at the border and within separate countries to facilitate movement of cargos, unofficial payment is inevitable. Border taxes are still high. Barriers in various countries of Central Asia are still different. In Kyrgyzstan and Tajikistan custom tariffs are considerably low. In Kazakhstan tariffs differ by their wide range of rate and high rates. In Uzbekistan the custom tariffs on imports are complicated. Besides, in all countries of the region tariffs are subject to frequent revision. The situation of custom tariffs is represented in Table 9.11.

Table 9.11 Custom tariffs in CARs[a]

Average	Kazakhstan	Kyrgyzstan	Tajikistan	Uzbekistan
Tariff range (%)	10.0	5.0	4.0	4.0
Maximum rate (%)	100.0	15.0	15.0	30.0

Note
a Data of official Custom Tariffs of the above-mentioned CARs.

Most of the exported goods from CARs are not subject to taxes. Custom tariffs of these countries are mainly on the imported goods. There also exist some non-tariff barriers on imported goods. In Uzbekistan the import of packed tea is banned. Imported country tea is packed at the local enterprises. In Tajikistan the import of tobacco goods and alcoholic drinks is completely licensed. In Uzbekistan the import of goods is restricted with the aim of encouraging domestic producers. The main part of imported goods of Chinese origin is brought to Uzbekistan by ways of contraband from Tajikistan, Kyrgyzstan, Kazakhstan and Afghanistan. In Uzbekistan the policy of limiting the import of consumer goods is aimed at protecting the domestic market and producers. The officials herewith refer to the need to protect local business from the illegal import of cheap products of low quality, coming from China, Iran, Turkey and other countries. Shuttle traders who bring most part of the consumer goods of Chinese origin are treated harshly. There are tough procedures of registration for shuttle traders. They have to be registered as individual proprietors at the local tax offices. Besides, they are obliged to be registered at the Ministry of Foreign Affairs as participants of foreign economic relations. Unlike other countries of Central Asia, shuttle traders in Uzbekistan must have an account in a bank, receive official licence for conducting export–import operations and retail trade. With the aim of limiting the import of consumer goods, Uzbekistan widely uses restrictive measures at border check points, situated at the Tajik–Uzbek, Kazakh–Uzbek and Kyrgyz–Uzbek borders. This is also directed to considerably limit import of consumer goods of Chinese origin.

Geographically speaking, Xinjiang occupies a special position in its relations with the CARs. It has a general extensive border with Central Asia. Between Xinjiang and the CARs there exist automobile and railway roads, built according to international standards. Transport and logistic expenditures in the structure of export and import between them will make up accordingly not more than 6 and 9 per cent. Reorientation of foreign trade of the CARs towards Xinjiang and other provinces of Western China would raise the economy of the region considerably. The largest chemical and oil processing factories, textile and leather productions are in Xinjiang. High technological industries in Urumqi will facilitate development of the CARs, so that this city becomes a continental open city with a huge port, fully serving trade with Central Asia and Russia. At present, such open border cities as Yining, Bole and Tacheng play an important role in the Central Asian trade. Kashgar is gradually becoming a large international trade centre oriented towards Kyrgyzstan, Uzbekistan, Turkmenistan, Tajikistan, Afghanistan and Pakistan.

In this connection it is necessary to pay attention to the fact that Xinjiang is a part of Greater Central Asia, including the CARs, Mongolia and Afghanistan. Among these countries Xinjiang differs by its high rate of economic, innovational, infrastructural and economic development. The high dynamics of economic development of Xinjiang are evident in Table 9.12.

This data shows that the volume of GDP in the period of 1990–2005 in Xinjiang grew 9.5 times, and per capita income by 7.3 times. Especially the processing industry grew at a high rate. During this period extracting fields increased the

Table 9.12 Dynamics of GDP in Xinjiang (100 million yuan)[a]

	1990	1995	2000	2005
Gross Domestic Product (GDP)	274	815	1,354	2,604
Primary branches of industry	95	241	288	494
Secondary branches of industry	84	284	538	1,165
Tertiary branches of industry	95	290	538	945
Transport, communication, maintenance	20	60	149	206
Trade	28	74	110	178
GDP per capita	1,799	4,701	7,372	13,108

Note
a *Xinjiang Statistical Yearbook, 2006*. Urumqi, 2006, p. 351.

volume of production 5.2 times, processing fields 13.9 times, transport, storing and communication 10.3 times, trade and public nutrition 6.4 times. This high economic development rate has taken place against the background of the general high rate of economic development of China. During this period, the volume of foreign trade ties of Xinjiang grew 19.3 times, the volume of export 15.0 times, the volume of import 38.7 times. The volume of border trade for the indicated period increased 49.1 times. The administrative centre of Xinjiang-Urumqi has become an enormous centre of foreign trade of Xinjiang. In 2005 its share in foreign trade circulation of Xinjiang was 30.1 per cent, in general volume of export 28.3 per cent, and import 33.2 per cent. In the structure of export of Xinjiang television sets, cotton yarn, packing materials, medicines, carpets, cotton fibre and so on prevail. In the structure of its import, raw oil, steel, minerals, fertilizers, cattle skin, oil products, medical equipment, timber and so on prevail.

The foreign trade of Xinjiang is mainly oriented towards Central Asia. As per estimates, in 2005 the general volume of trade between Xinjiang and the CARs was US$6,013.67 million. The volume of trade with the CARs made up 75.7 per cent of the total foreign trade of Xinjiang. Exports of Xinjiang to the CARs in 2005 reached 76 per cent, and imports from the CARs 75.1 per cent of the total volume of export and import of this Autonomous Region. Among the Central Asia trade with Xinjiang, Kazakhstan occupies the leading position. Out of 83.4 per cent of the total trade between Xinjiang and Central Asia, 79.4 per cent is the export of Xinjiang to the CARs and 90.5 per cent is the import from the CARs. The higher level of import from Kazakhstan is determined by the huge delivery of crude oil from Kazakhstan, on the basis of which the oil processing and oil chemical industry are developing at a high rate in Xinjiang. As a whole, trade between Kazakhstan and Xinjiang make up 63.1 per cent of the foreign trade of Xinjiang. Xinjiang's export to Kazakhstan is 60.3 per cent of its total exports, and its import is 68 per cent of the total imports of Xinjiang. This shows that other CARs have not yet fully used their potential of trade development with Xinjiang and with other parts of China. At the same time, the high volume of trade between Xinjiang and the CARs shows that these two economies can act as integrating and mutually beneficial economies. For further development of trade between Xinjiang and the CARs it is necessary to improve the effective work of custom organs. Custom services of the CARs have to gain experience in fast-tracking the customs clearance of truck loads waiting to clear the border control check point. Investigations by experts of the Asian Development Bank showed that the labour productivity of custom services on the frontier post Khorgos (Kazakh–Chinese border) is 12.5 times higher in comparison with the labour productivity of Tajik and Kyrgyz custom officials.

Conclusion

The directions of China's trade in the last 20 years consisted of trade of goods (80 per cent being Central Asian consumer goods). For the past few years, the volume of Chinese investments in the economy of Central Asia has been growing. Central Asian export to China is characterized mainly by delivery of raw material resources (hydrocarbons, chemical raw materials, cotton fibre, raw silk, scraps of ferrous and non-ferrous metals and so on). Oil, ferrous and non-ferrous metals are exported from Kazakhstan to China; cotton fibre, ferrous metals from Uzbekistan; cotton fiber, cotton yarn from Turkmenistan; cotton fibre, cotton yarn, silk cocoons from Tajikistan and so on.

In order to strengthen economic ties with the CARs, China pays special attention to the potential of Xinjiang carrying out huge quantitative and qualitative changes in their economy oriented towards development of ties with Central Asia. China is more and more involved not only as an important foreign trade partner of the Central Asian countries but as a huge investor. In Tajikistan, China invested more than US$600 million in construction of ETL-500 'North-South', ETL-220 'Khatlon-Lolazor', construction of the automobile road Dushanbe–Istravshan–Khujand–Chanak, construction of the auto-transport tunnel under the Shahristan pass and so on.

Until now the Central Asian countries were busy in the rehabilitation of processes and formation of market economy. Both these tasks are mainly settled. In the first stage, the issues of reform of economy, creation of market infrastructure, reconstruction of the system of state regulation of economy occupied the attention of state organs of power. Now all countries of the region look for new model of development, which would lead to dynamic structure of economic ties between China and the CARs. In the new model of economic growth serious attention is paid to regional cooperation. This also means that ties with some countries which are situated far from CARs, i.e. ties which are based on high transport expenses due to geographical factor, will be curtailed.

The processes of economic development going on in the CARs have a certain significance for China. Export-oriented development of the economy of Xinjiang is being carried out and directed towards the Central Asian region. In the CARs, Chinese goods have already occupied a firm and rather stable position. In the domestic markets of Central Asia, Chinese goods are more competitively capable than similar goods of Pakistani, Indian and Turkish origin. The price competitiveness of Chinese goods is higher in the majority of consumer goods, which has resulted in the decline in the import of such goods from other countries.

It is also necessary to note the country specialization of imported consumer goods in Central Asian markets. Iran maintains its position in a number of food products, building materials and cars; Turkey delivers footware, perfumes and cosmetics, men and ladies' clothing, some variety of office furniture. The Russian Federation maintains its position concerning agricultural machinery, locomotives and railway cars, building and sanitary technical materials, trucks and cars, technological equipments for industry and house construction, construction machinery, metallurgic steel frame works, minerals, fertilizers, chemical weed killers and pest killers, meat, dairy and fish products, and so on.

In the Central Asian market, Chinese goods compete with the goods of Russian origin as both the Chinese and Russian goods occupy various niches both according to their quality and price. Chinese goods play more important social role, as consumer goods of Chinese origin are used mainly by the low income group of the population. Russian goods are used by the middle and high income groups. However, this situation cannot go on for a long time. In the CARs, serious steps for reducing poverty are being undertaken. It means that in the structure of delivery of goods from China to the CARs, there should be gradual increase in the volume of consumer goods of higher quality with higher price; specific share of household articles for long-period usage, house and office electronic machines, scientific goods of private usage, complicated and scientific goods for improving teaching processes at schools, vocational schools, higher educational institutions has to increase; the volume of highly qualified decoration materials for house construction needs to grow; share of machinery, instruments, technological equipment imports from China has to grow.

The rapid rate of the development of economic ties between China and CARs can have a steady character and would be favourable for the socio-economic development of Central Asian countries. These ties favour rapid and effective development of western regions of China and first of all Xinjiang.

1   China will display more interest in the formation of highly developed economy of Central Asia.

2   To raise the level of economic development of the CARs, economic ties between China and CARs will develop both in qualitative and quantitative terms.

3   Economic ties between China and CARs need to be diversified. China must take measures for diversification of production and export of Central Asian countries.

4   The development of economic ties between China and the CARs will depend on the speed of carrying out of structural changes in the economy of the Central Asian countries and Xinjiang. As the economy of Xinjiang develops rapidly, it will lead to positive changes in the economic structure of Central Asian countries. The integration of the economies of these two neighbouring regions will take place not only due to interconnection but also the growth of inter-relations of the economies of Central Asia and Xinjiang.

Notes

1 B. Paramonov, A. Strokov and O. Stolpovsky, *Rossiyei Kitay v Centralnoy Azii: Politica, economica, bezopasnost* (Russia and China in Central Asia: Politics, Economics and Security). Bishkek, 2008, pp. 155 and 157.
2 Ibid.
3 Ibid.
4 Calculations are made on the base of official statistics of the Republic of Kazakhstan.
5 Calculations are made on the base of official statistics of the Republic of Kyrgyzstan.
6 Calculations are made on the base of official statistics of the Republic of Tajikistan.
7 Calculations are made on the base of official statistics of the Republic of Uzbekistan.
8 Calculations are made on the base of official statistics of the CARs.
9 See www.worldbank.org.
10 *Xinjiang Statistical Yearbook, 2006*. Urumqi, 2006.
11 Ibid.
12 Ibid.

10 Xinjiang factor in Kazakhstan–China relations

A.M. Yessengaliyeva and S.B. Kozhirova

Introduction

At the beginning of the 1990s after the adoption of the Development Strategy of China's western regions and the disintegration of the former Soviet Union, the Chinese authorities took active steps to expand trade in economic cooperation with the former Soviet republics. The latter, becoming independent states, also tried to establish political and economic relations with foreign countries, and especially with their neighbors. For a variety of geographical circumstances, the special role in these plans was assigned to China. The collapse of the Soviet Union led to the rupture of established economic ties between the former republics, regions, and even at the level of individual entities. This led to the widespread decrease in production. There was a question about the expansion of mutual trade turnover between Kazakhstan, Central Asia and China.

Mutual interest was the basis of various initiatives and practices aimed at expanding trade and economic relations between the countries of the region. Thus, in December 1992, an economic and trade agreement was signed between the governments of the Republic of Kazakhstan (RK) and the People's Republic of China (PRC), and it was followed by the signing of about 50 documents aimed at expanding this cooperation. The government of Kazakhstan provided China with customs preferential regime and goods imported from China were subject to preferential duty.

Since the mid-1990s a steady growth of trade began between the two countries. In the year 2000 the trade volume between the two countries amounted to over 1.2 billion dollars. Kazakhstan took second place among the CIS countries after Russia, thus becoming an important trading partner of China. During the negotiations at the highest level mutual interest was expressed in further enhancing economic ties and increase of trade. This approach was fully consistent with the long-term interests of both countries. The trade between the countries grew continuously, the representatives of the states met regularly and a number of agreements were signed in other business areas. China's share in foreign trade of Kazakhstan is about 6 percent. According to the official statistics, China ranked fourth in the list of trade partners of Kazakhstan.

During the visit of the Premier of the State Council Li Peng in April 1994 to Kazakhstan it was proposed to further the development of business ties and to focus on the supply of various goods in Kazakhstan directly by state producers that would allow the consumer to receive the goods, which will be more reliable in quality and cheap in price. With this statement, the Chinese government made it clear that China would go willingly to develop business cooperation on the basis of large enterprises with the participation and under the auspices of the governments of both countries.

During this visit, Li Peng signed an agreement which provided Kazakhstan with state loan of 50 million yuan and humanitarian assistance of 1.5 million yuan. Kazakhstan pledged to supply to Xinjiang 120,000 tons of iron ore worth about US$4 million and 60,000 tons of chemical fertilizer in exchange for Chinese textiles. Prospects for cooperation in the field of construction, production of construction materials, joint production of television sets were also discussed. Nevertheless, 91 percent of Kazakhstan's export to China accounts for commodities and strategic goods, one of the main product groups of Kazakhstan's export to China being ferrous metals (54 percent). In 2003, more than one million tons of ferrous and steel products were sent to China.[1] China continues to buy Kazakh rolled steel products due to its low cost. An agreement was signed between Ispat Karmet (Kazakhstan) and Computer Product Corporation (Guangdong Province) and JV Huante (Xinjiang Uyghur Autonomous Region) on the organization of the service center in Urumqi for processing, packing, sorting ferrous and upgrading its quality to international standards. Other important product groups of Kazakhstan's exports to China are: copper (9 percent), aluminum (11 percent), fertilizers (2 percent), cotton (0.5 percent) and wool (0.7 percent).[2] In 2004 in the structure of trade turnover iron and steel took the first place. According to economists' forecasts in the short term the export of Kazakh grain to China can be increased significantly.

China's export to Kazakhstan comprises mainly consumer goods. The structure of Kazakhstan's import from China in recent years has remained largely unchanged. It is based on consumer goods and food products, which together exceed 80 percent of Kazakhstan's import from China. Since 2002, the structure of import has changed and these include nuclear reactors and electrical equipment.

In the year 2000, the trade volume between the two countries amounted to US$1.9 billion, showing an increase of 80 percent against 1999. In 2004 the trade turnover between the two countries rose to US$2.7 billion.[3] Ten years later, in 2013, these figures increased by 11.3 percent to reach US$28 billion.

Present situation in Xinjiang

It is impossible to predict and evaluate the actual prospects of relations between China and Central Asia without an analysis of the situation in Xinjiang, which plays an important role both in Chinese and international economy. The region has experienced three waves of modernization during the "Great Leap Forward" and the Cultural Revolution during the reforms of the 1980s. In the planning of economic development of China, priority was always given to coastal provinces, and it was only in the eighth five-year plan (1991–5), that Xinjiang received a special status. Chinese economists believe that this is connected with plans to turn Xinjiang into a launching pad for Chinese penetration into Central Asia and the Middle East. However, it is believed that Xinjiang is experiencing more complex processes leading to its integration into the new international economic structures. China's economic strategy was primarily based on the development of the coastal provinces and their integration in the Asia-Pacific region, the so-called "Great international ring." At the end of the 1980s, Chinese strategy began to shift to new goals: the so-called "Great Northeast Asian Ring" (Russian Far East, Japan, Korea) and "The Great Islamic Ring" (Central Asia and the Middle East). Taking into consideration the fact that the South China Economic Ring (Hong Kong, Taiwan and Fujian Province and Guangdong) has already been built up, China is now setting up impact zones around its borders and its subordinate economic areas.

Xinjiang occupies a more prominent place in the economic and foreign trade policies of China. The region operates the formula of the "double openness" – internal and external. This means that Xinjiang remains a raw material supplier for the coastal areas, but on the other hand, it is involved in economic relations with Central Asia and according to the Chinese strategists through Central Asia with the Great Islamic Ring. New economic doctrine aimed at eliminating the imbalance in the development of coastal and inland areas was clearly formulated in the spring session of the National Assembly in 1988. Experts noted the discrepancy between the potential resources of Xinjiang and its industrialization degree.[4]

Prior to the beginning of the economic reform, special features of Xinjiang economy were the disproportion in the growth of industries, low development of Xinjiang, poor transport and communications network, technical and technological backwardness. In 1998 Xinjiang had 8,500 enterprises including 205 large and 13 medium ones. The value of their gross output was 58 percent of the total gross output value of industry and agriculture. In 1999 the share of state-owned enterprises accounted for 68.4 percent. In Xinjiang production structure the leading place belongs to three major industries: petroleum, chemical and light industries which lead to the development of other service and supporting industries. They provide Xinjiang's economic development strategy and the concept of creating a new open zone in the north. First place is the oil industry – 21.5 percent, followed by metallurgical, chemical and leather industries. Since 1949, China's investment policy was aimed at the development of heavy industry, as the basis of PRC export. Currently, the priorities have changed, and the leadership of the PRC provides comprehensive support to the development of light industry. The investment increase in heavy industry is lower as compared with light industry, though it still remains the priority. Power, mechanical and food industries are economically backward. Attempts are being made to increase industrial production in the field of power, the gold sector, and oil and metal industries.

However, the main place in the structure of the emerging national economy of Xinjiang is taken by the light industry. Xinjiang houses 38 types of light industry as against 44 types in China. Xinjiang has about 1,500 specialized light industry enterprises, including 33 large and medium size industries. Thus, one can say that the basis of regional economic complex is set up in Xinjiang. Xinjiang firmly occupies a market niche for some types of industrial products in the regional markets of the leading countries.

Xinjiang government adopted a special resolution on enhancing cross-border trade, creating special economic zones (SEZs) and other border crossings with Kazakhstan, Kyrgyzstan and Tajikistan. As for the SEZ, the central authorities have given Xinjiang all rights and privileges which are prevalent in similar zones established in other parts of China. The local authorities of Xinjiang took advantage of these rights and privileges and used in its relations with foreign investors and trade partners including the former Soviet republics.

In accordance with the concept of SEZs adopted in China, which takes into account economic factors and political considerations, and includes industrial parks, tourist areas, transportation hubs and other commercial activities and educational centers, all this provides not only joint industrial production facilities, construction of infrastructure facilities, tourist centers, professional training, etc., but also uses the advantages of cross-border economic ties for free flow of goods, services, assets and people.

Xinjiang belongs to the fourth economic zone. At the plenum of the CPC Central Committee in 1999 Jiang Zemin said that in the twenty-first century, Xinjiang will be one of the main vectors of strategic development of China. Therefore, there is a process of enhanced integration with other areas in the form of investment projects, inland laying of oil and gas pipelines and annually increasing trade relations in the region with Central Asian countries and the creation of new projects on energy security of China.

Economic relations between Kazakhstan and China's Xinjiang

Using the expertise and interest of both parties, as detailed in various documents, government organizations and private entrepreneurs have begun to actively develop these relationships. According to Chinese statistics, in early 1993, there were 95 joint ventures with foreign capital in China and Central Asian countries, and in 1994 the number increased to 453. In Kazakhstan this number increased from 57 to 313. The authorities have taken a number of measures to tighten the requirements for the registration of enterprises with foreign capital participation. As a result, in Kazakhstan, the number of Chinese–Kazakh joint ventures has decreased from 380 in the second half of 1995 to 73. In 1997, the five Central Asian republics had 115 joint ventures with Xinjiang Uygur Autonomous Region with the capital of about US$18 million, accounting for 74 percent of total investment by Xinjiang abroad. In their turn, the Central Asian republics established 22 companies (both mixed and fully foreign) in Xinjiang with a total invested capital of about US$9 million.[5]

One of the new forms of China's foreign trade with Central Asia is "shopping tourism" or "shuttle trade." Kazakhstan and Xinjiang signed the agreement on "shopping tourism" on July 31, 1991 in the city of Kuldzha, which stipulated that the payments are to be carried out only in a freely convertible currency. The volume of export-import operations in the cross-border trade with Xinjiang for the period from 1991 to 1997 amounted to US$3.68 billion.[6]

The city of Yining became one of the first trade centers in Xinjiang, located near the state border. Since 1991, hundreds of "shuttle traders" rushed here every day from both sides of the border. Monthly turnover here exceeded US$200,000. In 1992, when the State Council introduced special rights for this city to conduct foreign trade, there was a new surge in the activities of "shuttle traders." According to the estimates of Chinese economists, "shuttle trade" between China and Kazakhstan in 1996 amounted to US$200–300 million.[7]

In 1993, China and Kazakhstan introduced a visa regime for the citizens of the two countries, which adversely affected the "shuttle trade." Xinjiang and the Central Asian countries saw a positive role of "shuttle trade" (such as supply of the population with consumer goods, help in solving the problems of employment, replenish the coffers with customs duty, etc.). In this connection, in January 1997, Kazakhstan adopted a resolution aimed at alleviating the situation of "shuttle traders," freeing them from the payment of customs duties and taxes on importing goods weighing up to 70 pounds and costing up to US$2,000.

In 1995, in the district of Ili – the border crossing zone of Dulaty – Kolzhat free visit markets were opened for the residents living on both sides of the border. More than 50,000 people visited these markets within a period of five months and goods worth 120 million yuan were sold. Another example is the city of Khorgos. Khorgos border market occupies 30,000 square meters and daily volume of commercial transactions only in Chinese goods amounts to 400,000 yuan. Such free trade zones cater to transport services like railways or highways leading to the border. By the end of 1994 there were 58 open cities and counties that exceed two-thirds of their total number in Xinjiang. Since 1994 development zones of cross-border cooperation supported by various public policy benefits were functional in Xinjiang.

An important element in the development of trade relations in the region is the cross-border trade, especially at the initial stage of their development. This also relates to the fact that in Xinjiang there are ten national districts, 33 counties and cities comprising up to 60 percent of the district population that are situated on the border. In 1992 the CPC Central Committee and the State Council adopted a decision of an openness policy which started a new stage in the development of cross-border trade in Xinjiang: the trade volume totaled US$320 million, while the corresponding proportion rose to 42.7 percent.[8]

According to Xinjiang specialists, cross-border trade has made an important contribution to ensuring political stability and economic development of Xinjiang. The highest revenues from cross-border trade in the form of taxes and customs duties were in 1998, amounting to US$1.148 billion.[9]

Industrial enterprises created during this period with the participation of the PRC were characterized by small-sized invested capital and the number of employed workers as well as the use of relatively backward technology. Shops, restaurants, shipping and transport companies, etc. prevailed among these enterprises.

Due to the low quality of Chinese goods, there was public discontent in late 1993 over such economic cooperation with China. The mass media wrote about it and not only the press, but the official sources also claimed it. Being afraid of losing a promising market, Beijing took a series of measures to improve the situation. The PRC adopted a special law banning the production, import and export of low quality and fake goods, and also introduced penalties. Although this measure led to a reduction in trade for a while, it got positive response in the Central Asian countries. China's trade partners displayed a dissatisfaction that they were cut off from the central and eastern regions of China, where the export industry had reached Western standards, besides the weak participation of leading well-known Chinese companies in developing ties with regions.

Difficulties that Xinjiang and other provinces of northwestern China encountered in the quest to develop economic ties with Central Asian countries not to mention Europe, prompted Beijing authorities to develop a new strategic program for the western areas of the country. In 1999 the State Council decided to start the implementation of the program for the development of the central and western regions of China, and an Administrative Office was established to ensure the implementation of this program.

The reasons for the Chinese leadership to take such large-scale program were primarily related to address domestic problems, such as the elimination of the gap in economic and cultural development of the coastal and inner regions of the PRC. According to the developers of the program, the development of the western regions would provide a powerful stimulus for the expansion of market demand. Industrial development of western parts of the country would boost inflow of workforce to these regions that could ease the problem of unemployment in the country as a whole. The development of these areas would also lead to the growth of the living standards of the local population as minorities live compactly that would allow to reduce social tensions and ease the threat of separatism existing there. However, the development of the western areas of the program is closely linked with the strategy of the development of economic relations with foreign countries, as it envisages not only the involvement of foreign investment in these areas, but also the use of their geographical proximity to such regions as Central and South Asia, Southeast Asia for further expansion of China's foreign markets.

At its meeting in January 2000 the State Council took a decision on the "big development of the West," and this concept was approved by the third session of the 9th National People's Congress held in March 2000. The newly adopted concept of the "big development of the west" was unique. But unlike the previous years' concepts of the "west development," this concept had a unique character focused mainly on the economic development of the region. Its singularity was in the scale of prospective changes. The main task was not only to improve the development of the "western parts" of the country, but also to set up such economic environment that would allow them to continue the growth without large-scale support from the center. Consequently, these regions could be "supporting points" and produce any type of goods in nationwide scale.[10]

China's economic strategy fully applies to Xinjiang, as it specifies measures in the development of China–Central Asian economic relations. Taking into consideration the long-term program (2000–50) one should not expect any sudden changes in the economic policy of China in Kazakhstan in the near future. The priorities of the strategy development are to deepen the reform, improve management, enhance the districts' competitiveness and construct infrastructure financed by the state. The expansion of China's economic presence will increase gradually with the implementation of the changes in northwest China and the growth of economic power in the region and the country as a whole.

It is obvious that the "big development" of China's western regions will have an impact on neighboring states. And the main issue is what impact this will have and the extent of the impact on the security of the Central Asian region in general and for Kazakhstan in particular. The most important goals are to impart Xinjiang the status of a "land bridge" between Asia and Europe and turn the area into the main base for export with neighboring countries.

The PRC government, focusing on the development of Xinjiang in the context of the overall strategy of the development of the western regions (2001–5), invested about US$8.5 billion in its economy. As the situation is changing in Central Asia, Xinjiang's importance has increased in strengthening territorial integrity and national security of China. In this respect the Head of Xinjiang Administration was introduced to China's Politburo at the 16th Congress for the first time in the history of China. In addition, it was decided to include the candidate member of the Central Committee from Xinjiang Askhat Kerimbay (Kazakh by nationality) in the CPC Central Committee.

Nur Bakri, the regional governor, stated that, "Xinjiang will retain its openness to Central Asia and Europe and take the opportunity to contribute to the development of economic zones of the Silk Road." The "Silk Road Economic Zone" agreement was signed in November 2013 by the representatives of 24 cities in eight countries along the Silk Road. It aims to promote cooperation, development and prosperity of these countries. Xinjiang will promote the creation of a free trade zone with the countries along the Silk Route and strengthen multilateral cooperation in agriculture, energy, tourism and culture. At the same time, Xinjiang, according to Nur Bekri, will preserve open access to its domestic market and will prepare for the transfer of production from the eastern regions to the west.

The share of Xinjiang accounts for more than 75 percent of trade turnover between Kazakhstan and China. The volume of trade between Kazakhstan and Xinjiang in a short period increased several times. In 2007, this figure reached US$9.2 billion, and in 2008, US$12.24 billion.[11] The volume of trade between Xinjiang and Kazakhstan as of year-end 2012 increased by 10.3 percent and amounted to US$11 billion. The export from Xinjiang compared to the same period of the previous year increased by 15 percent, while import to Xinjiang decreased by 2.8 percent.

China's Vice Minister of Commerce Jiang Yaopin declared that "China is now the largest trading partner of Kazakhstan and Turkmenistan, as well as among the top three trading partners of Kyrgyzstan, Tajikistan and Uzbekistan." His words are quoted in the report of "Kazinform." In 2012, China's export to Central Asia accounted for only 1 percent, this region absorbed at least 83 percent of the export volume of Xinjiang region and 52 percent of its exports was sent to Kazakhstan.

The concept of the Silk Road economic zone was put forward by President Xi Jinping during his speech at Nazarbayev University in Astana, during his first state visit to Kazakhstan. According to the Chinese leader, for the benefit of the people and the structural development of the regional cooperation, first, it is required to strengthen political contacts, develop transport communications, ensure steady trade, strengthen the sphere of money circulation and also promote closer relations among the people of the regions. Experts believe that the establishment of the Silk Road economic corridor will unite the markets with three billion customers and provide new impulse for comprehensive economic cooperation in Eurasia.[12]

China's Silk Road super-project started with the organization of Chinese language centers in Russia, Kazakhstan, Kyrgyzstan, Tajikistan and Uzbekistan. Training base for the specialists of the former Soviet republics is located in the northwest of China including the Xinjiang Uygur Autonomous Region. Here China creates a "strategic pool of talented people in various fields" for the economic zone of the Silk Road.

According to the statistics, almost 90 percent of students in the Xinjiang Uyghur Autonomous Region are the citizens of Central Asian countries and other neighboring countries. During the last seven years more than 2,200 international students, over 60 percent of them being the citizens of the countries of the former USSR, studied in Gansu Province at Lanzhou University. Beijing's new policy on the development of northwest China includes the involvement of Xinjiang Uyghur Autonomous Region in the training of specialists for Russia and Central Asia. The Chinese claim that the Caucasian countries such as Armenia, Azerbaijan and Georgia have already been included in their integration plan. According to the official edition of the *People's Daily Newspaper*, the Caucasian countries hope that China's strategy in Central Asia will be able to reach out to the Caucasus. Universities of northwestern China are major sources of Chinese language and culture in Central Asia. Lanzhou University is one of ten universities in China authorized to promote the teaching of Chinese language in neighboring countries. The first Confucius Institute in Central Asia was opened in Uzbekistan in 2005 with the support of Lanzhou University. According to the Office of the State Steering Group for the expansion of the Chinese language abroad (Hanban) ten Confucius Institutes and 12 Confucius classrooms were opened in 2013 in Kazakhstan, Kyrgyzstan, Tajikistan and Uzbekistan. They trained about 23,000 students.[13]

Conclusion

Wang Weizhou, the specialist at the Shanghai Institute for International Studies, in his article highlights that the collapse of the USSR and the formation of independent Kazakhstan, Uzbekistan, Kyrgyzstan and Tajikistan have been very beneficial for China. First, because it significantly reduced direct territorial border contact between China and Russia, and three new Central Asian states set up a kind of safety pool that separates China from Russia on the 3,700-kilometer border. Wang Weizhou emphasizes that Russian pressure was reduced and consequently the Western influence on China.[14] Second, China can take advantage of the potential confrontation between Russia and the Central Asian countries, as for Beijing the use of the contradictions could help to develop China's relations with both sides. Such a situation is beneficial for China as it provides the best safety conditions and China gets "good environment to enter the Central and West Asian markets" and it can accelerate the reforms in western China (especially in Xinjiang). One can conclude that the Chinese strategy of "great international rings" and "great western development programme" are aimed at strengthening the role of the border areas in external integration with a view to stabilizing and increasing the economic power and influence of China, and in such Xinjiang factors importantly.

Notes

1 *Brief Statistical Yearbook of Kazakhstan, 2005*. Almaty, 2005, p. 158.
2 Ibid.
3 Ibid.
4 M.T. Laumulin, *Kazakhstan in Contemporary International Relations: Security, Geopolitics, Political Science*. Almaty, 2000, p. 359.
5 www.china.org.cn/russian/Sheng Xue. "China: Problem Areas. Xinjiang, Taiwan, Tibet," p. 56.
6 R. Rakhimov, "Integration Prospects of the PRC." *Sayasat*, 2004, No. 3, pp. 6–11.
7 Ibid.
8 K.L. Syroezhkin, "Some Results of the Reforms in Xinjiang and Kazakhstan." In *Russia and Central Asia: Migration and Security*. Barnaul, 2002, pp. 54–69.
9 I. Azovsky, "China and the Central Asian Countries: Economic Relations." *East*, 2005, No. 2, pp. 106–15.
10 K.L. Syroezhkin, *Problems of Modern China and Security in Central Asia*. Almaty, 2006, p. 110.
11 www.cc-sauran.kz-rubriki/economika/41-kazakhstan.
12 Zonakz, net-articles/75990: www.ami-tass.rureview/poleznye-stati/pekin-nachinaet.
13 "China in World and Regional Politics: History and Modernity." *Information Herald IFE*, No. 5. Moscow, 2005.
14 "Chinese Political Scientists about the Situation in CIS (Materials of Foreign Press)." *Express Information*, No. 3. Moscow, 2008.

11 Cross-border interaction between Xinjiang and South Siberia in Central Asia

The 'Big Altai' approach

Evgeny Vodichev

For a long time the historical development of the Russian empire and later the Soviet Union was connected with the growing role of the Asian direction in the Russian policy. The country was looking for new lands in Asia: in the east – in the Urals, in Siberia and the Far East, as well as in the south. These are the territories which previously were integral components of the Russian empire and then its successor, the USSR, but are now represented by independent Central Asian Republics. According to the approach widespread in Russian historiography, the contribution of Asiatic Russia to the development of the Russian state was enormous and multi-dimensional. Since the risks involved in the penetration of Russia into Asian territories were great, it did not manage to colonize in full. Even comparing gains and losses, achievements and prices paid for them makes considering Asiatic Russia not just as a fragment of the Russian state but as an important basis of national development.[1]

Territorial expansion into Asia was caused by objective factors rooted in the development strategy of a continental empire. However, this expansion led to a historical paradox. In many cases, when the Russian state was attempting to position itself as a European power, economic and geopolitical justification for this role was found in the east, in Asia. It seemed that in the east, and partially in the south, the country might obtain practically unlimited natural resources and geopolitical space. These territories provided with good possibilities for economic and political innovations, as due to specifics of colonization Asian regions were not burdened by traditional forms of Russian economy.

However, being global international actors, Imperial Russia and the former USSR tended to impose their socio-economic matrixes upon the colonized territories. In Asia, they tried to re-design a new socio-economic and socio-cultural milieu in an order acceptable for the national heartland. Russian continental empire both in its historical form and in a modernized form (the former USSR) behaved as a provider of the established economic and social order. It tried to obtain as much territories as it could, and also involve as many neighbours in its economic and political orbit as was possible. Doing that, it constructed new space which might well have agreed with the political ambitions of Russia but not with the socio-cultural environment.[2]

Central Asia in pre-Soviet, Soviet and post-Soviet connotations

In the twentieth century Soviet efforts to design and build a new space were specifically indicative in Asia. These processes got their reflection in terminology which received clear ideological meaning. Up to the beginning of 1990s, the category 'Central Asia' was rarely used in Russian history, geography and economics when applied to the territories belonging to the Russian empire and later to the Soviet Union. It is worth mentioning that by the beginning of the twentieth century all these territories were often addressed as Siberia, together with 'genuine' Siberian territories, the lands stretching from the Ural Mountains to Lake Baikal. Instead, in the Soviet epoch, especially since 1930s, the southern republics of the USSR with the exception of Caucasus have been attributed as 'Middle Asia and Kazakhstan' that contradicted the worldwide use of the term 'Middle Asia'. However, it could not change the objective reality: after going east and south the Russian state penetrated Central Asia and received some Central Asian 'essence' in return.

There were two reasons for this terminology game. On the one hand, in official historiography there was a tendency to draw a dividing line between the Soviet Republics belonging to the USSR, and those Central Asian territories which were not incorporated into the Soviet Union, such as, for example, Mongolia and Xinjiang. Thus, this terminology innovation was driven by political reasons. On the other hand, new approaches to economic and geographical division of the country were elaborated and accepted in social science. They divided the Central Asian part of the USSR into two big regions – Middle Asian economic rayon and Kazakhstan as separate economic entities. Simultaneously, the Urals economic rayon, West-Siberian, East-Siberian and Far-Eastern economic rayons were set up in Asiatic Russia. Evidently, only two of these territories were formally attributed as belonging to Siberia.

After the collapse of USSR in 1991, the term 'Middle Asia and Kazakhstan' rapidly disappeared from scholarly use and was substituted by the category 'Central Asia'. As previously, the reasons were mostly political. Former Soviet republics and now new independent states were eager to demonstrate their break with the Soviet past and return to their historical motherland – Central Asia. Another reason is rooted in the desire of these states to find new approaches for self-positioning in a modified system of international relations.

Today Central Asia is one of the most dynamic regions of the world which attracts the attention of all key geopolitical actors. High interest in Central Asia is explained by its strategic importance, growing economic meaning and provisions for international security and stability in one of the most turbulent parts of the world. It gives rise to new concepts of geopolitical design of the region. In parallel, new approaches are paving the way in terminology to describe changing reality. It may be pointed out that many of them are in fact 'new-old' approaches. For example, in the 1970s UNESCO initiated a huge cultural project referring to Central Asia. Understanding of the term 'Central Asia' established within the framework of this project, in geographical terms embraced territories of Mongolia, Xinjiang and Tibet in China, northeast of Iran, Afghanistan, Pakistan, some northern states of India, as well as Soviet (at that time) republics of Central Asia, Kazakhstan and southern part of the eastern regions of Russia.[3]

After 1991 the issue of borders of Central Asia as a geographical and cultural phenomenon and as a mega-region received specific importance in connection with changes on the political map of the world. Such factors as weight of some countries in the system of international relations, and struggle for influence over specific countries carried out by leading world and regional powers started to play a decisive role when impacting connotations. In other words, the category 'Central Asia' received an important geopolitical meaning. A connotation of the 'Greater Central Asia' was designed in American political science. Simultaneously, historical, political and philosophy discourse referring to the sense and borders of Central Asia as a scholarly connotation received a new push.

It is interesting to mention that two variants of translation of this term from English into Russian immediately appeared in the scientific literature – as 'Great Central Asia' emphasizing the importance of the region and its role in the world policy, and as 'Big Central Asia' as a mega-region with geographical and cultural specifics. According to the approach shared by many specialists, in this sense Central Asia incorporated north of Iran, Afghanistan, Xinjiang, Mongolia, five former Soviet and now independent Central Asian Republics, including Kazakhstan, as well as south of Siberia and Volga region in the Russian Federation.[4] Meanwhile, a more traditional and narrower connotation of Central Asia, which incorporates just Kazakhstan, Kyrgyzstan, Uzbekistan, Tajikistan, Turkmenistan and Afghanistan, still dominates in the Russian historiography and is presented as 'Minor Central Asia'. There is also the term 'Post-Soviet Central Asia' referring to former Soviet republics.

As a rule, the choice of connotations of Central Asia is determined by the assessment of processes ongoing in the region. One dimension lies in the classical triangle (Russia–China–Mongolia) that is used as a background for analysis of different civilization platforms which impact interactions in Central Asia. According to another dimension, the starting point for analysis depends on former belonging (or not belonging) to the territories of the Russian empire and then of the USSR. Respectively, most of the development there is interpreted through the prism of Russian (until 1917) and Soviet (up to 1991) impact.[5]

Connotations become methodology

It may be underlined that despite the variety of approaches, modern connotations do not draw an unbreakable line between Siberia, Xinjiang and Central Asia. While there is no historiography tradition of studying these regions together, new theoretical approaches are based on understanding of common entity on these regions as an integrated, multi-dimensional and multi-sided geographical, economic and socio-cultural thesaurus. Such interpretation brings us to the necessity of complex analysis of processes that took place in the past and are ongoing at the moment on trans-border territories of Central Asia. It also stipulates new researches with such interpretations of Siberia where this region is not seen as a 'random appendage' of Europe-oriented Russia, but represented as a part of the integrative Central Asian economic, geopolitical and socio-cultural space.

New connotations require updated methodology. According to such approach, Siberia is to be seen as a territory which embodies the Central Asian dimension of Russia. The south of Siberia is not considered as just a bridge to Central Asia any more: in many important respects it is Central Asia, both geographically and historically. In fact this is a reflection of the two-faced character of the Russian state – a country with mostly European facade and Asia backyard. Or vice versa, depending on the expert assessment of Russia's role in the world game. However, balancing interests in 'civilizationally' different parts of the world is not an easy task. For doing it, the country needs special 'moderators and facilitators', which, however, are to be found inside, not outside, the country.

One of the territories that claims to be such a moderator is the Altai region – a geographically unique territory that borders China (Xinjiang), Mongolia and Kazakhstan, the countries belonging in full or in parts to Central Asia. Historically and culturally Altai as a segment of South Siberia is a northern border of Central Asia itself, which, together with its surroundings including the scientifically and technologically sophisticated Novosibirsk and Tomsk and the industrially developed Omsk and Kuzbass area, can moderate and facilitate Russian contacts with Central Asia.

What should be mentioned in this connection is that Xinjiang in principle can play the same role for China, being its interface to Central Asia as well. For Kazakhstan and Mongolia the integrative functions of 'their Altais' are more organic as these two countries belong to Central Asia. It places the whole territory of Altai in a very special position of a bearer of specific identity as an integrator of different Central Asian cultures and traditions connected with Russia (Siberia), Kazakhstan, Mongolia and Xinjiang.

Collision of Russia's policy in Central Asia

It is not surprising that after the collapse of USSR and opening of the country to the global world, different ideas referring to utilization of these unique qualities of Altai for the benefit of the country and the region itself spread out across the academic milieu and among regional policy-makers. In Russia they were connected with the idea of new transport corridors based on connecting Asia (China) and Europe with a new highway and railroad to be built across the Altai Mountains.

The projects, however, were placed on hold. While quite a lot of construction has been made on the Chinese and Kazakhstan (an automobile road from the town of Ridder to the city of Gorno-Altaisk in Russia) territories, no real step forward was made on the Russian territory. The formal explanations are lack of appropriate funding in the federal and regional budgets for implementing these projects (which are very expensive due to very complex geographic and geological conditions) and environmental sensitivity of the road construction in the ecologically safe zone. Meanwhile, real explanations are to be looked for in the overall system of international relations of Russia in 1990s. Our assumption is that these are rooted in a lack of clarity in Russian geopolitical perceptions in this part of the world, if not in the lack of concept itself.

After the collapse of USSR because of political chaos and sharp economic crisis in the country, Russia lost Central Asia in about all possible respects – ideologically, politically and economically. In the beginning of 1990s Russia selected a Europe-centric focus in its international politics and proclaimed 'a drift to the West'. These accents on primarily, if not exclusively, the European identity of Russia together with economic and strategic weaknesses of the country entailed passive character of Russian policy in Central Asia in the beginning and middle of that decade.

In addition to that, within the framework of the 'empire type of thinking', Soviets traditionally considered Central Asia as a space for 'civilizing'. Within this paradigm, it is not a surprise that post-Soviet reformers used European identity as a cause for breaking with Central Asia, although such policy has never been made officially open to the general public. But the views according to which Central Asia was considered a burden for Russia, an obstacle for its return to the core of the European civilization, were rather widespread in some intellectual circles and impacted policy-making process. It should also be noted that to a certain extent such ideas touched upon Siberia as well, since these were connected with conservation of the traditional semi-colonial policy of central authorities regarding this part of the country.

On the other side, in the Russian policy of 1990s perceptions about 'objective' background for reintegration of Central Asia if not into the framework of one state with Russia but at least as highly integrated economic and political space were rather popular in political and intellectual discourse. Conclusions that result from such debate were the following: why should Russia articulate its policy in Central Asia as a priority if anyway Central Asian states would need to set up close economic and political relations with Russia?

As a result, for several years Russia forgot about its former 'south belt' which was not considered a priority area of its foreign policy any more. The country just reacted on what was going on in the region and did not try to effectively forecast and contribute to impacting political and economic processes in Central Asia. Up to the second half of 1990s, the Russian Federation did not have clear strategies focused on Central Asia, either on national or on regional levels. The attempt to formulate this kind of regional policy towards the Altai region was not supported at Russia's federal level at that time.

The niche opened by the collapsed Soviet Union was effectively filled in by its geopolitical rival, China.[6] Contrary to Russia, China specifically concentrated on former Soviet Central Asia. Initially, China was oriented towards maintaining equally good and balanced relations with all the five Central Asian Newly Independent States (CA NIS). Later necessity of making prioritization was realized, and major accents in the Chinese foreign policy were made on the countries with a common border, first of all on relations with Kazakhstan. Presumably, Chinese policy in this region was driven by its economic interests, preventing threats of terrorism and instability in its own Central Asian outskirts (Xinjiang), and efforts of the Western countries to reach a strategic dominance in the CA NIS region. Its attempts to accelerate cooperation with Kazakhstan met with success, and China managed to establish a strong presence in the whole of post-Soviet Central Asia.

By the end of 1990s, the attitude of the Russian Federation to the CA NIS region substantially changed. By that time Russia's relations with the West started deteriorating and brought disappointment in the possibilities of having close alliance with Western countries. That happened under the impact of the conflict in Chechnya, expansion of NATO to the East, and crisis in Kosovo in 1999. The change of strategy resulted in the formulation of more balanced international politics, and re-emergence of Russian interests in its traditional areas of influence in Central Asia. As a result, Central Asia reappeared as a sphere of Russian vital interests, and Kazakhstan took the lead in the list of new priority areas. Relations with Kazakhstan began to be considered as specifically important for Russian politics in the CA NIS region.

Trans-border cooperation across the Altai Mountains

If geopolitical perspectives of Russia are conceived not just as they are seen from Moscow but also from Siberia, regional integration of Siberia into the ongoing processes in Central Asia is seen as relevant and appropriate. While setting up a solid platform for cooperation on the state-to-state level takes time, trans-border (or frontier) region's trade demonstrated a good pace of development in the form of trans-border cooperation. Basically, trans-border cooperation is seen as a new type of interaction and integrative tendency. For Russia much of this cooperation concentrated in the Central Asian triangle is represented by the Altai region. It should be admitted that, historically, frontier cooperation on this territory was stimulated by the very effective engagement of Xinjiang Uyghur Autonomous Region of China (XUAR) and also by Kazakhstan. Russian (Siberian) regions initially lagged behind their neighbours.

Since the beginning of the 1990s Xinjiang has been carrying out a proactive policy in connection with frontier cooperation. In Urumqi – the centre of Xinjiang – some 60 per cent of gross domestic product (GDP) is produced in the services sector, represented mostly by trade. For the last 15 years Urumqi transformed into a huge logistical centre which now performs a function of distributing Chinese goods across the countries of Central Asia, to Russia and further to Europe. The annual rate of increase of the trade turnover in Urumqi in recent years is about 70 per cent. About three-quarters of its external trade is represented by the trade operations in the frontier regions. Most of the goods exported from Urumqi (about 75 per cent) are represented by clothing and footwear. It is worth mentioning that 90 per cent of these goods are produced not in Urumqi but in the inner China. It means that in reality Urumqi operates as a western gate of China, and this is a specifically designed accent in its economic policy.

Xinjiang effectively carries out Chinese trade and economic expansion in the countries of Central Asia. Its key partner is Kazakhstan, as their turnover increases by 100 per cent annually and currently reached 80 per cent of all international trade operations of Xinjiang. The major expectations are connected with importing oil by using a new oil pipeline from Kazakhstan to Xinjiang. In contrast to Xinjiang–Kazakhstan cooperation, turnover of Xinjiang and the Russian Federation is about ten times less. Russian import from Xinjiang is represented mostly by consumer goods and foodstuffs; export from Russia is basically wood, metals, plastics and aluminum. According to expert assessment, there is a demand from China for a broader import of wood, metals, construction materials, agricultural machinery, fertilizers, heavy tracks, electricity, etc., and certainly oil and gas. As the strategic decision of constructing a new oil pipeline to Xinjiang has been taken, these expectations are becoming more and more realistic. In principle, all these products could be exported from the Siberian regions as they possess the necessary production facilities.[7]

In an overall sense, since early 1990s trans-border cooperation of Russia with rest of the Central Asian actors on the south of Siberia has been rapidly developing. However, it was made on a bilateral basis without inter-regional and international mechanism of balancing interests of all the parties involved. Each country tends to pursue its own objectives which are not properly harmonized with other partners, and China is not an exception. Chinese economic activity in dealing with Russia and Kazakhstan through Xinjiang was very intensive in the first decade of the twenty-first century. Due to a strict vertical system of decision-making in this country trans-border trade became just a function of national strategy and was subordinate to its overall objectives.

According to the basic approach Xinjiang was supposed to become mostly a logistic centre and a kind of transitory warehouse for the export articles to be produced in the inner part of China. Chinese goods are supposed to be delivered to Russia and Kazakhstan and further to Europe through Xinjiang. The same approach is used for justifying the function of Xinjiang in delivering imported energy and raw materials to the Chinese economic heartland.

Such logic did not leave too much flexibility to Xinjiang's regional economy, making it in a way one-sided and underdeveloped. As compared with other parts of the country, Xinjiang is lagging behind in many important respects, including lack of complexity of the regional economic system. In principle, trans-border cooperation could have been used to soften economic asymmetry but it has not happened so far. Moreover, due to historical, socio-cultural and political specifics of Xinjiang, China seems to allow just a limited possibility for the regional cooperation in Xinjiang except for the economic aspects. Thus, it seems that there is a latent conflict of interests between the central authorities of China and the core regional interests of Xinjiang.

To a certain extent the same logic can be applied to the trans-border territories of Kazakhstan around the Altai region. On the one hand, Kazakhstan needs to expand its economic orientation to open new markets for its goods produced in heavily industrialized Eastern Kazakhstan region which has been in crisis for about two decades after the collapse of the former USSR. In addition to that, it would like to overcome its economic dependence on Russia based on complementarities of their economies previously belonging to one industrial complex. This is specifically the case for Eastern Kazakhstan, since regional complementarities of the economies of Ust-Kamenogorsk (now Oskemen, the centre of Eastern Kazakhstan region), the Altai territory with the cities of Barnaul, Rubtsovsk and Biysk, Novosibirsk and the Kuzbass area with the cities of Kemerovo and Novokuznetsk (all in Russia) are very high. However, there is enough evidence to conclude that Kazakhstan authorities would pursue a very prudent policy in connection with other aspects of trans-border contacts with Xinjiang, for example, remaining very cautious about possibilities of increasing influence of Uyghur liberation movement on the territory of Kazakhstan which can lead to intensified humanitarian contacts between trans-border regions of the two countries. The 16 million Uyghur population in China is a hidden bomb for the Chinese hegemony in the region. Though 400,000 Uyghur diaspora in the CA NIS countries is much less, it is still enough to destabilize the situation if something happens in the neighbouring territories.

The situation referring to trans-border cooperation in Russia is even more complex. On the one hand, it is very much favoured by both central and regional authorities of the country. Vladimir Putin, the former president of Russia, announced at one of the forums of the frontier territories cooperation of Russia and Kazakhstan which are organized on regular basis that frontier cooperation should be considered a 'school of integration', because the ongoing process in the framework of such cooperation is a good supplement to the inter-state efforts in developing bilateral relations.[8] However, many experts are much more sceptical in assessing the role of trans-border cooperation for Russia. According to one of them, Prof. Nikolay Grekov from the Siberian city of Omsk, expanded volume of trans-border trade is just an indication of the lack of clear objectives of the Russian policy towards the CA NIS countries. The central power could not produce a distinct policy with regards to Russia's neighbours in Central Asia and is utilizing trans-border cooperation as a spontaneous means of regulation of international problems which appeared after the collapse of the USSR. The expert believes, and one would tend to agree with him, that spontaneous development of trans-border trade leads to conservation of current economic asymmetry in the country, which can be specifically harmful for Siberia and cause serious geopolitical complications in future.[9] Although the expert's assumptions related mostly to the contacts of Siberian territories with Kazakhstan, one believes that these can be logically extended to relations with China through Xinjiang. This logic worked for the 1990s and the beginning of 2000s but is being reconsidered at the moment as the weight of Central Asia in Russia's international policy has clearly increased in recent years.

The 'Big Altai' approach

The statements above actualize two issues. The first is a necessity of reasonable balance of central and regional interests when implementing trans-border contacts and elaborating clear understanding how national interests are considered and harmonized with regional interests in every country. The second is harmonizing of interests of all the parties involved in trans-border cooperation, and setting up a proper mechanism of doing that.

The first project connected with economic development in the Altai trans-border region belongs to Chinese experts. It was a concept of the East-Central Asian economic zone proposed in 1996 and further developed in 1998 at the conference on inter-regional cooperation in the city of Rubtsovsk, Russia.[10] The project envisaged integration of economic capacities of the Altai territories of all the countries involved in order to accelerate the economic development of this region. There were proposals for setting up economic zones in Altai with special taxation regimes, joint utilization of natural resources, development of the trans-Altai system of communication and tourist infrastructure, and optimizing of the border check points system.

Whereas this project remained just a theory, the idea of integrated trans-Altai cooperation paved the way to further discourse on the advantages of the Altai region. As mentioned above, conceptualization of the role of Altai was also based on analysis of some economic and political practices in the region. In 1998 the declaration on sustainable development of Altai was accepted in Russia, and concept of global Altai Convention was proposed but not adopted so far. In the year 2000 Altai Mountains Forum took place in the Russian city of Barnaul. It was a step forward towards shaping the Big Altai approach as a political concept. Although, according to some experts, the concept was mostly driven by the Chinese side, the integrative approach was actively supported by many Russian specialists from the region, especially by the team of local political scholars from Barnaul.[11]

The concept was inspired by positive evaluation of outputs and expectation of further expansion of trans-border cooperation in the Altai region and pushing the idea of setting up a permanent cooperation network of economic actors and regional policy-makers with engagement of all four neighbouring countries. The idea was based, at least partially, on the positive evaluation of the experience of regional cooperation in the European Union and focused on complementarity of the economic complex in the Altai region.

Some first but important steps have already been performed to implement this plan. The process was stimulated by local initiatives supported by UNESCO and focused on designing of a number of environmental projects for the Altai territory, of which the concept of biosphere Altai zone for sustainable development was the most prominent. It pushed forward the initiative of the expert community, supported by local authorities of 'Big Altai' countries, to set up an institutionalized instrument for coordination of activities in the region. In the year 2002 the initiative resulted in setting up International Coordination Council

(ICC) 'Altai is Our Common Home'.[12] It embraced the Altai Territory and the Republic of Altai (Russia), Xinjiang Uyghur Autonomous Region (China), Bayan Ulgii and Hovd Aimaks (Mongolia), and Eastern Kazakhstan Oblast (Kazakhstan). The major purpose was to promote a dialogue between regional authorities of all the countries involved on the issues important for the whole trans-border territory of Big Altai.

The Council was supposed to tackle major problems of all the territories involved which required coordination of activities of local administrations, public institutions, expert communities from different countries; to provide assistance to all interested parties in arranging and preparing international conferences and workshops directed on cooperation issues in the Altai region, on preservation of the Altai ecosystem and developing their 'reasonable' economic utilization; to help in compiling data base on legislation for providing assistance to state administration of different levels, to commercial businesses, scientific institutions and NGOs which practically implement cooperation with their partners on the trans-border territory; to maintain an integrated information space in the Altai region. The Council has got a website hosted by the Russian partners.

However, after a good start further operation was not smooth enough. It became clear that effective development of this structure is impossible without political support from the central power level and its engagement in the operation of the new institution. It raises the question about the future of the 'Big Altai' mechanisms as a system integrator of interests of the 'neighbouring states' and as an interface of trans-border countries to Central Asia. Although the issue needs further investigation, one believes that in the long run the 'Big Altai' approach has good potential for transformation into an effective mechanism of balancing interests of all countries involved. However, it depends on their political will, readiness to harmonize central and regional economic policy and overcome centre–periphery asymmetry in the decision-making process. In this projection Xinjiang in China constitutes the most difficult case because of specific position of this 'trouble-making region' 'enjoying' a very suspicious attention and strict control from the central authorities.

Economic cooperation in the region is also considered as not sufficient so far. The progress is hindered by a number of factors, which are different for each of the countries involved and some of them are of objective character. We will address just two of them which do not cover the whole issue. From the Russian dimension one such limiting factor is a weak export base of the Altai territory. Russia exports those goods via Altai which are considered strategically important for the country (metals, fertilizers, wood, etc.) and imports just food and consumption goods. Neither the region, nor the country at large, are satisfied with the structure of export but it cannot be changed when relying just on local capacities.

Another point is the problem of transportation. The road construction projects across Altai are being discussed for many years but the issue is not resolved so far. As mentioned above, China has made good steps forward. Some road construction has also been done by Kazakhstan. Russia is clearly lagging behind in this respect, which leads us to suspect that insufficient or lacking investments are not enough to explain the situation. It seems that from the geopolitical point of view Russian strategies still lack clarity in the region, and it works as a hindering factor.

Despite all the problems, cooperative processes are developing in the region. In addition to the 'big policy game', for further success much will depend on regional actors involved in the activity of the ICC and supporting agencies. Meanwhile, according to our vision, the impact of this institution in the short run should realistically be limited to the following:

- Setting up a common communication forum for intellectual regional elites and contributing to construction of image of the 'Big Altai' region as a territory with a specific local identity facilitating not just regional cooperation but also being an interface to outer Central Asian space. To achieve this, economic cooperation should be effectively supplemented with science, education and cultural contacts across all trans-border territories. Existing practices should be substantially expanded.
- Contributing to performing expert functions referring to trans-border activities and realities including initiating research and expertise on comparative analysis and harmonization of regional legislation, regulation and practices to facilitate contacts and exchange of people and goods.
- Considering, summing up and lobbying trans-border interests and defending them before central and regional authorities when national economic, science, educational and cultural strategies are debated and formulated. This is clear that effective operation of this structure is impossible without political support from the central power level.

Thus, the 'Big Altai' approach is getting more and more popularity as a theory but remains of limited use as a practical tool. The theoretical potential of this approach is substantial but it remains underestimated and not widely utilized by policy-makers in all countries involved so far. However, the ongoing processes in the frontier Central Asian region provide for some positive expectations regarding further development of the 'Big Altai' approach both as a theory and a practice. Much will depend on harmonizing and compromising Russian, Kazakh and Chinese national strategies in Central Asia, especially in transborder areas that seem to become one of the important issues in their international politics agenda. In the meantime, the contradictory economic and political situation in Xinjiang will remain the crucial issue that may limit the possibility of effective utilization of the 'Big Altai' approach in the short run and in a longer perspective.

Notes

1 V.V. Alekseyev, Ye. V. Alekseyeva, K.I. Zubkov and I.V. Poberezhnikov, *Aziatskaia Rossiia V Geopoliticheskoy I Tsivilizatsionnoy Dinamike. XVI–XX veka* (Asian Russia in Geopolitical and Civilisation Dynamics, 16–20 Centuries). Moscow, Nauka, 2004, p. 586.

2 Ye. G. Vodichev and V.A. Lamin, 'Russian Identity and Siberia's Self-Identification: Historical Traditions in a Global World', in Douglas W. Blum (ed.), *Russia and Globalization: Identity, Security and Society in the Era of Change*. Washington, DC, Woodrow Wilson Center Press, and Baltimore, Johns Hopkins University Press, 2008, pp. 170–3.

3 A.A. Ulunian, 'Geopoliticheskiy Neoconcept 'Bolshoy Tsentralnoy Azii': Funktsionalizatsia Protiv Ideologizatsii' (Geo-Political Concept of Greater Central Asia: Functionalism Against Ideology), *Istoricheskoe Prostranstvo. Problemy Istorii Stran SNG*, 2. Moscow, 2007, p. 173; A. Ulunian, 'Bolshaia Tsentralnaia Aziia Ili Vneshnepoliticheskiy Instrument?' (Big Central Asia or Foreign Policy Instrument?), available at www.centrasia.ru/newsA.php?st=1207304460.

4 V.S. Boyko, 'Rossiiskiy Altai V Geopolitike Tsentralnoy I Vnutrenney Azii V 1990-e – Nachale 2000-kh Godov (K Postanovke Problemy)' (Russian Altai in Geopolitics of Central and Inner Asia in 1990 – beginning of 2000s), in V.A. Moiseev (ed.), *Tsentralnaia Aziia I Sibir. Materialy Konferentsii*. Barnaul, AzBuka, 2003, pp. 219–26.

5 See S.G. Luzianin, 'Rossia – Kitay – Tsentralnaia Aziia: Problemy Migratsiy I Regionalnoy Bezopasnosti' (Russia – China – Central Asia: The Problems of Regional Security), *Bezopasnost V Kontaktnykh Zonakh: Opyt I Praktika Regulirovaniia Etnopoliticheskikh Napriazheniy*. Barnaul, AlGU, 2002, p. 23.

6 See B.K. Sultanov (ed.), *Sotrudnichestvo I Bezopasnost V Tsentralnoy Azii: Sostoianie I Perspectivy* (Cooperation and Security in Central Asia: Present Status and Perspectives). Almaty, KISI, pp. 136–54.

7 Galina Kovaleva, 'Sosedey Ne Vybiraut', available at http://expert-sibir.ru/journal/read/1852.

8 See on www.kremlin.ru/text/2006/10/11.

9 N.V. Grekov, 'Bezopasnost Rossii I Sibirsko-Kazakhstanskie Prigranichnye Sviazi' (Security of Russia and Siberian-Kazakhstan Border Links), *Dnevnik AShPI № 20. Sovremennaia Rossiia I Mir: Alternativy Razvitiia*, available at http://ashpi.asu.ru/prints/dn19_20.html.

10 O.N. Barabanov, 'Altaiskii Region: Problemy I Perspektivy Mezhregionalnogo Prigranichnogo Sotrudnichestva Na Styke Tsentralnoy Azii I Sibiri' (Altai Region: Problems and Perspectives of Inter-Regional Border Cooperation on the Juncture of Central Asia and Siberia), in O.N. Barabanov and S. Yu. Nozhkin (eds), *Rossiiskaia Zapadnaia Sibir – Tsentralnaia Aziia: Novaia Regionalnaia Identichnost, Ekonomika I Bezopasnost. Materialy Mezhdunarodnoy Konferentsii*. Barnaul, 2003.

11 See O. Barabanov, 'Bolshoy Altai: Proekt Transgranichnogo Regionalnogo Sotrudnichestva Na Styke Tsentralnoy Azii I Sibiri' (Big Altai: A Project of Trans-Border Regional Cooperation on the Juncture of Central Asia and Siberia), *Tsentralnaia Aziia I Kavkaz*, Moscow, Vol. 5, No. 23, 2002, pp. 78–85; *Altay Daily Review*, 29 August 2006, available at www.bankfax.ru/page.php?pg=37216?8ce29758.

12 www.altaiinter.info/council/.

12 Economic and social development in Xinjiang

Chen Xi

The year 2009 marked the sixtieth anniversary of the establishment of the People's Republic of China and Xinjiang's peaceful liberation. However, this year also witnessed seriously violent incidents in Urumqi on 5 July 2009, astonishing the world (see Chapter 16). Facing the double impact of the 7/5 incident and the international economic crisis, Xinjiang tried to overcome the difficulties in order to maintain its stability and improvement in the economic situation.

Economic situation in Xinjiang

After 65 years of development, Xinjiang's gross economy has developed and its industrial structure has been reasonably adjusted. Besides, its position in the national economic development strategy has improved considerably. Xinjiang has now become an important production base of foodstuffs, cotton, fruits and livestock besides being the production and reserve base of energy and mineral resources in China.

Substantial funds have been invested by the Centre and the Autonomous Region to strengthen the basic industries and building infrastructure in agriculture, irrigation, transport, energy, education, etc., thus laying the firm foundation for the sustainable growth of Xinjiang's economy. Especially, with the implementation of the Western Development Strategy, investment of funds in Xinjiang has been increased resulting in the rapid improvement in the building of infrastructure in Xinjiang.

Xinjiang's agricultural resources are abundant. Industrialization of agriculture has been expedited in Xinjiang with the development of foodstuffs, cotton, fruits and high-quality livestock and Xinjiang's basic agriculture, so that the advantageous position of farm products is sustained.

While entering the twenty-first century, Xinjiang's industrial development has led to the formation of a completely modern industrial system in sectors like oil, coal, steel, chemical, electricity, construction materials, spinning and some other industries. Industrial cluster areas such as 'Northern-Hillside Mountain, Tian Economic Belt', 'Urumqi-Changji Integrative Zone', 'Kuerle – Kuche Petroleum Chemistry Industry Belt', along with 32 national and regional industrial parks have been developed. These clusters play an important role in driving and expanding economic and social development in the whole of Xinjiang. The Region pays much attention to the development of the three counties in Southern Xinjiang, by investing funds, by reducing the gap in regional development, and improving the living standard of all nationalities in Southern Xinjiang.

Xinjiang follows the opening up strategy of 'external opening up, internal communication, eastern connection, western exports, west coming and east going' to form the all-round, multi-layered, wide-range opening pattern, and to stimulate the inner-regional communiation. The geographical and regional advantages of westward opening of Xinjiang are utilized fully, tapping both the domestic and international markets and carrying out intensive cooperation with the surrounding areas to explore the Central Asian, West Asian, South Asian, East European and Russian markets.

Though the year 2009 was a hard year in the economic development of Xinjiang, the growth rate of Xinjiang's economy reached 8 per cent. Industrial development has been largely responsible for the considerable improvement of Xinjiang's comprehensive economic power since the implementation of the Western Exploration during the past ten years. However, the occurrence of the 7/5 incident in Urumqi adversely affected Xinjiang's economic development.

Economic growth has now stabilized after a steep decline. The actual GDP of Xinjiang whole area in the first three-quarters of 2009 was 282.493 billion yuan, showing an increase of 6.4 per cent over the same period. The total value of primary industry was 64.974 billion yuan, which showed an increase of 4.6 per cent; that of the secondary industry was 117.115 billion yuan, showing an increase of 6.5 per cent; and the tertiary industry was 100.404 billion yuan, which rose by 7.5 per cent.

Agricultural production has been stable, leading to increase in farmers' cash income. In the first three-quarters, the whole region realized 113.319 billion yuan of gross yield from farming, forestry, stockbreeding and fishing showing an increase of 4.8 per cent. The whole-year gross foodstuff yield created a new historical record, reaching 12 million tons. In 2009, the net per capita agricultural income was estimated to be 4,000 yuan. Xinjiang farmers' cash income per capita from January through September 2009 was 2,983 yuan, showing an increase of 380 yuan, or 14.6 per cent.

Industrial growth has shown an upward trend after reaching the bottom. The raw oil yield and manufactured goods in the first three-quarters of 2009 was 8.5 per cent and 2.1 per cent respectively, while the profit of the petroleum industry declined, resulting in a 5 per cent fall in industrial growth rate. However, local industry is still strong, the petroleum industry has begun to recover, and the industrial economy has started moving up. Under such circumstances, the added industrial value over the certain scale is 91.122 billion yuan, which shows an increase of 4.5 per cent.

In 2009, driven by the national domestic-demand-dragging policies, consumer market in Xinjiang continued to grow at a slow rate, while the rural market consumption increased due to the rise in the rural consumption.

By the end of September 2009, the balance of various deposits of Xinjiang's financial institutions was 658.424 billion yuan, showing an increase by 118.001 billion yuan than the beginning of the year. Xinjiang's financial institutions issued loans of 360.207 billion yuan, showing an increase by 77.469 billion yuan than the beginning of the year. Considerable increase in the loan size inspired the market confidence, expanded domestic demand, hindered the sliding down of economy, and promoted the stabilization and slow recovery of the economy.

In 2009, the disposable income of Xinjiang's urban and rural residents was estimated to be 12,120 yuan. As such the disposable income of the urban residents (9,022 yuan) increased by 5.6 per cent, whereas the income of urban low-income households (2,682 yuan) increased by 28.2 per cent.

Problems in Xinjiang's economy in 2009

The economy is weak, being much reliant on the petroleum industry. In the first three-quarters of 2009, influenced by the international economic crisis and Production Reduction Plan in the Middle East, the petroleum industry suffered a 10 per cent drop in its industrial added value, resulting in the overall industrial growth rate of 5 per cent for the whole region. The sharp decline in petroleum taxation led to the fall of 2,060 million yuan in the whole regional general local budget income, accounting for a decline of 80 per cent in the local taxation. Therefore, Xinjiang's economic structure is not sound, as it is too much reliant on such resource industries as oil, natural gas and coal. As the oil price is affected seriously by the international markets, Xinjiang's economic development remains vulnerable to instability and uncertainty.

The problems in the middle and small scale enterprises are still outstanding, and the environment of enterprises needs further optimization. The middle and small scale firms lack funds, and face the difficulty in financing. The loans are mainly invested in building infrastructure with other fields contributing less to the short-term economic growth. The loans invested in sectors such as industry,

Table 12.1 Financial income increase and GDP increase in Xinjiang, 1999–2008

Year	Financial income increase (%)	Local financial income increase (%)	GDP increase (%)
1999	7.80	9.05	7.40
2000	22.59	10.88	8.70
2001	19.60	20.26	8.60
2002	31.22	22.48	8.20
2003	13.20	10.09	11.20
2004	26.44	21.43	11.40
2005	18.97	15.81	10.90
2006	21.89	21.71	11.00
2007	32.03	30.26	12.20
2008	27.91	26.31	11.00

consumer, small and middle-size enterprises, are relatively less, resulting in serious problems for these enterprises in their development, thus weakening the foundation of Xinjiang's economic growth to a certain degree.

Income difference is becoming bigger. The farmers' per capita income in Xinjiang is listed as the second worst, and the difference with the national level still remains big. Meanwhile, the income difference between the urban and rural residents and between different regions has become bigger and bigger, leading to common social complaints, which have a negative impact on Xinjiang's social stability.

Under the conditions of slow recovery of the world economy, the stabilization and recovery of the national economy, Xinjiang's economy can step out of the bottom of the economic cycle, as its stabilization and recovery trend is becoming more and more obvious. However, due to multiple effects of the international economic crisis, the 7/5 Urumqi incident and the deficient self-sufficiency of Xinjiang's economic development, the stabilization and growth of Xinjiang's economy is still a slow process. As compared to the year 2009, Xinjiang's economic development in 2010 witnessed positive trend in the international macro-environment and the national macro-regulation policies, further enforcement of additional support by the country to Xinjiang, further allotment of resources and geographical advantages through large batches of infrastructures, energy and chemical industry projects. One believes that Xinjiang's economy can step out of the bottom, stabilize and then recover quickly.

Social development and associated problems

People's living standards have improved considerably. In the countryside, besides the food, cotton and other traditional crops, horticulture and some other businesses have become the new channels to increase farmers' income. With the local labour going out of their homeland, especially those going to East China, they have got another means to increase their income. The development of tourism drives the production and sales of handicrafts thereby facilitating the development of national handicrafts, leading to the employment of hundreds of thousands of people directly or indirectly. With the modernization of transport, travel has become more convenient and quick. In the early period of reform and opening up, it took nearly one week from Urumqi to Beijing by rail, whereas now it takes only over three hours by air. The residential situation has improved. Housing area per capita in the countryside has increased from 10.20 square metres in 1983 to 22.79 square metres in 2008, while in the urban area it has increased from 11.90 square metres in 1983 to 27.30 square metres in 2008. In recent years, more than 300,000 households in Kurla, Hotan, Kashgar, Atushi, Aksu and some other areas of Southern Xinjiang make use of clean and cheap natural gas.

Education has developed. Before 1949, there was only one university, nine middle schools and 1,355 elementary schools in Xinjiang, and the enrolment rate for the children going to school was only 19.8 per cent, with the illiteracy rate throughout Xinjiang being over 90 per cent. Through the 65 years of development, historical achievement has been made in the field of education. Nine years' education has been made compulsory, and illiteracy has been eliminated. Various kinds of higher education and vocational education have been started, and are developing stably. Currently, there are 4,159 elementary schools, with the number of students in schools being 2,012,000, the enrolment rate for children suitable for elementary education being over 99.6 per cent; 1,973 middle schools, with 1,722,000 students; 32 ordinary higher schools (universities or institutes) with 241,000 students, and 10,300 postgraduates. Minority education is being encouraged through the implementation of special national policies. To ensure that the minority examinees can receive higher education, there exist preferential policies for the minority examinees for the colleges and institutes since the 1950s. Senior-level minority talent is cultivated by the implementation of 'Special Cultivation of Xinjiang Minority Science and Technology Talents' project, bursary for minority students abroad, etc. Third, with the development of the economy and society, communication between the nationalities has become more frequent, and more and more minorities are eager to learn the Chinese language. The Xinjiang government decided in 2004 to boost the 'bilingual' education, so that the minority students graduating from senior high schools are able to 'know both the Chinese and the Uyghur'. The implementation of 'bilingual' education policy helps increase understanding and communication between the nationalities, development of equal, solid, interdependent and harmonious nationality relations, and promotion of common prosperity and development between different nationalities. Fourth, in order to let the minority students in the remote areas have access to the high-level elementary education, Xinjiang Senior High School was started in 13 middle schools in 12 economically advanced provinces and cities including Beijing and Shanghai, since the year 2000. Until now, the Xinjiang Internal Senior Class has finished the target of recruiting 29,600 students in ten sessions, and the on-school size has reached 20,000. The number of cities holding the class has increased from 28 in 2008 to 29 in 2009, and the schools holding the class increased from 50 to 52. As regards the entrance examinations to the college in recent years, the undergraduate enrolment rate of the Internal Senior Class has reached over 90 per cent.

The science and technology venture in Xinjiang which was absent before 1949 is developing and innovating. After 65 years, reasonably professional science research and development system with the regional characteristics has been established in Xinjiang, and a multi-national science research team with academic attainment has been cultivated. The innovation capability of scientific and technological enterprises has been enhanced, and a group of internationally famed brands, such as 'Golden Wind', 'TEBA', have been created.

Cultural activities are becoming richer and more colourful. Before 1949, there was no professional cultural group or art research institute. Through 65 years' development, various types of cultural facilities were established in Xinjiang. By 2008, there were 119 art performance teams, two cultural science research institutes, two art creation institutes, 15 folk art museums and 94 cultural centres in Xinjiang. The number of cultural workers of nationalities engaged in professional performance was 4,355. Besides, there are 93 public libraries, 47 museums, six regional-level broadcasting stations and eight television stations.

The medical institutions keep increasing. Before 1949, the medical and sanitary service was much lower in Xinjiang. During the past 65 years, there has been considerable investment in medicine and sanitation. Currently, there are 7,238 medical institutions of different kinds, including 1,629 hospitals, 936,000 beds and 43,800 doctors. The health and epidemic prevention capacity have been improved considerably.

The employment policies keep improving. During the past few years Xinjiang has promoted the increase of employment through the rapid and sustainable economic development, increasing jobs and expanding employment size through various measures. Since the implementation of the Western Development Strategy, over 300,000 persons get re-employment annually in Xinjiang. Employment is determined by the market-oriented mechanism in human resource allocation. In recent years, the labour export has become a new path to secure employment, solving the problem of low income in farmers' income of such people in such remote farming and pasturing areas as Southern Xinjiang and the difficulties in poverty alleviation. Labour export which started from the Jiashi County of Southern Xinjiang has covered the whole of Xinjiang. The farmers and herdsmen of Xinjiang voluntarily select the employment units from domestic firms with job requirements, and then, accompanied by the Muslim priests and cooks selected and funded by the government, join these jobs.

Social safeguard system has been established. Currently there are 799 community service facilities of all types in urban areas of Xinjiang. Over tens of thousands of persons participate in the five most important types of insurances, that is, basic endowment insurance, unemployment insurance, medicare, industrial accident insurance and procreation insurance.

After the 7/5 Urumqi incident, the Party and the government paid attention to Xinjiang's social development. First, the central government paid much attention to Xinjiang. In 2009, Hu Jintao, Xi Jinping, Zhou Yongkang, Meng Qingzhu and other national leaders made investigations and reviews, and several declarations were made to direct Xinjiang's reform, development, stability and the treatment of the 7/5 incident. Second, the 27th Nationality Unity Education Month was implemented. A series of propaganda and educational activities were implemented on the theme 'thanksgiving of the great homeland to construct harmonious Xinjiang'.

New progress has been made in the religious sphere. A considerable percentage of the religious circles played an important role in the promotion of social harmony. After the 7/5 incident, a number of Xinjiang Islamic priests condemned the violent and terrorist activities, standing on the first line of antiseparatist and extremist violence, and leading the crowd of believers to maintain social stability and nationalities' unity. Second, the Muslim priests direct the followers to work hard for their economic upliftment. In 2009, Xinjiang's main media devoted special columns 'directing the patriotic and religious people to get rich by hard work', reporting continuously on the typical cases of the religious people getting rich by working hard in Xinjiang in recent years. Muslim priests conducted preaching activities in Kelamayi, Tacheng, Changji, Turpan, Aksu, etc., educate their followers on AIDS and national AIDS prevention and cure policies in local languages, thereby urging the Muslim priests in the whole of Xinjiang to adopt AIDS prevention and cure campaign into their daily sermons. Good preparations are made for organizing Hajj pilgrimages. Four meetings were held in Xinjiang to decide and allocate the seats for Hajj pilgrimage in 2010.

Equalization of education opportunities is promoted through bilingual education, especially in the training of pre-school-enrolment education, middle vocational education and teacher team construction in schools in order to keep the number of bilingual teachers in vocational institutes and schools increasing, besides upgrading the quality of the teaching stuff.

Urban and rural medical service system has been strengthened, with the construction of 38 county-level hospitals, 209 central-village hospitals and 39 community sanitation service centers. Since 1 October 2009, all the relevant departments in Xinjiang implemented the newly issued 'Advice on Employment Promotion by the Regional Party Committee and People's Government', and four special policies were implemented to promote employment.

By the end of September 2009, there were 2,310,000 persons enrolled in the basic endowment insurance, 2,750,000 in urban employees' basic medicare, 2,280,000 in urban residential basic medicare, 1,683,800 in unemployment insurance, 1,630,000 in vocational injury insurance and 1,750,000 in procreation insurance.

Conclusion

The 7/5 incident caused psychological estrangement and adverse relations between the Han and Uyghur people. The people also began to doubt the government's ability to govern, leaving much space for rumours, resulting in the further decline in the prestige and authority of the government. Therefore, strengthening of the nationalities' unity and rebuilding harmonious and friendly relationship between various nationalities has been the key target for the post-7/5 Xinjiang.

With the fiscal investment in Xinjiang's people's livelihood having increased ten-fold during the past ten years, the condition has improved considerably. However, the problem of the people's livelihood is still serious, as much remains to be done to support the poor population, to improve social safeguards, to resolve the unemployment problem, to improve public service, etc. The employment situation is still difficult, and the overall level of the basic public service is still lower.

In recent years, the hostile powers at home and abroad have been spreading the separatist ideology through broadcasting stations, Internet, books, magazines, vocal and visible products, besides propagating religious extremist ideas under the cover of academic and cultural activities, thus stirring up religious fervour among the people.

The 7/5 incident reflects the gaps in the understanding and management of the floating population, house renting, etc. in some communities. In these communities the floating population is big and the floating frequency is much higher, the composition is complex, which makes it difficult for the community commissioners to investigate. Keeping watch over the community house renting and management of floating population, updating of residential information and communication with the public would help in implementation of community stability.

To conclude, the year 2010 was an important year for Xinjiang, as Xinjiang's economic and social development stepped into an uncommon opportunity following the Central Working Conference on Xinjiang issue in May 2010. However, Xinjiang is still vulnerable to sudden accidents, and there are still big challenges for social stabilization and control. Separatism still remains the main threat to Xinjiang's social stability.

13 China's Western Development Programme in Xinjiang

Wang Jianming

China's Western Development Programme is a specific geographical concept, as it caters to five southwest provinces: Sichuan, Yunnan, Guizhou, Tibet, Chongqing; and five northwest provinces of Shanxi, Gansu, Qinghai, Xinjiang and Ningxia. It also includes Inner Mongolia, Guangxi and Xiangxi Autonomous areas of Hunan province and Enshi Autonomous area of Hubei province. The nationalities of Tujia and Miao autonomous areas are located in these two areas. This region has an area of 6.85 million square miles which accounts for 71 per cent of the whole of China and nearly 30 per cent of the population of China. The region has borders with many countries, including Mongolia, Russia, Tajikistan, Kyrgyzstan, Kazakhstan, Pakistan, Afghanistan, Vietnam, Bhutan, Nepal, India, Burma and Laos. The border runs to about 18,000 miles which accounts for 91 per cent of the borders of whole of China. Western China has many resources, big territory, complex nationalities and many neighbours. It holds the position of the centre of Eurasia, thereby occupying a very important strategic position. The development of the western part is important for the modernization of China.

When, in July 1998, the former president of China Jiang Zemin visited Xinjiang, he stressed that Xinjiang is the most important province in the western part of China. 'We should do everything we can to make Xinjiang developing fast not only in politics but also in economy', he said. In November 1999, the Central Communist Party and State Council held an economic conference in which the Chinese government decided to carry out the Western Development Programme. In September 2000, former Premier Zhu Rongji visited Xinjiang and made a specific announcement for Xinjiang's development. The local government declared its goal that by the year 2020 the GDP of Xinjiang would reach 720 billion yuan (according to the price in 2000), which would be twice that of 2000, so that Xinjiang develops at the same pace as other provinces and becomes an important pivot of twenty-first-century economic development of the country.

Due to the activities of last ten years of China's Western Development Programme, Xinjiang, which was Western China's economic 'depression' in the past, has become China's 'bridgehead' open to the countries in Central Asia, South Asia and Eastern Europe. Being rich in natural resources makes Xinjiang the most attractive 'treasure land' for the large domestic enterprises and groups.

Table 13.1 Development of industry structure in Xinjiang (%)

Primary industry	16.4
Secondary industry	49.7
Teritary industry	33.9

Source: Information Office of the State Council of the People's Republic of China, Development and Progress in Xinjiang, September 2009.

The past ten years of China's Western Development Programme witnessed largest investment and fast growth, which proved to be most effective and beneficial for the common people in the history of Xinjiang.

Xinjiang Uyghur Autonomous Region accounts for about one-sixth of the country's land area. Over the past 60 years, under the leadership of the Communist Party of China and the central government, and with the support of other parts of China, people of various ethnic groups in Xinjiang have made progress. The region has made a historic leap out of under-development, with tremendous changes taking place in the areas north and south of the Tianshan mountains.

Since 1949, particularly after China's reform and opening-up in the late 1970s, Xinjiang has entered an era of rapid economic and social progress and comprehensive growth, with the local people enjoying tangible benefits. Proceeding from the state development strategy, the Chinese government has paid attention to the development and construction of Xinjiang. It has made a national policy to help the frontier areas develop their economy and worked out a series of strategic decisions to promote Xinjiang's development. Xinjiang has been given priority in the national strategy launched in the year 2000 to develop the western regions.

Over the years, Xinjiang has made full use of its own advantages, and has focused on economic restructuring and changing the modes of economic growth, infrastructure construction and environmental protection, along with the improvement of people's livelihood and basic public services, so as to keep the development of Xinjiang at pace with the national development, and to have a balance between the development of southern Xinjiang and that of northern Xinjiang. The local GDP in 2008 stood at 420.3 billion yuan, which is 86.4 times higher than that of 1952, three years before the establishment of the Xinjiang Uyghur Autonomous Region, that is up by 8.3 per cent on average annually.

In the year 2000, the social welfare expenditure in Xinjiang's general budget expenditure was 3.7 billion yuan, accounting for 40 per cent of the total budget,

Table 13.2 Xinjiang government expenditure, 2009 (%)

Transport	Public service	Agriculture	Social security	Education	Medical	Others
15	17	18	12	8	3	27

Source: www.xjcz.gov.cn/web/xjft/czzl_new/czys_new/.

Table 13.3 Deposited savings of Xinjiang residents (in yuan)

1955	1978	2000	2008
14	52	4,913	11,972

Source: Information Office of the State Council of the People's Republic of China, *Development and Progress in* Xinjiang, September 2009.

Table 13.4 Consumption of Xinjiang residents (in yuan)

1952	1978	2000	2007
122	181	2,662	4,890

Source: Information Office of the State Council of the People's Republic of China, *Development and Progress in* Xinjiang, September 2009.

which rose to 72 billion yuan (68.6 per cent) in 2008 and 94 billion yuan, i.e. over 70 per cent, in 2009 respectively.

Xinjiang got a 5.5 billion yuan loan from the central government, of which two billion was used in education, 1.5 billion in the construction of social welfare housing, 500 million in the construction of hospitals, one billion in rural roads construction and 500 million yuan were spent on renovating old and dilapidated houses in Kashghar.

The general living standard of urban and rural residents has also improved. Average income of urban and rural residents for one year rose to 11,432 yuan in 2008 from 5,645 yuan in 2000. The average net income of the rural people increased to 3,503 yuan in 2008 from 1,618 yuan in 2000. The average net income of the rural people in 2009 was about 4,000 yuan. However, people in the Ruoqiang county in Xinjiang have an average annual income of over 10,000 yuan.

Xinjiang's transport infrastructure is the microcosm of the basic infrastructure in Xinjiang. During the last ten years of China's Western Development Programme, the government has invested over 66.4 billion yuan in building the transportation infrastructure. By the end of 2008, Xinjiang highway mileage reached over 150,000 kilometres.

Xinjiang's railway construction has registered an impressive growth. In October 2008, the construction of Lan(Lanzhou)–Xin(Xinjiang) second railway was started with a total investment of 145 billion yuan. After its completion, the time from Beijing to Urumqi that presently takes nearly 42 hours, will be reduced to 11 or 12 hours. It means that if one starts travel in the morning, one will reach Beijing in the evening. The number of airports in Xinjiang province increased from 14 to 17 in the year 2010.

Being rich in mineral resources, in recent years, Xinjiang has set up a number of pillar industries relying on oil, natural gas and coal resources which drive the economic development of Xinjiang. Now Xinjiang has become China's major important oil and natural gas production base and petro-chemical industrial base. The production of crude oil increased from 18.484 million tons in 2000 to 27.151 million tons in 2008, thus becoming the second biggest area of crude oil production in China. The production of natural gas increased from 3.539 billion cubic metres in 2000 to 23.589 billion cubic metres in 2008, becoming the biggest natural gas production area in China from the year 2006. The coal-fired power projects and chemical projects relying on coal resources are also being developed.

The strategy of utilizing Xinjiang's advantageous resources has attracted many enterprises and groups to invest in Xinjiang. There are 89 enterprises having their affiliate organizations in Xinjiang. In the year 2009, these enterprises and groups invested about 100 billion yuan in Xinjiang, thus playing an important role in the development in Xinjiang and overcoming the financial crisis.

In order to maintain a balance between the Western Development Programme and environmental protection, Xinjiang has followed the principle that basic infrastructure and environmental protection is the fundamental prerequisite for Xinjiang's development and resources exploitation. There are several ecological landmarks in the Western Development Programme, such as the comprehensive improvement of Tarim River, for which a total investment of 10.7 billion yuan has been made. By the end of 2009, 8.6 billion yuan were invested to build more than 200 ecological projects at the lower reaches of the Tarim river. In this manner, the ecological damage to the lower reaches of Tarim river which has had discontinuous flow for 30 years, has been contained.

As regards the return of cropland to forestland, Xinjiang has completed 10.63 million acres. During the past ten years, Xinjiang has been taking up forest protection projects and 120 million acres of natural grassland have been restored. In Tianshan and Altai mountain and other major forest areas, Xinjiang has banned logging, and forestry workers have now turned into plantation workers.

In the year 2000, Xinjiang's sand desertification speed was two million square miles per year. After the implementation of ecology project, the sand desertification has been contained effectively. By the year 2009, the sand desertification speed declined to 0.8 million square miles per year.

Xinjiang is the first province in China where cost of books and incidental expenses, besides the living expenses of the students living in schools have been waived. By the end of 2009, after the efforts of 15 years, nine-year compulsory education has become a reality in Xinjiang. The government of Xinjiang Autonomous Region made a one-time allocation of two billion yuan to rebuild or repair the school buildings for implementing the policy of nine-year compulsory education in order to give the students a safe and comfortable studying environment.

From the year 2006, Xinjiang introduced the policy of bilingual education for children. By the year 2012, bilingual education will be popularized among 85 per cent of pre-school children (children who receive two years' pre-school education before they come to elementary school), which will make the 11-year compulsory education a reality. However, the compulsory education of high school students in southern Xinjiang, remains to be completed. Once implemented, it will be 14-year compulsory education in Xinjiang. That will be a big change and improvement. At the same time efforts are also being made to protect the traditional culture of ethnic minority groups.

Xinjiang has now become an important energy base in China and an important area of the Western Development Programme. At the same time, people have realized its important role of being rich in resources, and have also discovered the advantage of Xinjiang's geographic location. Seventy per cent of the goods exported from Xinjiang abroad are from inland China and Xinjiang has become the bridgehead or forward-post of China open to the western neighbours.

During ten years of the Western Development Programme in Xinjiang, the construction of roads has been a priority, which facilitates export of Xinjiang's local products to the markets of neighbouring countries and helps in Xinjiang's sustainable development. Xinjiang shares its borders with eight countries and there are 15 national ports. The products come from the markets of 1.3 billion people in China and go to the markets of 1.3 billion people of Central Asia, West Asia and South Asia.

Conclusion

National unification, ethnic unity, social stability, besides the coexistence and development of harmony of all the peoples of Xinjiang are the lifeblood for the region's development and progress. The people of all ethnic groups in Xinjiang strive for common prosperity sharing a common destiny, and consolidating and developing socialist ethnic relations characterized by equality, unity, mutual assistance and harmony. Though the events of 7/5 caused a huge shock, these did not affect the overall unity and stability in Xinjiang and the pace of Xinjiang's reform and development.

14 China's nationalities and religious policies in Xinjiang

Wang Qinji

Xinjiang has been a conglomerate region of numerous nationalities and religions for a long time. After the establishment of the New China, the nationality and religious policies were implemented in accordance with Xinjiang's reality so as to ensure the territorial integrity, stability and development of Xinjiang.

Status of nationalities in Xinjiang

Xinjiang has multiple nationalities. According to the fifth national general population census in 2000, 55 nationalities live in Xinjiang, that is, Uyghur, Han, Kazakh, Hui, Mongols, etc. By the year 2008, the population of Xinjiang stood at 21,308,000. The number of non-Han nationalities is 12,945,000, accounting for 60.8 per cent of the whole population. In 2007, the nationalities with a population of over million included the Uyghurs (9,651,000), Hans (8,239,000) and Kazakhs (1,484,000).

Various nationalities migrated to Xinjiang during different periods in history. In 101 BC, the military of the Han dynasty started to station itself in Xinjiang. The Western Region Office (called *Duhufu*) was established by the central government of the Han dynasty in 60 BC. Thus the Han immigration in Xinjiang started. By the end of the Han dynasty, the Hans had penetrated throughout Xinjiang to form the pattern of wide distribution while being concentrated around the military stations.

Table 14.1 Xinjiang nationalities population change (in thousands)

Year	Total population	Han	Uyghur	Kazakh	Hui	Mongol
1949	N/A	291	3,290	443	122	52
1990	N/A	5,690	7,190	1,100	681.5	137
2000	N/A	7,500	8,350	1,250	840	150
2003	19,339.5	7,711	8,823.5	1,352.1	866.7	166.9
2004	19,631.1	7,802.5	8,976.7	1,381.6	876.3	169.6
2005	20,103.5	7,956.6	9,235	1,413.9	893.5	171.7
2006	20,500	8,121.588	9,413.796	1,434.969	909.6	174.641
2007	19,339.5	8,239	9,651	1,484	943	177

After the unification of Xinjiang under the Qing dynasty, the Qing government organized its military composed of the Manchu, Mongol, Xibo, Dawoer, Han and Hui nationalities, who entered and were staioned in Xinjiang to garrison the frontier and explore Xinjiang, thus encouraging the Hans and Huis in the mainland to migrate to Xinjiang. From the late nineteenth century until the early twentieth century, the Russians, Uzbeks and Tatars also entered Xinjiang and settled down. By 1949, when the People's Republic of China was established, there were 13 nationalities in Xinjiang.

After the establishment of the New China, especially since the reform and opening up, influenced by the market-orientation, the spontaneous and voluntary population movements aimed mainly at study, commerce and farming became frequent between Xinjiang and the mainland. The population flow driven by the economic and social development changed the composition and distribution of nationalities in Xinjiang, leading to an increase in the number of nationalities. All the 55 nationalities except the Jinuo settled down in Xinjiang for livelihood. Second, the number of all nationalities keeps increasing. The population of the top four nationalities, that is, the Uyghur, Han, Kazakh and Hui, increased by 74, 61, 81 and 78 per cent respectively between 1978 and 2007. Third, the mixed settlement of nationalities in the urban areas and towns has become more obvious. There are 52 nationalities in Urumqi, and the proportion of minorities in its population increased from 18 per cent in 1978 to 27 per cent in 2007.

Religious policies in Xinjiang

Many religions coexist in Xinjiang and main religions include Islam, Buddhism, Christianity, Catholicism, Taoism, etc. Earlier, before the introduction of Islam, several religions, such as Zoroastrianism, Buddhism, Taoism, Manicheism, Jingism, had been introduced into Xinjiang along the Silk Road, and were propagated along with the local indigenous religions.

Before the introduction of foreign religions, the indigenous people in Xinjiang believed in local religions and Shamanism. Even now some minorities still retain the ideas and customs of their original religion and Shamanism. Around the fourth century BC, Zoroastrianism was introduced from Central Asia. And around the first century BC, Buddhism was introduced from Kashmir (India), and it emerged as the main religion in Xinjiang as it was promoted by the supervisors of all the regions. Around the fifth century AD, Taoism was introduced in the mainland. Around the sixth century AD, Manicheism was introduced from Central Asia. From the late ninth century until the early tenth century, Islam was introduced into Southern Xinjiang from Central Asia. In the middle of the tenth century, the Kala Han dynasty believing in Islam started a religious war with the Yutian Buddhist Kingdom, which lasted for 40 years. Thus Islam was forced into the Hetian region. From the middle of the fourteenth century, Islam gradually became the main religion and was followed by the Mongols, Uyghurs, Kazakhs, Khalkhas, Tajiks, etc. living in the Chahetai Han Kingdom through its forced propagation. By the early sixteenth century, Islam substituted Buddhism to become the major religion in Xinjiang. Currently there are ten minority groups believing in Islam, and their population is over 11.3 million.

A policy of freedom of religious belief has been implemented in Xinjiang to promote the healthy and orderly development in religious spheres:

1   Freedom of religious belief is a fundamental right enjoyed by the citizens in the Constitution which states:

> the citizens in the People's Republic of China have the freedom of religious belief ... any county authority, social group, or individual cannot force the citizens to believe or not in the religions, and not discriminate the citizens with religious beliefs or not.

China emphasizes the equality of individuals under its laws.

2   The freedom of religious belief is respected and normal religious activities are protected by law. By 2008, there were 24,800 mosques, churches, temples or similar religious places in Xinjiang, and 29,000 missionaries, 91 religious teams and two religious institutes. The number of Muslim mosques increased from 2,000 at the beginning of the reform to 24,300 now. The number of missionaries increased from over 3,000 to 28,000. Since the 1980s, the number of persons going for Hajj pilgrimage to Saudi Arabia has accumulated to over 50,000 and about 2,700 have been going for Hajj pilgrimage annually in recent years.

3   The religious believers enjoy full suffrage and policy discussion rights. By 2008, there were over 1,800 religious personages participating in the people's representative committees and the political negotiation committee and taking positions at each level. They participated and discussed the policies representing the believers, and even supervised the implementation of the policy of freedom of religious beliefs.

4   The Xinjiang Autonomous Region People's Representative Committee and the government constitute and issue the 'Provisional Prescriptions on the Management of Religious Activity in Xinjiang Uyghur Autonomous Region', which stipulates China's policy on the safeguarding of normal religious activities. It states that the religious groups, religious activities and religious citizens should abide by the laws, maintain the unity of China, unity of the nationalities and stability of the society. Any organization or individual cannot engage in the activities destroying the social order, hurting citizen's physical health, hindering the national education system and indulge in other activities hurting the country's interests, social commonwealth and citizen's legal interests by misusing religion to interfere in the national administration, judiciary and other national activities.

5   The religious policy seeks to ensure that the religious personages acquire lectures or other religious works. The Quran, the Woerci Selections, new

edition of *Woerci's Lecture Collections*, and other Islamic classics, religious books, magazines and the Buddhist classics or other religious works are translated, published and issued in the Uyghur, Kazakh and Chinese languages.

6   Since the establishment of the Xinjiang Islamic Institute, 489 imams, Hatifu or religious teachers have been trained in Xinjiang. From 2001 to 2008, the Xinjiang Islamic Institute produced over 20,000 religious missionaries. Since 2001, 47 persons were sent by Xinjiang to the advanced Islamic institutes in Egypt, Pakistan and other Islamic countries for further study and research, in order to become high-grade Islamic missionaries.

Nationality policies in Xinjiang

Since the establishment of the People's Republic of China, the Chinese government initiated a series of nationality policies to realize equality, unity and development. Being one of the regional nationality autonomous regions in China, all the nationality policies of the central government are implemented in Xinjiang to provide benefits to all nationalities, to form, develop and consolidate the new-type nationality relationship of equality, unity and mutuality.

1   Admitting the existence of the nationalities, and safeguarding equal rights in each aspect, is the basic principle and fundamental policy to solve the nationality problem. The Constitution of China stipulates:

> All the nationalities within the People's Republic of China are equal. The country will safeguard the legal rights and interests of all the minorities, maintain and develop the equal, united and mutual relations between all nationalities. Discrimination and oppression of any other nationality are forbidden, any behavior destroying the national unity and causing national splittism is forbidden.

The citizens of any nationality in Xinjiang enjoy equal rights endowed by the Constitution and the laws, including the suffrage and the eligibility for election, the right to participate in the administration of national affairs, etc. Adequate quota is reserved for the minorities in Xinjiang at the sessions of the National People's Representative Congresses. The Xinjiang representatives at the 11th session of National People's Representative Congress are 60, composed of 11 nationalities, where the minority representatives account for 60 per cent. Currently, the minority representatives from Xinjiang are among the leading members of the Standing Committee of the National People's Representative Congress and the national political negotiation committee. There are also certain representatives from each minority cluster area in the regional people's representative congress.

2   Regional autonomy is implemented in the minority cluster regions, that is, letting the minorities manage their internal affairs by themselves, which is

the fundamental policy to solve China's nationality problems. The equality between the nationalities in Xinjiang is realized through regional autonomy for nationalities. The Xinjiang Uyghur Autonomous Region was established in 1955, which is a nationality autonomous region with the Uyghurs being the main nationality. Moreover, five Autonomous Prefectures were established for the Kazakhs, Huis, Khalkhas and Mongols, six Autonomous Counties for the Kazakhs, Huis, Mongols, Tajiks and Xibos, and 43 Autonomous Townships for other nationalities in other minority cluster areas besides the Uyghur. As for the representative composition of the People's Representative Committees and the allocation of the departments at different levels, the principle of equal participation, common management between the nationalities is followed to ensure the implementation of management right for the nationalities. The autonomous authorities at all levels have the rights to constitute and implement the autonomous laws, local codes and the decisions with legal binding, and to safeguard the autonomous rights over the local nationality. By the end of 2008, the Regional People's Representative Committee and the standing committee enacted 127 local laws, 28 legal decisions and resolutions, and adopted 100 local laws for the Urumqi City, and bylaws for all the autonomous prefectures and counties.

3   Selection, grooming and use of the minority leaders are the key to the nationalities policy. The regional government has nurtured and created a number of excellent minority leaders so that the number and quality of the minority leaders team has improved greatly. In 2008, the minority leaders in the whole of Xinjiang were 363,000, accounting for 51.25 per cent of the whole-Xinjiang leaders. Currently, the Chairman of the Autonomous Region, the executive of each Autonomous Prefecture, the head of each Autonomous County, and the Director of the Regional People's Representative Committee, the Dean of the People's Court, the Chief of the Procuratorate are all appointed from the nationalities implementing the nationalities policy and regional autonomy. The commissioners and chiefs of most regions and prefectures, are headed by the minority leaders.

4   The principle of equality between the nationality languages and scripts is followed, thus opposing the privilege of any form. The Autonomous Region government issued the 'Provisional Prescriptions On Nationality Languages Utilization in the Xinjiang Uyghur Autonomous Region', and 'Bylaw on Languages and Scripts in the Xinjiang Uyghur Autonomous Region' to safeguard the freedom and rights on the use of their own language by the minorities systematically. Currently there are ten languages and scripts used by 13 generation-residential nationalities. The Chinese and the local language scripts can be used simultaneously in the Autonomous Region, and certain Autonomous Prefectures and Counties. The minority languages and scripts are used widely in news, press, broadcasts, movies, TV, etc. The *Xinjiang Daily* is issued in the Uyghur, Chinese, Kazakh, and Mongolian

languages. The Xinjiang TV station telecasts in Uyghur, Chinese, Kazakh and Mongolian. Xinjiang People's Press publishes books in Uyghur, Chinese, Kazakh, Mongolian, Khalkhas and Xibo.

5 Respecting the minority customs and habits is one of the important means to safeguard equal rights of all nationalities. A series of policies and laws are constituted by the country and the governments at different levels to respect and care about the minority customs and habits on catering, dress, festivals, marriages, etc. For example, the Marriage Law of the People's Republic of China stipulates that the male citizens' marriage age should not be earlier than 22 years old, and of the female 20 years. But historically and traditionally the marriage age of some minorities has been lesser. In order to take care of such tradition, the Autonomous Region's People's Representative Committee constituted the Supplementary Prescriptions on the Marriage Law of the People's Republic of China in the Xinjiang Uyghur Autonomous Region. It stipulates that the marriage age of the male minorities should not be earlier than 20 years and for the females 18 years. The Autonomous Region government carries out the special arrangement on the production and supply of minority necessities annually, and special attention is paid to the ten nationalities who follow Islam. In Xinjiang, the people of all nationalities believing in Islam can enjoy the holidays on the *Roza* and *Guerbang*.

6 More flexible procreation policies are implemented for the minorities. According to the national family planning policy, the People's Representative Committee of the Xinjiang Uyghur Autonomous Region constitutes the Provisional Prescriptions on the Minority Family Planning in the Xinjiang Uyghur Autonomous Region in accordance with the actual situation prevailing in Xinjiang, implementing more flexible procreation policies than the Hans in favour of the minorities. The detailed stipulations include: each Han couple in the urban area can have one child, while a minority couple can have two children; each Han farming or pasturing couple can have one or two children, while a minority couple can have three. Thus the increase in the minority population is ensured so as to make their natural population growth rate higher than that of the Hans.

7 Strengthening the unity of nationalities safeguards the real equality between the nationalities. Special importance is given to the strengthening of the nationalities unity in Xinjiang. The Autonomous Region government has been advocating the nationalities unity policy for years, underlining the importance of 'three interdependencies' principle, that is, 'the Han cannot be independent without the minorities, the minorities cannot be independent without the Han, and all the nationalities cannot be independent of each other'. This principle is followed by the nationalities in Xinjiang in their practices. Xinjiang is the first to implement the nationalities unity advancement awards in China since 1982. The nationalities unity education activities have been held every May since 1983. The nationalities unity and relevant knowledge education courses have been introduced at each level of

the school education. The unity and mutuality idea between the nationalities has deep roots in the hearts of each nationality through years of consistent efforts on the nationalities unity education.

To conclude, the nationality and religious policies implemented in Xinjiang are consistent with the actual situation in Xinjiang, receiving support of the nationalities promoting all-round development in Xinjiang, and laying good foundation for the long-term and sustainable development and stability in future.

15 Ethno-religious separatism in Xinjiang and China's response

K. Warikoo

Continued inter-ethnic conflict in Xinjiang and Tibet and the questioning of Chinese sovereignty by ethnic-religious minorities in these regions is seen as a major challenge to the nation-building process in China. Chinese scholars now advocate reconsideration of Chinese nationalities policy, which they believe is based on the Soviet (Marxist-Leninist) theory of nationalities and which proved a failure with the disintegration of the former USSR.[1] They argue that the Chinese Communist Party (CCP) adopted the Soviet nationalities policy, recognizing various ethnic groups of China as nationalities. Following the Soviet Union, which was established as a multi-national federation of various nationalities controlled by Moscow, 'China launched a campaign in the 1950s that recognized 56 nationalities having common territory, language, economic mode and culture',[2] and established various autonomous regions. However, the China model does not offer the formal right of political secession to its nationalities, as was provided in theory by the Soviet model.[3] Chinese scholars believe that the special policies and concessions in terms of family planning programmes, university admissions, administrative positions in autonomous areas and dual school system for local minorities favouring ethnic minorities in China, are the roots of ethnic conflicts today as these have only 'strengthened and politicized minority group identity'.[4]

Due to its geo-strategic location, and abutting the borders of India, Pakistan, Afghanistan and the Central Asian Republics of Kazakhstan, Kyrgyzstan and Tajikistan, Xinjiang is the important strategic frontier of China in its northwest. With the main overland trade routes connecting China with Central and South Asia passing through Xinjiang, it is China's bridge to Central Asia and South Asia. Xinjiang is also vital for China's quest for energy security. China views Xinjiang as a continental bridge which 'extends China's reach to Central Asia and simultaneously serves as a security buffer to China proper'.[5] Besides being used as the site for nuclear testing, Xinjiang is a region of vast unexploited petroleum and mineral reserves and immense agricultural potential. Following the disintegration of the USSR, China's position in Central Asia and the Middle East has been enhanced by its possession of Xinjiang. China has been following the time-tested policy of large-scale Han settlement in Xinjiang 'as a means to work towards regional stability and bring the new Central Asian republics and peoples of Xinjiang closer to China's world view'.[6] However, the main hurdle in achieving China's economic, political and strategic objectives in this region is the ethno-religious resurgence which feeds the Pan-Turkic and Islamic secessionist movement in Xinjiang.

Xinjiang region of China presents a case of geo-cultural diversity. Whereas the lofty mountain ranges of Altyn Tagh, Kuen Lun, Karakoram, Pamirs, Ala Tau and the Altai virtually encircle the region, the great Taklamakan desert to the east cuts it off from the mainland of China. And the Tien Shan range of mountains cuts the region into two distinct but unequal parts, the northern region traditionally dominated by the pastoral nomads and the southern region or the Tarim basin possessing numerous fertile oasis-settlements dominated by the Uyghurs. Different ethnic groups are settled/concentrated in different geographical areas such as Uyghur Muslims dominating southern parts of Xinjiang (*Alty Shahr*), Kyrgyzs settled in Kizilsu Prefecture in the south, Tajiks living in the mountainous Tashkurghan County, and Mongols, Kazakhs and Huis living in their distinct traditional habitats in northern Xinjiang, with the Hans dominating both the northern and eastern parts of Xinjiang. These ethnic groups retain their distinct ethno-cultural identity which has been consolidated by the creation of separate Autonomous Prefectures and Counties for respective ethnic groups in their respective territorial loci, within the overall framework of Xinjiang Uyghur Autonomous Region of China. These ethnic groups speak different languages – Uyghur, Kyrgyz, Tajik, Kazakh, Mongol and Chinese Mandarin.

Whereas Muslim Uyghurs are predominant in the southern part of Xinjiang particularly in Kashghar, Khotan, Aksu and Turfan Autonomous Prefectures, the Muslim Kazakhs are concentrated in Ili Kazakh Autonomous Prefecture (adjoining Kazakhstan), Mori Kazakh Autonomous County of the Changji Hui Autonomous Prefecture, and Barkol Kazakh Autonomous County of the Hami Prefecture.[7] Similarly the Muslim Kyrgyzs inhabit the Kizilsu Kyrgyz Autonomous Prefecture (adjoining Kyrgyzstan) and the Muslim Tajiks have been provided an Autonomous County of Tashkurghan (adjoining Tajikistan) within the Kashghar Prefecture.[8] Mongols reside mainly in Bayangholin and Bortala Mongol Autonomous Prefectures and Hoboksar Mongol Autonomous County. In fact these divisions were created during 1954, that is more than a year before Xinjiang was declared as the Uyghur Autonomous Region.[9] Uyghurs are in majority in the southern parts of Xinjiang (Kashghar, Khotan, Aksu) as well as in Turfan, which has turned this region into a centre of separatist forces. Hans are in majority in northern and eastern parts of Xinjiang, mainly concentrated in urban areas. Notwithstanding their intra-ethnic differences, most of the non-Han population of Xinjiang are of Turkic stock and are Muslims by faith sharing their religion, Turkic language and culture with their counterparts in the neighbouring Central Asian countries. Given China's tenuous historical position in this region, any cross-border fraternization on ethnic-religious grounds between the Muslims of Xinjiang with their Central Asian, Afghan and Pakistani neighbours is a potential source of instability for China in its strategic frontier.

Inter-ethnic relations

From the cultural and racial point of view, Uyghurs and other Muslim groups like Kazakhs and Kyrgyzs belong to the Turkic Islamic groups and they see Chinese Hans and even Chinese Hui Muslims as alien ethnic group and race. The local Muslims speak Turkic (Uyghur, Kazakh, Kyrgyz) languages, whereas Chinese Hans and Huis speak Mandarin. There is a communication gap between the Han Chinese and local Turkic racial groups. All Uyghur, Kazakh and Kyrgyz Muslims in Xinjiang observe local Xinjiang time which is two hours behind the Beijing time. This is in marked contrast to various offices and institutions and the Han Chinese people settled in Xinjiang who observe Beijing time. Few Uyghurs can speak Chinese and very few Chinese know the local language.

There exist separate hostels for Han and Muslim students in universities and institutes as well. Similarly, there are exclusive restaurants for Muslims and Hans. In Muslim restaurants, smoking and drinking are not allowed. During a visit to Beijing, this author was told by Prof. Wu Hongwei that in Ili city, an Uyghur Muslim killed a neighbouring Han (even though both lived together for long) at the instigation of some Uyghurs to kill the Hans as it would be tantamount to making Hajj pilgrimage. Prof. Wu affirmed that religious extremists are exclusive, aggressive and opposed to non-Muslims and even opposed to other sects of Muslims. Few Uyghurs can speak Chinese and very few Chinese know the local language. Dru Gladney found during his visit to Kashghar Teachers College that 'young Uyghurs would rather learn Urdu than Chinese', as it would facilitate their trading with Pakistan.[10] Hans find it inconvenient when passing through the localities dominated by the Turkic peoples. The Kazakhs in Ili region of northern Xinjiang still retain their bitter memories of 1960s when about 100,000 Muslim Kazakhs and Uyghurs migrated to the neighbouring region of Kazakhstan, then part of the former USSR. There are about one and a half million Kazakhs in Xinjiang and about 200,000 Uyghurs in Kazakhstan, maintaining family and ethnic ties across the border. Besides, several hundred Uyghurs have settled in Pakistan-occupied Kashmir (PoK), where they use the Karakoram Highway to keep their family ties and trading connections alive with Xinjiang.

Though there is an aura of peace in Xinjiang, relations between Uyghurs and Hans or elsewhere in Xinjiang are not cosy. Rather both communities maintain adversarial race relations. They do not eat together and have separate restaurants/eating places. However, Hans and Hui Muslims (who speak Chinese language and eat Chinese food excepting pork) maintain good relations. Hui, Kazakh and Kyrgyz communities of Xinjiang are reported to have remained aloof from the 5 July 2009 Urumqi riots, which involved mainly Uyghurs and Hans. As such, mutual distrust between Uyghurs and Hans remains. The majority of the Uyghurs in southern Xinjiang (Kashghar, Khotan, Aksu) do not know Chinese. However, as compared to the past, many Uyghur parents now send their children to cities to learn Chinese languages, as it provides them higher education, jobs and better opportunities. Uyghurs now seek to adapt to the new reality. However, there is shortage of teachers to train Uyghurs in Chinese language. The central government realizes the urgency of this problem and seeks to resolve it as soon as possible. New government policy is to encourage the Hans to learn the Uyghur language. Those Hans who understand Uyghur language are given preference for jobs. Similarly, from kindergarten onwards, bilingual education (Chinese and Uyghur) is imparted to children. Over 300,000 Uyghurs and Kazakhs are scattered in mainland China (Beijing, Henan and some other places), working mainly in restaurants, bakeries and labour. They continue to live in ghettos even while staying outside Xinjiang. Few of them have been found involved in petty crimes and also in extremist and terrorist activities. Professor Ilham Tohti, a prominent Uyghur economist and scholar, who taught at the Central University of Nationalities in Beijing, was detained by security agencies in January 2014.[11]

Way back in 1955, China declared Xinjiang as Uyghur Autonomous Region, in cognizance of its main Uyghur nationality. It also established Autonomous Prefectures for Kazakh, Hui, Kyrgyz and Mongol nationality areas; and Autonomous Counties for Kazakh, Hui, Mongolian, Tajik and Sibo. The regional concentration of various ethnic-religious groups has been consolidated by the Chinese policy of creating separate administrative divisions – Autonomous Prefectures, Autonomous Counties and towns within Prefectures, where a particular ethnic or religious group is in majority. In this manner, China has set up necessary administrative mechanisms to take care of other non-Uyghur minority nationalities in Xinjiang. China has successfully followed the policy of Han settlement in Xinjiang as a means towards social and political stability and territorial integrity. The immigration and settlement of Hans, Huis and others from mainland China, has resulted in the increase of the share of the Han population from 6 per cent in 1953 to about 40 per cent in 2007 and sharp reduction of the Uyghur population from 80 per cent in 1941 to 46 per cent in 2007 (see Tables 15.1, 15.2 and 15.3). Despite several attempts by the local Uyghur Islamic radicals to intimidate and shoo away the Han settlers in Xinjiang, the authorities have not only foiled all such attempts but even reinforced the Han presence in Xinjiang. The problem gets accentuated by the large concentration of Muslim Uyghurs in the southern part of Xinjiang (to the extent of about 90 per cent) (see Table 15.4) whereas they constitute only about 46 per cent of the total population in the entire province.

Ethnic-religious separatism

Xinjiang, being the only Muslim majority province in China, has been home to ethnic-religious separatist movement for a long time. Uyghurs in Xinjiang continue to nourish aspirations of ethno-political independence and have not come closer to the Chinese national mainstream, notwithstanding some economic upliftment due to increased Chinese investment and cross-border trade. Riots occurred in Aksu in April 1980 when Han settlers were beaten up, their homes looted and a factory run by them damaged.[12] The Aksu riots, in which several

Table 15.1 Population of main ethnic groups in Xinjiang

Ethnic group	1941[a]	1953[b]	1964[b]	1982[b]	1990[b]	2000[c]
Uyghur	2,984,000	3,640,000	4,021,200	5,995,000	7,195,000	8,345,622
	80%	74.7%	54%	45.8%	47.5%	45.21%
Han	187,000	299,000	2,445,400	5,284,000	5,696,000	7,489,919
	5%	6.1%	32.9%	40.4%	37.6%	40.6%
Kazakh	326,000	492,000	501,400	903,000	1,106,000	1,245,023
	8.7%	10.1%	6.7%	6.9%	7.3%	6.74%
Hui	92,000	150,000	271,100	567,000	682,000	839,837
	2.5%	3.1%	3.6%	4.3%	4.5%	4.55%
Kyrgyz	65,000	68,000	69,200	112,000	140,000	158,775
	1.7%	1.4%	0.9%	0.9%	0.9%	0.86%
Others (Tajik, Mongol, etc.)	76,000	225,000	133,500	220,500	337,900	368,674
	2%	4.6%	1.8%	1.7%	2.2%	2.04%
Total	3,730,000	4,874,000	7,441,800	13,081,500	15,156,900	18,459,511

Sources: a Chang Chih-yi, 'Land Utilisation and Settlement Possibilities in Xinjiang', *Geographical Review*, Vol. 39, 1949. b Yuan Qingli, 'Population Changes in Xinjiang Uyghur Autonomous Region (1949–1984)', *Central Asian Survey*, Vol. 9, No. 1, 1990. Xinjiang Uyghur Autonomous Region Bureau of Statistics, *Xinjiang Statistical Yearbook*, 1996, Beijing, 1996. c Department of Population, Social, Science and Technology Statistics of the National Bureau of Statistics of China, *Tabulation on Nationalities of 2000 Population Census of China*, Beijing, 2003 (http://en.wikipedia.org/wiki/Xinjiang#Demographics).

Table 15.2 Population of main ethnic groups in Xinjiang (1949–2007)[a]

	1949	1955	1960	1970	1975	1985	1995	2007
Total	4,333,400	5,117,800	6,863,300	9,765,800	11,545,300	13,611,400	16,613,500	20,951,900
Uyghur	3,291,100	3,726,500	3,991,200	4,673,300	5,266,400	6,294,400	7,800,000	9,650,600
Hans	291,000	550,500	1,944,500	3,861,200	4,780,100	5,349,200	6,318,100	8,239,300
Kazakhs	443,700	508,300	541,600	616,300	751,400	987,200	1,237,700	1,483,900
Hui	122,500	147,900	199,600	383,300	477,100	599,600	747,600	943,000
Kyrgzs	66,100	68,500	67,300	80,100	94,200	123,500	157,800	181,900
Mongol	52,500	60,500	67,300	88,400	1,00,300	123,300	152,800	177,100
Sibos	11,700	13,800	15,700	20,800	23,900	29,200	38,200	42,400
Russians	19,500	7,800	2,900	700	700	4,300	9,000	11,600
Tajiks	13,500	15,200	15,100	18,300	20,500	28,900	38,200	44,800
Uzbeks	12,200	10,900	7,300	6,500	7,400	9,300	13,300	16,100
Tatar	5,900	3,700	2,500	2,100	2,800	3,300	4,700	4,700
Manchu	1,000	1,200	1,500	2,800	3,500	9,500	19,900	25,600
Daur	1,800	2,100	2,700	3,200	3,700	4,800	6,200	6,700
Others	900	900	4,100	8,800	13,300	44,900	70,000	124,200

Note
a Wu Fuhuan (ed.), Xinjiang Shaoshuminzu Fazhan Bagogao, 1949–2009 (Xinjiang Minority Nationalities Development Report, 1949–2009) (in Chinese). Urumqi, September 2009, pp. 26–9.

Table 15.3 Population of main ethnic groups in Xinjiang, 2007[a]

Ethnic group	Total	Percentage of total population
Uyghurs	9,650,600	46.06
Hans	8,239,300	39.33
Kazakhs	1,483,900	7.08
Hui Muslims	943,000	4.50
Kyrgyzs	181,900	0.87
Mongols	177,100	0.85
Tajiks	44,800	0.21
Sibos	42,400	0.20
Manchus	25,600	0.12
Russians	11,600	0.06
Daurs	6,700	0.03
Uzbeks	4,700	0.02
Others	124,200	0.59
Total Population	20,935,800	99.90

Note

a Wu Fuhuan (ed.), *Xinjiang Shaoshuminzu Fazhan Bagogao, 1949–2009* (Xinjiang Minority Nationalities Development Report, 1949–2009) (in Chinese). Urumqi, September 2009, pp. 26–9.

hundred civilians and soldiers were reported to have been killed or wounded,[13] terrified the local Chinese settlers forcing thousands of them to demonstrate and demand permission to return to their homes.[14] And by early 1981 more than 30,000 Hans were reported to have left Xinjiang for Shanghai.[15] In October 1980 an accident in which an Uyghur pedestrian was killed by a Chinese truck driver provoked local unrest, particularly after the Chinese police refused to execute the driver even though the local court had sentenced him to death.[16] Further trouble was averted when the sentence was commuted. In June 1981 Uyghur demonstrators attacked the Han settlers and even a PLA army base in Kashghar.[17] The inter-ethnic discord between Uyghurs and Han Chinese did not leave the Provincial Communist Party unaffected. The situation worsened in August 1981 when the Uyghur Provincial Committee members virtually revolted against the Chinese ruling majority which forced the then Vice Chairman, Deng Xiaoping, to visit Xinjiang for nine days to resolve the political crisis. Deng ordered a reorganization of the Provincial Committee and Xinjiang's First Party Secretary, Wang Feng (1978–81) was replaced by Wang Enmao who had worked in Xinjiang from 1949 to 1969.[18] Wang Enmao's task was to re-establish political stability and strengthen security in Xinjiang. In 1985 and 1986, Uyghur students organized public demonstrations in Urumqi demanding a ban on nuclear testing in Lop Nor and settlement of Hans in Xinjiang.[19] It was in May 1989 that Muslim students in Xinjiang University at Urumqi protested against the application of Chinese policy of birth control to non-Han peoples also. Slogans like 'Han people leave Xinjiang' were also raised then. Despite such incidents, Xinjiang remained quiet and peaceful and China continued with its liberalized policy of allowing freedom of religion, restoration of old mosques and

Table 15.4 Population of major ethnic groups in Xinjiang (area wise), 2007*

	Total	Minorities	Uyghurs	Hans	Kazakhs	Hui	Kyrgyzs	Mongol	Sibos	Tajiks
XINJIANG UAR	20,951,900	12,712,655	9,650,629	8,239,245	1,483,383	942,956	181,862	177,120	42,444	44,824
URUMQI	2,312,964	625,172	284,058	1,687,792	63,275	237,730	1,514	9,088	4,757	3,353
KARAMAY	267,174	65,486	40,512	201,688	10,684	6,352	133	2,293	868	24
DIRECTLY ADMINISTERED AREAS (XPCC)										
Shihezi City	636,090	35,238	7,648	600,852	3,957	16,402	60	838	179	23
Aral City	166,544	11,332	6,719	155,212	206	996	33	272	10	6
Tumushuke City	147,804	94,279	93,053	53,525	—	586	—	32	1	—
Wujiaqu City	72,782	2,433	72	70,349	103	1,475	9	196	14	—
HAMI	546,169	182,057	110,220	364,112	49,663	16,226	17	2,452	171	—
Barkol Kazakh Autonomous County	101,310	36,445	150	64,865	34,406	290	1	1,424	8	—
CHANGJI HUI AUTONOMOUS PREFECTURE	1,353,742	346,707	61,646	1,007,035	132,582	130,793	152	6,544	598	7
Mori Kazakh Autonomous County	87,229	29,612	4,964	57,617	22,425	821	28	7	7	—
ILI KAZAKH AUTONOMOUS PREFECTURE	4,342,166	2,438,415	702,219	1,903,751	1,139,293	368,474	19,371	72,570	33,884	152
Qapqal Sibos Autonomous County	184,057	119,425	48,450	64,632	37,433	9,582	305	511	20,804	1
Hoboksar Mongol Autonomous County	51,634	33,144	1,034	18,490	14,558	477	23	16,646	55	—
Altay Prefecture	645,057	373,747	9,777	271,310	328,610	22,853	210	5,890	101	1
BAYINGHOLIN MONGOL AUTONOMOUS PREFECTURE	1,224,080	520,830	400,528	703,250	1,197	61,892	216	48,886	191	3
Yanqi Hui Autonomous County	129,897	73,032	39,276	56,865	39	29,570	104	3,171	—	—
BORTALA MONGOL AUTONOMOUS PREFECTURE	472,918	154,656	60,149	318,262	44,664	17,814	90	27,833	409	5
KIZILSU KYRGYZ AUTONOMOUS PREFECTURE	500,007	463,150	317,540	36,857	126	594	139,042	70	27	5,199
KASHGHAR	3,694,349	3,423,137	3,367,013	271,212	230	5,805	6,438	534	113	37,084
Tashkurghan Tajik Autonomous County	34,612	32,553	1,759	2,059	2	17	1,986	3	5	28,751
AKSU	2,203,077	1,748,101	1,718,270	454,976	190	14,826	9,422	760	107	75
HOTAN	1,883,894	1,818,716	1,814,785	65,178	82	1,471	795	106	10	919
TURFAN	600,610	462,865	423,212	137,745	270	37,778	1	186	36	—

Note

* Department of Population, Social, Science and Technology Statistics of the National Bureau of Statistics of China, *Tabulation on Nationalities of 2000 Population Census of China*, Beijing, 2003 (http://en.wikipedia.org/wiki/Xinjiang#Demographics).

construction of new mosques. The number of new mosques being built with the help of voluntary donations in various settlements increased manifold. In 1988, their number was reported to have reached 24,000.[20] Uyghur and Arabic editions of the Quran, besides other Islamic scriptures, have been circulated in hundreds of thousands after 1980, when the Regional Islamic Association resumed its activity.[21] Hajj pilgrimage to Mecca is also allowed and thousands of Xinjiang Muslims have undertaken the Hajj pilgrimage. Most of the mosques in Muslim-dominated areas have *madrassas* attached for teaching the Quran, Arabic and also for training of young ones in Islamic doctrine. This has had a considerable impact on the society and politics in the region.

Uyghur academics, intellectuals and literary figures have been voicing their dissenting views on historical, cultural and socio-economic aspects of Xinjiang. Three books, namely *The Uyghurs*, *A Short History of Xiongnu (Turk)* and *The Literature of the Uyghurs* written and published between 1986 and 1989 by Turghun Almass, an Uyghur expert on local history and culture, created ripples in Xinjiang. Almass describes the Uyghurs as 'indigenous nation' which was 'independent of China' in the past.[22] Referring to the Great Wall being the national boundary of China, he described the area highlighting the inter-ethnic/racial conflict between Turkic peoples and the Hans. Almass espouses the case for an 'independent state' of all 'Turkic people'.[23] By eulogizing the conversion of Uyghurs from Buddhism to Islam, which in his opinion turned them into a 'powerful and unified nation', Almass sought to link Pan-Islam to Pan-Turkism.[24] As expected, Almass's books evoked sharp reaction from Chinese party and government circles and Han academics. He was accused of twisting and fabricating Xinjiang's history and threatening national unity.[25] Almass's works were dubbed as a 'vain attempt to incite racial conflict and fan flames of Xinjiang's independence'. He was accused of manipulating history to incite 'secession of Xinjiang from China'.[26] Even though Turghun Almass's three books were banned by the Chinese government, his books were sold at premium due to large demand among the Uyghurs, particularly after the ban. This author was informed by an Uyghur teacher in Urumqi (during a visit in 1998) that almost every Uyghur household possesses his books. This indicates the sustenance of popular Uyghur dissent and opposition to Chinese control in Xinjiang.

To meet this ideological threat, Xinjiang Academy of Sciences published the *Educational Textbook of Atheism* for use by the young masses in Xinjiang. This book, which highlights the negative role of religion in the long history of Xinjiang, nevertheless foresees a 'long struggle to eliminate religion'.[27] However, Chinese books on history, culture and traditions of Xinjiang provoked strong reaction from the Muslims in Xinjiang. In April 1987 several Kazakh students in Ili went on strike to protest the publication of novel *White House in the Distance* (in Chinese), describing it as a distortion of Kazakh customs and an insult to the national pride of Turkic people.[28] Similarly, in December 1988, Uyghur students staged a protest march in Beijing against the exhibition of two historical films which they found 'disrespectful to their race'.[29] The publication of *Sex Habits* by the Shanghai Cultural House caused resentment among the Muslims throughout

China and protest marches were organized in Beijing, Lanzhou and several cities in Xinjiang.[30] Taking advantage of the freedom of religion and culture allowed after 1978, there has been rise in ethno-nationalist tendencies in Xinjiang, often using Islam as a means of common identity and a rallying point to forge unity among diverse Muslim ethnic groups. A report from Turfan, which is predominantly Muslim, suggested that more than 25 per cent of local party members were taking active part in religious activities since 1990. And 40 per cent of such members were of rural background. Chinese efforts to reduce the number of such Islamic party members were not bearing any fruit.[31]

Increased trans-border trade and traffic between Xinjiang and adjoining region of Kazakhstan, Kyrgyzstan and Pakistan (via Karakoram Highway passing through Pak-occupied Kashmir) has resulted in greater interaction between the Turkic peoples of Xinjiang and their ethnic counterparts and co-religionists in Central Asia, Pakistan, Turkey and Saudi Arabia. Uyghur and Kazakh exiles from Xinjiang settled in the Middle East, Turkey, Europe, the United States and Australia have been keeping close contacts with their counterparts in Xinjiang and have been running scores of organizations aimed at achieving the goal of separation of Xinjiang from China. A publication, *Voice of Eastern Turkestan*, was being published from Istanbul, the headquarters of the East Turkestan Liberation Front which had been led by the old Uyghur politician in exile, Isa Yusuf Alptekin. Isa Alptekin mobilized diplomatic support in Turkey for the independence of Eastern Turkestan. Alptekin even met the Organization of Islamic Conference (OIC) leaders during the Islamic Foreign Ministers' meeting at Istanbul in August 1991, and asked for an Observer status for Eastern Turkestan in the OIC. Subsequently, he met Turkey's leaders including former President Turgut Ozal and Prime Minister S. Demirel, seeking their support.

Uyghurs settled in Turkey, Western countries, Central Asian states of Kazakhstan, Uzbekistan and Kyrgyzstan revitalized their activities soon after the independence of these former Soviet Republics. An International Uyghur Union of CIS was set up in early 1992 in Almaty with the objective of protecting human rights and seeking self-determination for Uyghurs in Xinjiang. The Nevada Semipalatinsk Movement in Kazakhstan had a separate department to mobilize opinion against the Lop Nor nuclear tests. In Kyrgyzstan a new Uyghur party, 'For a Free Uyghuristan', was set up in June 1992 aimed at the creation of Independent State of Eastern Turkestan. Besides, several newspapers in Uyghur language such as *Uyghur Awazi* (Voice of Uyghur) were being published in Almaty. A number of Uyghurs have been reported to be migrating to Turkey, Middle East and Central Asian states from Xinjiang. This is in addition to the defection of more than 100 prominent Xinjiang Muslims to Turkey during the decade of 1980–90.[32] Following the dismantling of the USSR, China's borderlands attracted renewed Western interest. In Munich (Germany), the Eastern Turkestan Cultural and Social Association was established in January 1991 by Erkin Alptekin, son of late Isa Alptekin. It published a periodical, *Eastern Turkestan Information*. Earlier in February 1990, Erkin Alptekin became the founding

Vice Chairman of Unrepresented Nations and Peoples Organization (UNPO) which seeks self-determination for Eastern Turkestan and Tibet, among others.

Piqued at the ethno-religious resurgence in Xinjiang and taking an alarmist view of ethnic conflict and Islamic resurgence in the newly independent Central Asian states across the border, the Chinese authorities, party functionaries and officially controlled educational and media establishment in Xinjiang openly denounced the 'infiltration, subversion and sabotage by hostile foreign Islamic elements' for fanning the separatist movement in Xinjiang.[33] A local newspaper, *Xinjiang Ribao*, in its editorial dated 9 February 1990 called for an end to religious interference in matters pertaining to education, judiciary and administration and stressed the need to prevent all 'unfriendly foreign organizations and individuals and their local supporters from using religion for their dangerous designs'.[34] A local Chinese commentator, Shi Jian, writing in the same paper on 18 March 1990, ascribed the rise of ethno-religious separatism in Xinjiang to lax control on religious activities of mosques and *madrassas*.[35] The Deputy Secretary of Xinjiang Region CPC Committee, A. Niyaz, who led a fact-finding visit to various areas in Xinjiang, while emphasizing the need to follow strictly the 'Policy of Freedom of Religious Beliefs', warned that religion would not be allowed to interfere in state affairs, administration of justice, education and culture, marriage, public health and family welfare and the system of privileges or discrimination.[36] Niyaz also held the foreign hostile Islamic groups responsible for infiltration and internal subversion.[37] The 7th Xinjiang Uyghur Autonomous Regional People's Congress held in March 1990 at Urumqi identified the ethno-religious separatist movement as the greatest danger facing Xinjiang.[38] Earlier in August 1989, the Chinese Minister of Public Security, Wang Feng, had held the 'conspiratorial separatist elements' responsible for instability in Xinjiang.[39] Gorbachev's policy of perestroika and glasnost were also seen as a contributory factor for ethno-religious resurgence in Central Asia. Tomur Dawamat, the former head of Xinjiang government, cited 'global changes in pursuit of bourgeois liberalisation', alluding to Gorbachev's reforms in the ex-USSR, as one of the factors behind unrest in Xinjiang.[40] Speaking at a news conference in Beijing on 24 March 1990, Tomur Dawamat confirmed the arrest of some separatist activists belonging to the East Turkestan Liberation Front for 'distributing reactionary leaflets and raising slogans'.[41]

However, it was after the violent riots that rocked the Baren township in Kashghar district of south Xinjiang in early April 1990, that the Chinese authorities made a thorough reappraisal of the situation. The anti-Chinese riots, which were reportedly sparked off after the local authorities banned construction of a mosque near Kashghar airport, coincided with *Ramzan* – the month of fasting for the Muslims.[42] The riots, which soon fanned to other towns, were described as 'armed counter revolutionary rebellion' by local television broadcasts. Activists and supporters of the Islamic Party of Eastern Turkestan, which has a declared object of establishing an independent Islamic Republic in Xinjiang, proclaimed *jihad* to 'eliminate infidels' from Xinjiang.[43] The Chinese language channel of Xinjiang Television showed on 22 April 1990 a video film of Uyghur language documents which it claimed gave instructions for a *jihad* combined with an armed Turkic nationalist uprising for an East Turkestan Republic. General Wang Enmao, who headed the region for three decades, later confirmed that seven separatist groups, some with foreign links, had been uncovered.[44] Banners of 'Revive Islam' and 'Independent East Turkestan Islamic Republic' were raised during these disturbances. It was believed that the arms for the uprising came from the Afghan *Mujahideen* routed through Pakistan via the Karakoram Highway. In fact two Pakistani nationals alleged to be operatives of Pakistan's Inter-Services Intelligence (ISI) were reported to have been arrested for fanning unrest in Xinjiang.[45] Karakoram Highway was also closed by the Chinese for some time, so as to curb the influx of Islamic militants from the Pakistani side.

The issue of ethno-religious separatism in Xinjiang predominated the 15th session of the Regional Party Central Committee on 19 July 1990. In their speeches, both Tomur Dawamat, the head of the Xinjiang government and Janabil, the Deputy Secretary of Xinjiang Regional Communist Party, exhorted the delegates to 'take clear-cut stand against separatism and defend country's integrity'.[46] While referring to misuse of religious slogans for anti-Chinese and secessionist activities, Tomur condemned the Islamists' opposition to tapping Xinjiang's resources for its development and also to family planning practices. Janabil was more forthright in admitting that the separatist campaign inside and outside Xinjiang was 'rampant'. He stated that some foreign organizations would use visits to China to see relatives, or to do business, as opportunities for sending subversive agents into Xinjiang and to incite local people against Hans. Also that some local scholars, educationists, artists and littérateurs have been using their lectures, articles, discussions and works of art and literature to 'distort history' and propagate about independence of Xinjiang.[47] Janabil was particularly distressed about the increasing influence of Pan-Islamic and Pan-Turkic elements over young generations. He condemned the slogans – 'Exclusion of Hans', 'eradicate infidels', 'East Turkestan Islamic Republic', that were witnessed in the April 1990 riots. The common features of the May 1989 and April 1990 disturbances in Xinjiang were the unfurling of Islamic banner, war cry of *jihad* (holy war), demands to expel the Hans and open call for establishing the Independent Eastern Turkestan Islamic Republic.

Incidents of bomb blasts were reported to have occurred in Urumqi (February 1992), Ili, Khotan, Kashghar, Kucha, Korla and Bortala (5–8 March 1992), wounding a number of people and causing substantial damage to property. Tomur Dawamat, the Uyghur Chairman of Xinjiang Regional Government in a statement in March 1992, accused the Muslim separatists of sabotage and subversion. That 1993 also witnessed bomb blasts in Kashghar and some other towns indicated the persistence of organized movement of Islamic militants against the Chinese authority in Xinjiang. In 1996, there were several reports of bomb blasts and clashes between the Muslim separatists and security forces in Xinjiang. Chinese authorities responded firmly by arresting about 3,000 Uyghurs and seizing arms and ammunition. A big riot took place in Yining (Ili) town near the Kazakhstan border on 5–6 February 1997 during the Muslim festival of *Ramzan* when more than 1,000 youth demanding independence and shouting anti-China and Islamic slogans took to streets and indulged in arson and beating/ killing of Hans. Over 100 persons (all Hans) were injured and ten Hans were beaten to death.[48] Subsequently there were a number of bomb blasts in Urumqi on 25 February 1997, that is on the day of funeral of Deng Xiaoping, killing nine and injuring 70 persons. This was followed by a bomb blast in Beijing on 7 March 1997 injuring 30 persons. Uyghurs in exile pressing for independence of Eastern Turkestan claimed the responsibility for these attacks.[49] Chinese authorities took quick action by arresting thousands of Uyghur Muslim activists. Summary trials were organized to award punishments to those found guilty of terrorist activities. Qio Shi, head of China's parliament and top political leader, made an unscheduled visit to Urumqi in mid-April 1997. Expressing concern over the worsening situation in Xinjiang, he declared China's firm resolve to 'oppose national separatism and religious extremist forces'.[50] Chinese official sources reported in May 1997 about the execution of eight members of Muslim Uyghur separatist group for being involved in terrorist activities, bomb blasts and other criminal acts.

The surge of ethnic-religious separatism in Xinjiang is also linked to the part played by Uyghur ranks along with the Afghan *Mujahideen* in the *jihad* against Soviet forces in Afghanistan. According to a Pakistani analyst, many Uyghur Muslims were trained by Afghan and Pakistani fundamentalists during the Afghan war in the 1980s.[51] One of the Uyghur youths who received training in one of the *madrassas* in Pakistan, vowed that after his return to his hometown in Khotan he would cleanse it of communism. 'We want to make a new Islamic state for Uyghurs and leave China', he declared.[52] Hundreds of Uyghur Muslims from Xinjiang were reportedly sponsored by Pakistan's Jamaat-e-Islami and Tablighi Jamaat for educating and training them in *jihad* at the Islamic University, Islamabad, Syed Mawdudi International Institute, Lahore and other *madrassas* and training centres. China took up the issue with Pakistan protesting against Pakistan's Islamic parties' involvement in infiltration of Islamic militants into Xinjiang.[53] China's tough stand on this issue paid dividends, when the Pakistani authorities arrested 12 Chinese Muslims who had sought asylum in Pakistan after sneaking through Gilgit. These Uyghurs were handed over to the Chinese authorities.[54] That a ringleader of Pakistani Islamic group operating in Xinjiang was executed in mid-1999[55] further establishes the Pakistani connection of Islamic militancy in Xinjiang.

In an interaction with the Chinese specialists in Beijing in December 2005 including those from Xinjiang Uyghur Autonomous Region, this author was told that 'Xinjiang is a hotbed of separatists, terrorists and foreign Islamic extremists'. The number of mosques in Xinjiang has increased to 25,000. This author learnt that some extremist imams preach violence and hatred and some good imams have even been assassinated by the extremists. Prof. Pinyan of Urumqi stated that the separatists act in the guise of religion, killing innocent people. The suicide bombers are convinced that they would go to heaven after their sacrifice.

While highlighting the problem of religious extremism in Xinjiang, Prof. Pinyan pointed out that though there are very few extremists, yet there are very few Muslims ready to stand up against such extremists. From the 1980s onwards, the religious situation in Xinjiang has become more tense. Eighty per cent of villagers go to mosques and there is social pressure on people to attend mosques, as the extremists try to isolate non-followers from the community. Religious extremists are gaining foothold in Xinjiang, and they advocate violence, causing tension.

Dr Zhao Shuqing, Director, Institute of Ethnic Minority Groups Development Research, Beijing informed that Islamic groups which penetrated Xinjiang in 1980s and joined ethnic separatists, pose a great threat to stability in Xinjiang. These Islamist extremist groups have set up Islamic schools, where extremist ideology is taught and arms training is also given. These groups have broadcasting stations and also publish books to disseminate *jihadi* ideology. Even handwritten material is circulated among the Muslims in Xinjiang, advocating *jihad* and for establishing an Islamic state. They encourage the people to join this movement. In some cases, school teachers and headmasters from other Muslim countries preach in these schools. Some students are even sent abroad for training, and on their return become the backbone of the *jihadi* movement. Some religious schools in the name of Arabic teaching recruit Uyghur students. Neighbouring countries provide hospitality to the Uyghur Muslims. High-tech means are employed to promote *jihad* in Xinjiang. Hizb ut-Tahrir, the transnational Islamist group, has also penetrated Xinjiang, particularly in schools and universities. Whereas in mainland China, administration is separate from religion, in Xinjiang administration at the grassroots is linked with religion. Islamic extremism is being used as a weapon against Hans and other non-Muslim groups and administration. Islamists believe that it would take them 30 years to achieve their goal of Islamic state in Xinjiang, out of which the first ten years would be utilized for indoctrination. Even Muslims advocating good Islam are targeted and killed. If Islamist extremists gain strength in Xinjiang, it would cause instability and hamper economic development and even lead to the exodus of the Chinese business community from Xinjiang.

Prof. Jin Yijiu, a veteran Chinese expert on Islam, stated that Osama bin Laden will continue to influence the Muslims around the world. 'As war against terrorism continues, Islamic extremism will also continue.' Pointing to the existence of religious seminaries in Peshawar, Prof. Yijiu stated that these Islamic militants are sent to Kashmir for *jihad*. In Prof. Yijiu's assessment, 'radical Islam will be transferred from generation to generation. Jihadis will train female jihadi soldiers. They will attack Western targets and also expand their targets.' He stressed that the

radical forces in Kashmir have been thinking of an Islamic state from Kashmir to Central Asia. The Islamist organizations want to set up Islamic state in South and Central Asia and also in Xinjiang province of China where *Eastern Turkestan Islamic Movement* has forged links with Al Qaeda.

The State Council of China released an official report on 21 January 2002 detailing the terrorist incidents involving East Turkestan separatist forces in Xinjiang from 1990 to 2001 in which 162 persons were reported to have been killed and 440 injured.[56] The report stated that

> in the 1990s, under the influence of extremism, separatism and international terrorism, part of the East Turkestan forces inside and outside the Chinese territory turned to splittist and sabotage activities with terrorist violence as the main means, even brazenly declaring that terrorist violence is the only way to achieve their aims. The programmes of the *East Turkestan Islamic party* and the *East Turkestan Opposition Party* seized by the police clearly point out that they will take the road of armed struggle and conduct various terrorist activities in densely populated regions. In a booklet *What is the Hope for Our Independence* compiled by them, they openly declared that they would create a terrorist atmosphere at kindergartens, hospitals and schools at any cost.[57]

That the Uzbek authorities arrested in March 2006 an ethnic Uyghur Hussein Celil who holds Canadian citizenship and later extradited him to China to face charges of 'terrorism',[58] is evidence of close cooperation between Uzbekistan and China on the issue of religious extremism and terrorism. Similarly, Kazakhstan denied one Uyghur, namely Ershidin Israel, an exit visa after the UNHCR had granted him refugee status in mid-March 2010 and secured a resettlement offer for him from Sweden. Israel had fled Xinjiang to Kazakhstan in September 2009 and applied for asylum there. Kazakh authorities later arrested Israel after the Chinese authorities had made an extradition request based on terrorism charges against him.[59]

China put pressure on the Saudi government not to issue Hajj visas to those Uyghur pilgrims who applied for their visas in their Embassy in Pakistan.[60] As a result, over 6,000 Uyghurs were stranded in Pakistan due to the denial of their visas by the Saudi Embassy in Islamabad.[61] The Uyghur separatists in Xinjiang were reported to be involved in a series of terrorist acts to coincide with the opening of Olympic Games in Beijing. On 4 August 2008, in one such terror attack in Kashghar, 16 police personnel were killed. In another attack on 10 August 2008, the terrorists, who included two Uyghur women, targeted supermarkets, hotels and government offices in Kuqa town.[62] Xinjiang Communist Party Secretary Wang Lequan was quoted as saying that 'the fight against separatist forces in Xinjiang is long term, arduous and complex'.[63] On the eve of Pakistani President Asif Ali Zardari's visit to Beijing in third week of October 2008, Chinese authorities listed major terrorist leaders of the East Turkestan Islamic Movement (ETIM). The United Nations has listed the ETIM as a terrorist group, which is reported to be headquartered in Federally Administered Tribal Areas (FATA) of Pakistan.[64] China indicated that most of the Uyghur terrorists operating in Xinjiang have close links with similar groups in Pakistan.[65] Mushahid Husain, the Pakistan Muslim League (Quaid-e-Azam) [PML(Q)] leader who visited China in April 2009, confirmed that the Chinese officials told him that 'the ETIM has its military headquarters in (the tribal areas) and is planning to attack China on the 60th anniversary celebration of the Communist revolution in October'.[66] Husain further revealed that Meng Jianzhu, Chinese Minister for Public Security, had flown from Beijing to Shanghai to discuss the threat with Pakistan's President Zardari during the latter's visit to China in late February 2009.[67] That the Uyghur radicals get arms training in Pakistan and are even involved in the ongoing fighting in Syria, was revealed by the Syrian Ambassador to China, Imad Moustapha, in July 2013. He stated that 'around 30 Uyghur men went to Pakistan to receive military training and then went to Turkey. They are now most probably fighting in the northern city of Aleppo.'[68] The Chinese official media also underlined the Pakistani links of China's separatist leader Memetuhil Memetrozi, co-founder of ETIM. The state-run *China Daily* published, in December 2013, the confessions of Memetrozi, who was handed over by Pakistan to China, admitting that he had been indoctrinated in a *madrassa* in Pakistan.[69] Concerned over the threat of terror attacks from the territory of Pakistan, China has been pressing Islamabad to take action against the Islamist militants plotting attacks inside China from within Pakistan.

July 2009 Urumqi riots

While the Uyghur resentment against the Han Chinese presence in Xinjiang is increasing, China's sovereignty is also being challenged by Uyghur Muslim separatists. The 5 July 2009 riots in Urumqi in which over 200 persons, mostly Hans, were killed, sent shockwaves across China. The worst ethnic violence in decades that erupted in July 2009 between the Han Chinese and Muslim Uyghurs in Xinjiang, coincided with the sixtieth anniversary of communist rule in China. The simmering tensions between the two communities broke into full blown riots in Urumqi on 5 July 2009, when over 10,000 Uyghurs demonstrated to protest against the death of two Uyghur workers in a brawl between migrant Uyghur workers and Han Chinese in a toy factory in south China's Guangdong province in late June 2009. According to Human Rights Watch:

> in the evening hours of July 5, large group of Uyghur youth, armed with knives, and stones launched brutal attacks in parts of the Uyghur quarter and in poor mixed areas of south Urumqi. They randomly attacked Han Chinese residents, including women, children, and elderly, leaving scores dead or injured. The attackers also set dozens of houses, businesses, buses and cars on fire, and ransacked shops.[70]

The casualty figures, released by the Chinese authorities in August 2009, put the death toll at 197 people – which included 134 Han Chinese, ten Uyghurs and 11 Hui Muslim, and one from the ethnic Manchu group and over 1,600 were injured in these ethnic clashes.[71] Thousands of Han Chinese living in Urumqi responded by organizing counter protests smashing Uyghur stores and restaurants and seeking revenge for the Han deaths. The Chinese authorities, which put the blame for the riots on the 'separatist forces', were quick to impose a curfew and arrested hundreds of Uyghur suspects in Urumqi. The Chinese foreign ministry, which also distributed videos of the violence depicting gruesome scenes of people being beheaded and set on fire, accused the World Uyghur Congress and its US based head Rebiya Kadeer as being behind these riots.[72] Chen Guangyuen, President of the Islamist Association of China (IAC) in his statement issued at Beijing condemned the riots as a 'serious crime and against the basic doctrine of Islam'.[73] He stated that it was 'a violent crime which was instigated and directed by separatist forces abroad, and carried out by outlaws inside the country'.[74]

Worried over the alarming situation in Xinjiang, Hu Jintao, the President of China and Secretary General of Communist Party of China, cut short his visit to the G-8 summit in Italy and rushed back to Beijing to deal with the crisis.[75] That Hu decided not to attend the G-8 summit and also postponed a subsequent state visit to Portugal indicated China's concern and also its resolve to defuse the crisis in Xinjiang, before it got out of hand. At the same time, Chinese foreign ministry sought the cooperation of several countries including Afghanistan, Pakistan, Kazakhstan, Turkey, Germany and the United States to help unearth links between their citizens and the World Uyghur Congress.[76] The Chinese government had earlier issued a white paper, which claimed that several Xinjiang terrorists were trained in bases in Pakistan.[77] An urgent nine-member Politburo Standing Committee meeting led by President Hu Jintao asked the Communist Party members and officials at all levels to mobilize and restore order.[78] It promised punishment to rioters and leniency to those 'misled by agitators'[79] in a bid to isolate the hardcore separatist elements from the common masses. Zou Yonghong, Press Officer at the Chinese Embassy in New Delhi, in his signed article explained the role of World Uyghur Congress and its leader Rebiya Kadeer, stating that the Urumqi riot was 'premeditated and remotely manipulated and instigated by separatist forces from abroad'.[80]

There was renewed unrest in Urumqi following protests by thousands of Han Chinese in the capital city of Xinjiang in the first week of September 2009, demanding security. According to Bingtuan Television, a Xinjiang based station, reports of syringe attacks were coming from local disease control centres since 20 August 2009.[81] Local officials stated that over 500 people, mostly Hans, were stabbed with needles,[82] rumoured to have been infected, triggering panic and fresh unrest. Massive protests by Han Chinese in Urumqi on 2–4 September 2009, accusing the local authorities of failure to prevent the mysterious 'syringe attacks' on them, forced the government to sack two senior officials. Xinhua news agency announced on 5 September 2009 that Li Zhi, Secretary of the Urumqi Municipal Committee of the Communist Party of China and Liu Yaohua, the provincial Director of Public Security Department, were replaced. Simultaneously, trial of detainees, mostly Uyghur suspects, was initiated. The Xinjiang People's Procuratorate followed the 'three fast principle (*san kuai yuanze*): fast review, fast arrest and fast prosecution' in dealing with the suspected rioters. The Intermediate Peoples Court in Urumqi sentenced six Uyghurs to death and one Uyghur with life imprisonment for their involvement in the 5 July ethnic riots. At the same time, a court in Guangdong sentenced to death a Han Chinese for his role in violence on Uyghur workers which sparked the Urumqi riots.

In Xinjiang, Uyghur extremists used modern means of communication, Internet services, etc. to spread anti-Han hate mail and separatist agenda during the course of Urumqi riots in July 2009. Soon after, China snapped all communication links in Xinjiang, which has seven million Internet users, to prevent the expansion and recurrence of violence as the riots were fanned and orchestrated by the Uyghur separatists via Internet, text messages and long distance telephone calls. Internet and mobile services were resumed in Xinjiang in May 2010, that is ten months after the July 2009 riots.

The magnitude and intensity of ethnic clashes in Xinjiang came as a rude shock to Chinese leadership. China's response to the crisis has been swift, tough and calibrated – taking security measures to control the situation, detaining hundreds of people, summary trials and deterrent punishment to the convicted rioters, restricting Internet and telephone communication, controlling the flow of information on the riots to the media and the outside world, taking steps to reassure Han Chinese settlers in Urumqi and reaching out to Muslim countries in Central Asia and South Asia seeking their cooperation. Squarely blaming the three forces of 'extremism, separatism and terrorism' for the riots, the Chinese leadership reaffirmed the existing policies in the region. That Cambodia, ignoring US pleadings, deported back to China 20 Uyghur Muslims in December 2009, who had sought asylum in Cambodia and were under the protection of the UNHCR following the July riots in Urumqi,[83] on the eve of a visit to Phnom Penh by Chinese Vice President Xi Jinping, points to the success of China's diplomacy.

Notwithstanding China's claims, Uyghurs continue to challenge Beijing's authority in Xinjiang. The Uyghur Muslim separatists have adopted a new modus operandi of soft terror, that is spreading social hatred, intimidating and threatening the local Han Chinese settlers, discrediting the Chinese security agencies and creating scares like the 'syringe attacks', which is somewhat similar to the anthrax scare in the United States after 9/11. In July 2011, around 18 people reportedly died in Khotan following the attack by armed extremists. The year 2013 witnessed several incidents of violence between the Uyghurs and the authorities in Xinjiang. In April 2013, 21 persons died in the violent clashes between the Uyghurs and the police in Kashghar. In late June 2013, at least 35 people were killed in violence in Lukqun, about 200 kms from Urumqi, after the Uyghur extremists allegedly attacked the police station and government offices.[84] Eleven persons were killed in November 2013, when armed Uyghurs clashed with police in Maralbashi County in southwestern Xinjiang. Earlier the Chinese authorities had blamed the separatist ETIM for organizing an attack in Tiananmen Square in Beijing on 28 October 2013, where a jeep carrying three Uyghurs drove into a crowd and burst into flames killing five persons including the three occupants.[85]

The year 2014 witnessed a spate of terror attacks both within and outside Xinjiang. On 1 March 2014, an Uyghur group of masked assailants armed with knives went on a stabbing spree in Kunming railway station killing 29 people and injuring over 100.[86] The attack in Kunming, which is the provincial capital of Yunnan and a popular destination for Chinese tourists, was well organized and was described by a Chinese party-run newspaper as 'China's 9/11'.[87] Less than two months later, a similar attack on 30 April 2014 on Urumqi railway station left at least three people dead and 79 injured.[88] This attack was significant as it came on a day when China's President Xi Jinping addressed a meeting in Urumqi while concluding his four-day visit to Xinjiang. The Xinjiang provincial government identified the two attackers as Uyghur extremists. President Xi urged the troops to 'strike crushing blows against violent terrorist forces and resolutely strike against terrorists'.[89] While blaming ETIM for these terrorists attacks, the Chinese sources stated that the group was operating from North Waziristan in Pakistan. Yet another terror attack took place on 30 May 2014, killing 39 people and injuring over 100, when five suicide bombers drove two explosive-laden vehicles through a crowded market in Urumqi and blew up the vehicles and also themselves.[90] Fresh violence erupted in July 2014 when around a dozen men drove a truck into the local police station and detonated explosives in Yercheng, a town north of Kashgar. The local authorities claimed to have killed 13 'mobsters'. This was followed by another terror attack in Shache County (Yarked) on 28 July 2014, when a group armed with knives and axes attacked a police station, government offices and majority Han Chinese residents, damaging cars and killing 35 Han Chinese. Local police claimed to have shot dead 59 terrorists and arrested 215 others.[91]

The Chinese response to this violence has been swift and heavy-handed, as most of the armed Uyghur attackers were shot dead by the police. Besides, China's central bank has taken steps to freeze the assets of domestic terrorist groups and their 'overseas affiliates', underlining China's concern over the activities of Uyghur extremists and terror groups abroad, particularly in Pakistan.[92] Chinese authorities also banned the wearing of Islamic veils in public in Xinjiang. A rare mass trial was held in May 2014 in front of 7,000 people in a sports stadium in Ili prefecture, where the court convicted 55 persons on the charges of 'splitting the country and organising and taking part in terrorists activities' sentencing them to imprisonment.[93] Over 40 Uyghurs have been executed since June 2014 for their involvement in terror attacks in Xinjiang. The Uyghur scholar Ilham Tohti, who voiced his criticism of Chinese policies in Xinjiang through his website Uyghur online, was on 23 September 2014 sentenced to life imprisonment by a Urumqi court for fanning separatism. It remains to be seen if the swift and punitive measures seeking to curb extremism and terrorism in Xinjiang will eradicate the menace or further complicate it by radicalizing even those Uyghurs who might be moderate and on the fringe. Developments in Xinjiang will definitely be influenced by the proximity of Uyghur separatists to the extremist and terrorist organizations operating from Pakistan and also with ISIS.

China's policy in Xinjiang

Consolidating Chinese presence by elaborate communication network

Soon after the incorporation of Xinjaing into China in 1949, the outlying periphery was brought close to the mainland by building roads. China has through history been acutely conscious of building large highways to connect cities and towns, this tradition being traced back to Chin emperor (270 BC). The Chinese government has started a large-scale project to upgrade air, rail and road transport infrastructure costing billions of dollars in Xinjiang and Tibet regions, with a dual purpose of integrating the two peripheral regions with the mainland, reducing both distance and time of travel, speeding up development along the new tracks, and enhancing the People's Liberation Army's (PLA) mobility and capacity to bring troops to border areas. The PLA is also building a 'digital great wall' (a network of fibre optics which would improve the PLA's command and control mechanism and communication) along the borders in Xinjiang and Tibet.[94]

Donkeys, the traditional mode of transport in vogue earlier in Xinjiang, have given way to motor cars/carriages. Bicycles have been replaced by motorcycles, battery run small bikes and cars. Foreign brands like Honda, Daewoo, Toyota, Volkswagen, Mazda and Mitsubishi cars manufactured within China are order of the day. Even in southern Xinjiang, one finds these cars plying the roads.

Urumqi airport is the most modern and spacious airport, with three terminals. There are direct flights from Urumqi to Islamabad, Tehran, Dushanbe, Tashkent, Baku, Novosibirsk, Moscow and other international destinations. In the domestic sector, there are regular flights from Urumqi to Beijing, Xian, Chengdu, Shanghai, Kunming and almost all destinations in China. Besides, at the provincial level, flights operate from Urumqi to Kashghar, Khotan, Aksu, Kuqa, Korla, Ili, Altai, etc. The Urumqi airport is full of activity, and provides the evidence of easy mobility of Han Chinese to and from various provinces of China into Xinjiang and vice versa. Over 15 flights to Beijing operate per day, and similarly to other destinations in China. Beijing to Urumqi takes about four hours. The flights are almost always full, with Han Chinese constituting about 85–90 per cent of the passengers. Air China, Southern China, Henan Airlines, Shenzhei Airlines operate flights to and from Urumqi.

Kashghar airport is modern, though not newly built. Southern China, Henan Airlines fly from Urumqi to Kashghar about 12 times a day, which reflects the mobility of people. Kuqa and Aksu airports are small, but well organized. The government is planning to build a new modern and big airport at Baicheng, i.e. midway between Kuqa and Aksu. Under the new Xinjiang development plan, six new airports are proposed to be built in Xinjiang. Southern China Airlines signed an agreement with Xinjiang government on 28 May 2010, for further developing communication in Xinjiang.

That China opened a new high-altitude airport at Ngari in Tibet (4,300 metres), claimed to be the highest airport in the world, demonstrates China's determination to integrate and consolidate its physical presence in outlying provinces of Xinjiang and Tibet, by building quick and efficient means of air communication. Air China flight (Airbus 831) which flew from Chengdu to Ngari, proposes to have flights between Ngari and Lhassa and southern Xinjiang soon.

China has linked the mainland with the outlying and distant province of Xinjiang through rail links, thus overcoming the huge distance and Taklamakan desert. A rail route connects Beijing, passing through Lanzhou, to Urumqi, and further the railway line goes across the border into Kazakhstan and beyond via Alashankou, which has been developed as a big port to facilitate cross-border trade. At present, it takes about 40 hours to cover the distance between Urumqi and Beijing by train. Both goods and passenger trains run on this route. A new express high speed train track costing 21 billion yuan is being built from Urumqi to Lanzhou to connect it onwards with Beijing. The new express train will take only 12–14 hours from Urumqi to Beijing. It is a giant step towards integrating Xinjiang with the mainland.

The railway line has been extended from Urumqi to Kashghar in southern Xinjiang. Whereas it takes only over one hour from Urumqi to Kashghar by air, it takes 32 hours by a normal passenger train to reach Kashghar from Urumqi. However, the high speed express train covers the distance in only 23 hours. From Kashghar railway station, trains go to Urumqi, Korla, Aksu, Turfan and Daochi (in Shaanxi province). People can change trains at Urumqi for their onward journey to Beijing, Shanghai, etc. The railway has recently been extended from Kashghar to Khotan and train service on this route has been started. It takes only 2–2.5 hours from Kashghar to Khotan by this high speed train. By 2020, Xinjiang will have 8,000 kms of railway network, as it is being connected with Central Asia.

Economic development

China has followed a well calibrated policy of development – railways, roads, telecommunications, buildings, high rise residential apartments, industries, oil refineries and so on in Xinjiang. Xinjiang is very rich in oil, gas and mineral resources. It possesses high quality oil reserves which accounts for 30 per cent of China's oil reserves. It has natural gas reserves of trillions of cubic metres, accounting for 34 per cent of China's natural gas reserves. Xinjiang has coal reserves of two trillion tons, accounting for 47 per cent of China's coal reserves. Xinjiang ranks second in China's wind energy resources. In 2008, Xinjiang ranked second in China by producing 27.22 million tons of crude oil, and first by producing 24 billion cubic metres of natural gas.[95] Xinjiang produced three million tons of cotton in 2008, ranking first in China.[96] Local revenue of Xinjiang crossed 36 billion yuan in 2008.[97] With the revised resource tax of 5 per cent being levied on prices instead of production volume, from mid-2010, CNPC and Sinopec, China's top two oil companies, are expected to generate additional five billion yuan (US$732 million) in annual tax revenue for Xinjiang.[98] Per capita income of rural households in Xinjiang was 3,503 yuan in 2008, which was less than the national average of 4,140 yean. Per capita income of urban residents was 11,432 yuan as compared with the national average of 15,780 yuan. Chinese government has acknowledged the imbalance due to the lower standard of living in Xinjiang than in other parts of China.

Even though vast deserts intervene between the settled oasis towns and cities, a number of settlements, small industries, hotels, restaurants and other service centres have come up along the railway line and highways (wherever there is some settlement/oasis). Most of these businesses, shops, hotels, services, etc. are manned by Han Chinese or even Hui Muslims. China Mobile, China Telecom, Sinopek, Petro China, major Chinese companies and banks have set up big establishments in various parts of Xinjiang. And Han Chinese run most of those offices, shops and establishments, with some Chinese and English speaking educated Uyghurs also working there.

Whereas Urumqi, the capital of Xinjiang, is highly developed with massive industrialization, Uyghur-dominated southern Xinjiang, like Kashghar, Khotan, etc., are also undergoing development. High rise buildings are seen everywhere. Wide highways, amusement parks and public facilities have been built. Kashghar is nearly rebuilt, with old mud houses giving way to modern high rise residential and commercial buildings. Public transport is very good and cheap.

China has evolved a ten-year (2011–20), partner assistance programme of involving 19 affluent regions including coastal and central provinces and big cities to accelerate the socio-economic development of various areas in Xinjiang.[99] For instance, Beijing Municipality is spending 7.26 billion yuan (about US$1.06 billion) for housing and protected agriculture in Khotan city, Khotan County, Moyu County and Lop County of Khotan Prefecture over a period of five years. Anhui Province along with Beijing and Tianjin municipalities are investing in the construction of railways, roads, fruit processing and protected agriculture in Khotan. Guangdong Province will spend 9.6 billion yuan (US$1.41 billion) on infrastructure and public services in Kashghar Prefecture.

Hebei Province is partnering with No. 2 Division of the Xinjiang Production and Construction Corps (XPCC) and Bayingolin Mongol Autonomous Prefecture with an investment of 1.8 billion yuan (about US$263.62 million) in agricultural technologies, housing, employment and education. Hubei Province is also developing agriculture, tourism and education in Bole city, Jinghe and Wenquan Counties of Bortala Mongol Autonomous Prefecture in partnership with No. 5 Division of the XPCC. Jiangxi Province is investing 2.03 billion yuan (US$303.16 million) in Akto County of Kizilsu Kyrgyz Autonomous Prefecture. The three northeastern provinces of Heilongjiang, Jilin and Liaoning will partner with Tacheng and Altay in northern Xinjiang as they have similar climatic conditions. They will invest in mining, flood prevention, disaster relief and job training.

It means direct involvement of experts, officials and other Hans from mainland China in giving their professional expertise and economic support to develop/implement various projects in Xinjiang. This practice not only enables other provinces/Han experts to acquire direct first-hand knowledge of Xinjiang affairs, but also promotes cross-regional contacts, besides paving the way for

Han penetration into the Uyghur-dominated areas. That Xinjiang Production and Construction Corps (XPCC) is the local partner/implementing agency in most of these programmes, ensures that the overall Chinese security concerns and objectives are met in the process of execution of such projects in Xinjiang.

Beijing has plans to develop Kashghar as the second Shenzhen (which is the most advanced region in China). The face of south Xinjiang is going to change into an ultra-modern city by the year 2020. This region, being Uyghur-dominated, will thus be converted into a modern multi-ethnic territory (like what has been achieved in Urumqi, Korla and other parts of north Xinjiang). More importantly, Uyghur Muslim ghettos/clusters in various cities and towns of south Xinjiang will be eliminated altogether.

Jolted by the 5 July 2009 riots in Urumqi, the Chinese government has been taking direct and serious interest in Xinjiang affairs. China has taken an all-round view of the Uyghur unrest, social, educational and economic issues in Xinjiang. The Chinese central government held a comprehensive high level conference on 17–19 May 2010 in Beijing to assess the socio-economic situation in Xinjiang and finalize the new development plan for Xinjiang. The conference was addressed by President Hu Jintao and Prime Minister Wen Jia bao. The President stressed the need to reduce the existing gap in GDP growth in Xinjiang and the rest of China. He emphasized the importance of social stability and national unity in Xinjiang. He urged the national banks in China to invest in Xinjiang. After the conference, China announced a new development policy for Xinjiang. China has implemented its decision to charge a new Resource Tax of 5 per cent on oil and gas produced in Xinjiang, which is expected to boost Xinjiang's physical revenue by 25 per cent (i.e. about five billion yuan) for oil and two billion yuan for gas per year, which will be used for development projects in Xinjiang.

China opened a new 1,833 km gas pipeline on 14 December 2009 connecting Turkmenistan, Uzbekistan and Kazakhstan with Xinjiang. This pipeline will deliver 40 billion cubic metres of gas per year, more than half of China's current annual gas consumption, once it reaches full capacity by 2013. The gas will be pumped from Saman-Depe in Eastern Turkmenistan and delivered all the way to Xinjiang. China's President Hu Jintao and the presidents of Turkenistan, Uzbekistan and Kazakhstan opened the new pipeline together, by turning a symbolic wheel to open a valve on the pipeline. This gas will reach Shanghai through another pipeline (over 4,500 km) between Urumqi and Shanghai.

Foreign companies investing in Xinjiang get more trade concessions than in Shanghai. Carrefour (a French department store chain), which has opened several stores in Beijing and other parts of China, has also opened several stores in Xinjiang. Super 8 Hotel chain, which is one of the world's largest economy lodging operators with almost 2,100 hotels worldwide, has three hotels in Xinjiang.

The Chinese government accords priority to social stability and feels that development will come with it. China is injecting US$1.5 billion into Xinjiang starting in 2011, to remove economic disparity and social instability. Kashghar is going to be developed as a Special Economic Zone, in order to forge close ties between Kashghar and other regions of China, which in turn will mean settlement of more Hans in Southern Xinjiang. The May 2010 Beijing conference on Xinjiang marks a new thrust in China's policy towards Xinjiang, by increasing investment, pace of development, technological innovation, ethnic-religious stability, employment and security.

China's cultural policy

China and its people have through history been conscious of its history and civilizational importance. Xinjiang remains embedded in Chinese memory and consciousness since ancient times, as various Chinese annals have recorded numerous episodes of China's forays and feats in this remote northwestern outlying border area. The main elements of this policy have been examined in Chapter 2.

China's security arrangements

China considers religious extremism, separatism and terrorism as three evil forces, and has taken a set of elaborate, practical and concrete steps to root out these evils. Southern Xinjiang, which has the majority population of Uyghur Muslims, has been the cause of concern.

China is quite conscious of this threat to its territorial integrity. China has secured its frontiers and neutralized this threat by consolidating its military presence and Han settlement in Xinjiang. However, very few security forces are visible in the streets in affected areas in Xinjiang. China installed 50,000 CCTVs in Urumqi to monitor the movements of suspected Uyghur activists. On the diplomatic front, China has not only warded off any Islamic criticism of its policies in Xinjiang, but has succeeded in having its position legitimized and endorsed by Muslim countries like Iran, Pakistan, Central Asian Republics and other Middle Eastern countries. The Central Asian countries have even undertaken not to allow any anti-China movement by the Uyghurs living within their respective countries.

Chinese scholars and authorities are conscious of the potential threat from the conservative and extremist sections of Uyghurs. Their policy is to isolate the extremist and separatist elements from the general Uyghur population, by removing the economic disparities between southern Xinjiang and rest of China. Since economic development is accompanied by the ingress of Hans, Huis and other nationalities, plans for changing the face of south Xinjiang have been set in motion.

The Chinese government shifted Wang Lequan (Secretary, Communist Party of China in Xinjiang from 1985 to April 2010), from Urumqi to Beijing, as he was seen by the Uyghurs as a hardliner following a military approach towards the separatists. He was posted as the Deputy Chairman, Supervision and Inspection Committee of CPC, in Beijing. Wang was replaced by Zhang Chunxian as the new CPC Secretary in Xinjiang. Zhang, who was earlier CPC Secretary in Hunan province, is known as open-minded, soft and ready to listen to the local problems. He is also called as Internet Party Secretary. Wang's shift from Urumqi to Beijing and new development plan for Xinjiang, represent a calculated policy aimed at containing religious extremism and separatism in Xinjiang, and promoting socio-economic stability.

Elaborate security measures including installation of over 50,000 CCTVs in Urumqi alone, have been taken to maintain normalcy and law and order in Xinjiang. Another important step taken is the policy of eliminating the Uyghur Muslim ghettos/clusters, which are the centres of religious extremism and separatism. Many old houses in southern Xinjiang have been demolished to create big public spaces, parks, roads and for construction of high rise residential buildings. Then the concerned families are allotted flats in these buildings in a proportionate manner, so that the particular high-rise building has an mixture of various communities, which have equal stake in the safety, security and welfare of their residential complex. Thus this housing complex remains immune to any ethnic riots outside the complex.

China allows legitimate and normal religious activities in Xinjiang, which has about 25,000 registered mosques and 29,000 imams, etc. About 3,000 Muslims from Xinjiang go to Hajj pilgrimage each year. However, all religious activities including speeches/sermons of imams are monitored by the government under its law on 'Prescriptions on the Management of Religious Activities in Xinjiang', which stipulates that all religious groups and activities should be undertaken within legal norms, maintaining social stability and the unity and integrity of China. Misuse of Islam for politicization and for interfering in the government, society, administration, judiciary and other activities is not allowed. The Xinjiang Islamic Institute has been established to train imams and religious preachers for various mosques in Xinjiang within the prescribed norms.

Conclusion

The demise of the former USSR and establishment of independent Central Asian Republics which share their history, religion, culture and above all the Silk Route connection with Xinjiang created a new awakening among the indigenous Muslims of Xinjiang (both Uyghurs, Kazakhs, Kyrgyzs, etc.) about their Islamic and Pan-Turkic identity. Being conscious of the strategic position of Xinjiang as the hub of trans-Asian trade and traffic and also about its huge economic resources, the Muslims of Xinjiang seek to assert their socio-economic and political position. Liberalized Chinese policy towards religion, new initiatives for modernization and economic development, better communication, linkages with Pakistan, Turkey and Central Asian states, and developing cross-border trade of Xinjiang with its neighbouring Muslim countries, have resulted in greater mobilization and assertion by the Muslims of Xinjiang on an ethno-religious basis.

That the Uyghurs in Xinjiang, particularly Kashghar, Yarkand, Khotan, Bachu, Kucha, Turfan and even Urumqi, give the credit for Chinese liberalized policy towards Islam to Pakistan's former President Zia-ul Haq was explained to this author during his visit to these areas in June 1994. Local Muslim perception was based on the fact that Zia-ul-Haq who timed his visit to Kashghar in July 1984 to coincide with Friday, persuaded the local Chinese authorities to unlock the big Friday Mosque in Kashghar to enable him offer prayers. The lock was duly opened and he offered prayers along with local Muslims in the Kashghar mosque, which had remained locked since long. Besides, Pakistani traders, travellers and Islamic activists who have been thronging the towns of Xinjiang, have been contributing by financing the construction of mosques and distributing Islamic literature. In fact, this author witnessed a sort of co-relation between the extent of Pakistani influence particularly in Kashghar, Yarkand, Khotan, Turfan etc. to the degree of Islamic resurgence in these areas. Pakistani presence in Xinjiang is quite visible in the form of businessmen, traders and visitors who fly to Urumqi from Islamabad or come from Gilgit via the Karakoram Highway. Pakistan's Jamaat-e-Islami, Tablighi Jamaat and other fundamentalist groups have easy access to and influence over the anti-Chinese Muslim separatists in Xinjiang.

The emergence of independent Central Asian states, ethnic-religious resurgence particularly in Tajikistan and Ferghana valley of Uzbekistan and mobilization of Uyghurs in these states, caused discomfitures in China. The fear of rise of Islamic fundamentalism and Pan-Turkic consciousness in Xinjiang is compounded by the recurrent clashes between Han Chinese and local Uyghur/ Kazakh/Kyrgyz Muslims in Xinjiang since 1980s. Han settlers are being browbeaten in southern Xinjiang where Uyghurs are in majority. New Chinese policy of giving preferential treatment to local Muslims in admissions, employment, etc. is yet another source of anxiety for the Han settlers. Finding themselves in an uneasy situation these Hans are keen to leave the area and go back to their original homes or migrate to these areas where Muslims are not dominant. At the same time, Hans have consolidated their position in north and east Xinjiang and Han traders/businessmen are making profits due to Chinese 'open door policy' and encouragement of cross-border trade with the CIS countries.

China considers itself to be an important player in the new geopolitics of the region not only because it shares nearly 3,000 km of its strategic frontiers in Xinjiang with the Central Asian states of Kazakhstan, Kyrgyzstan and Tajikistan, but also due to cross-border fraternization of Muslim–Turkic population inhabiting this area, which makes China's borders vulnerable to ethnic religious separatism.

The Chinese are concerned over the issues of Islamic fundamentalism, Pan-Turkic revivalism, cross-border infiltration of drugs, arms and subversives, external initiatives to resurrect the movement for 'Independence for Eastern Turkestan', which question China's sovereignty over Xinjiang. Use of arms and ammunition and involvement of foreign subversives from Turkey, the Taliban and Pakistan's Jamaat-e-Islami and other Uyghur groups in Central Asian states, whose activists have been working in Xinjiang to propagate Pan-Turkic and Pan-Islamic views, has lent extraneous dimension to the domestic Muslim resentment against Han Chinese. That China was incensed over the activities of the Pakistani Islamic parties in Xinjiang and expressed its concern to Pakistan describing these as interference in its internal affairs, was reported by Pakistani press itself.[100]

Many Uyghurs have been counting on the negative impact of the Soviet break-up on the domestic politics of China, Western, Turkic and Islamic support to their independence movement, the growing indiscipline in the PLA, people's emerging disaffection with the communist system, particularly among the younger generation of China, and the desire of the Han settlers in Xinjiang to go back to their original place of birth as key factors which could assist the process of secession of Xinjiang from China. Uyghur separatists hope that growing economic disparity between the coastal and economically rich provinces of China and the backward inner and central provinces is likely to contribute to the weakening of Central authority in China.

China on its part is quite conscious of the new threat to its territorial integrity as a result of the changed geopolitical situation in Central Asia. China has been pursuing an elaborate set of policies in Xinjiang to ensure its political stability. The main elements of this policy are:

1   Special economic zones have been created to facilitate the cross-border trade of Xinjiang with adjoining Central Asian Republics and the CIS, in a manner that most of the business and trade remain in the hands of Chinese. This has also provided economic incentive to sustain the increasing influx of Hans into Xinjiang. Not only that, Xinjiang is used as a springboard to penetrate and influence Central Asian economy, polity and society. In fact China's 'open door policy' for promoting Xinjiang's foreign trade is designed to carve out a definite Chinese influence in the Central Asian Republics. Chinese consumer and other goods are flooded into Central Asia. Thousands of Chinese Hans are reported to have migrated to the Central Asian states of Kazakhstan, Uzbekistan and Kyrgyzstan for trade and business purposes. They are reported to have married local girls, purchased properties, shops and business and mixed with the local population. This has made these republics apprehensive of big Chinese influx, which they see as a repetition of 'Russian colonialism' in the past and the extension of Chinese 'colonialism' in Xinjiang at present. Though at the official level, Central Asian Republics maintain close ties with their giant neighbour, at the popular level, the Muslim population of these republics empathizes with the Uyghurs, Kazakhs and Kyrgyzs of Xinjiang due to their common ethnicity, religion and culture.

2   China seeks to secure its troubled frontiers and to neutralize the threat to political stability in Xinjiang by consolidating its military presence and by encouraging more Hans to settle there. On an average, 250,000 to 300,000 Hans are reported to be immigrating to Xinjiang each year in search of better fortunes.[101]

3   China has declared Xinjiang as its core strategic area, which is non-negotiable. China brooks no international interference in its internal affairs in Xinjiang. China has to a great extent influenced the Muslim countries like Iran, Pakistan, Central Asian Republics and in the Middle East with the sale of arms and other incentives in return for their dollars

and has succeeded in securing their political support for China's presence in Xinjiang. Several Muslim leaders and high power delegations from Iran, Pakistan and the Central Asian Republics have visited Xinjiang during the past few years. During Iranian President Rafsanjani's visit to Xinjiang it was decided to create a direct trans-Asian railway between Beijing and Iran through Central Asia. During the fourth ministerial meeting of China–Arab League Summit held on 13–14 May 2010, China pressed its position on Xinjiang, Tibet and Taiwan affairs, seeking Arab support for China's stand on these issues. China's Defence Minister, who visited Pakistan on 24 May 2010, worked out an intelligence-sharing mechanism with Pakistan to deal with terrorism. This visit was followed by the visit of Pakistan's Army Chief, General Ashfaq Kayani, to Beijing in June 2010, during which both countries reaffirmed their strategic and security ties. Both China and Pakistan conducted joint anti-terror military exercise in Ningxia Hui Autonomous Region to coincide with the sensitive first anniversary of Urumqi riots. The drill, named 'Friendship 2010', which was conducted between 1 to 11 July 2010, was the third of its kind and it took place against the backdrop of heightened security measures in Xinjiang. China's Defence Minister, Liang Guonglie pressed the visiting Pakistani General Kayani for cutting off links between Uyghur separatists and Islamic fundamentalist groups in Pakistan. China is seeking Pakistan government's support to fight the Uyghur separatists. China and the Central Asian Republics have taken a common stand against trans-border terrorism, Islamic extremism, ethnic-religious separatism, drugs and arms trafficking. And China has institutionalized this process of cooperation through the setting up of Shanghai Cooperation Organization (SCO).

4   China sees religious extremism, terrorism and separatism as the main challenges to its security. Concerned that separatists are using religion as a banner to seek separation or independence of Xinjiang, China is firm in its resolve to maintain its territorial integrity using both its security forces and its economic, political and diplomatic prowess to retain its position in Xinjiang.

5   Following a series of violent terror attacks during the period 2013–14, that resulted in over 30 deaths and hundreds of injured, China launched a year-long 'strike hard' campaign to hunt down terrorists, simultaneously stepping up security in major cities across the country.

Notes

1 Ma Rong, 'The Soviet Model's Influence and the Current Debate on Ethnic Relations'. *Global Asia*, Seoul, Vol. 5, No. 2, Summer 2010, pp. 50–5.
2 Ibid.
3 Ibid.
4 Ibid.
5 Lillian Craig Harris, 'Xinjiang, Central Asia and the Implications for China's Policy in the Islamic World'. *China Quarterly*, March 1993, p. 115.

6 Ibid., p. 116.
7 Yuan Qingli, 'Population Change in the Xinjiang Autonomous Region (1949–1989)'. *Central Asian Survey*, Vol. 9, No. 1, 1990. p. 59.
8 Xinjiang Government, *Xinjiang: A General Survey*. Beijing, 1989, pp. 28–43.
9 Ibid.
10 K. Warikoo, 'China and Central Asia: A Review of Ching Policy in Xinjiang, 1755–1884'. In K. Warikoo and Dawa Norbu, *Ethnicity and Politics in Central Asia*. New Delhi, 1992, pp. 2–20.
11 Ananth Krishnan, 'China Detains Prominent Uighur Scholar'. *The Hindu*, 17 January 2014, p. 14.
12 *Washington Post*, 12 September 1981.
13 Donald H. McMillen, 'Xinjiang and Wang Enmao'. *China Quarterly*, September 1984, pp. 575–6, 581.
14 *Los Angeles Times*, 4 November 1981.
15 Ibid.
16 *Washington Post*, 12 September 1981.
17 Ibid.
18 Ibid.
19 Yan Dig, 'Nuclear Pollution and Violation of Human Rights in Xinjiang'. *Minzhu Zhongguo*, Paris (in Chinese), February 1992, pp. 19–21.
20 Dru Gladney, 'The Muslim Face of China'. *Current History*, September 1993, p. 280.
21 *Far Eastern Economic Review*, 25 August 1988.
22 *JPRS-CZR*-91–009, 25 February 1991.
23 Ibid.
24 Ibid.
25 Ibid.
26 Ibid.
27 *Eastern Turkestan Information*, Munich, January 1992, p. 5.
28 *Eastern Turkestan Information*, Munich, October 1992, p. 1.
29 Ibid.
30 Ibid.
31 *Xinjiang Ribao*, Urumqi, 27 September 1996.
32 Ibid.
33 *JPRS-CAR*-90–035 dated 7 May 1990.
34 Ibid.
35 Ibid.
36 Ibid.
37 Ibid.
38 *Xinjiang Ribao*, 18 March 1990.
39 *Far Eastern Economic Review*, 19 April 1990.
40 Ibid.
41 Ibid.
42 *FBIS-CHI*-90–070 dated 11 April 1990.
43 *Far Eastern Economic Review*, 3 May 1990.
44 *FBIS-CHI*-90–070 dated 11 April 1990.
45 Ibid.
46 *Xinjiang Ribao*, 20 July 1990.
47 *Xinjiang Ribao*, 2 August 1990. See also *JPRS-CAR*, 90–073 dated 28 September 1990.
48 *Ming Pao*, Hong Kong, 10 February 1997.
49 *International Herald Tribune*, 10 March 1997, p. 4.
50 Cited in *The Hindu*, 15 April 1997.
51 Ahmed Rashid, 'The Chinese Connection'. *The Herald*, Karachi, December 1995.

52 Ibid.

53 *Hindustan Times*, 13 August 1997.

54 *Pioneer*, 6 May 1997.

55 *China Daily*, 28 June 1999.

56 China State Council '"East Turkistan" Terrorist Forces Cannot Get Away With Impunity' (21 January 2002) (reproduced in *News from China*, Beijing, 29 January–11 February 2002), p. 8.

57 Ibid., p. 7.

58 See statement by Rebiya Kadeer, President, World Uyghur Congress at the 4th Session of UN Human Rights Council, Geneva, 12–30 March 2007, p. 3.

59 See Martin Scheinin, *Report of Special Rapporteur on Promotion and Protection of Human Rights and Fundamental Freedoms while Countering Terrorism*. UN General Assembly Document A/HRC/16/51/Add.1 dated 14 February 2010, pp. 25–7.

60 Ibid.

61 Ibid.

62 'Xinjiang Attack: China Looking at Qaida Link'. *Times of India*, New Delhi, 12 August 2008.

63 Lindsay Beck, 'Xinjiang: China Admits "Life and Death Battle"'. *Indian Express*, New Delhi, 15 August 2008.

64 Saibal Dasgupta, 'China Finds Pak Link to UyghurTerror'. *Times of India*, 23 October 2008, p. 23.

65 Ibid.

66 Cited in *Indian Express*, 10 April 2009.

67 Ibid.

68 'Pak-Trained Chinese Muslims Fighting in Syria'. *Hindustan Times*, 3 July 2013, p. 14.

69 'China Jihadi Outfit Leader Admits to Pak Terror Links'. *Times of India*, 28 December 2013, p. 20.

70 Human Rights Watch, 'We Are Even Afraid to Look for Them'. New York, October 2009, p. 12.

71 Xinhua News Agency, 5 August 2009. See also Zou Yonghong, 'What Really Happened at Urumqi on July 5'. *The Hindu*, 12 July 2009, p. 9.

72 See *Times of India*, 8 July 2009.

73 Cited in *The Hindu*, 8 July 2009.

74 Ibid.

75 *Hindustan Times*, 9 July 2009.

76 *Times of India*, 9 July 2009.

77 Ibid.

78 *Hindustan Times*, 10 July 2009.

79 Ibid.

80 Zou Yonghong, 'What Really Happened'.

81 Cited in *Hindustan Times*, 4 September 2009.

82 *The Hindu*, 5 September 2009.

83 *Times of India*, 23 December 2009.

84 Ananth Krishnan, 'Security Tightened in Xinjiang Amid Reports of Violence'. *The Hindu*, 30 June 2013, p. 15.

85 Ananth Krishnan, 'Tiananmen Terror Attack Poses "New Challenge"'. *The Hindu*, 2 November 2013, p. 15.

86 Ananth Krishnan, 'Xinjiang's Cycle of Violence'. *The Hindu*, 24 March 2014, p. 8.

87 Ibid.

88 Ananth Krishnan, '"Religious Extremists" behind Xinjiang Attack'. *The Hindu*, 24 May 2014, p. 13.

89 'China Blames Extremists for Attack'. *Indian Express*, 2 May 2014, p. 12.

90 Ananth Krishnan, '31 Dead as Blasts Rock Market in Xinjiang'. *The Hindu*, 23 May 2014, p. 12. Ananth Krishnan, 'Involvement of Foreign Groups Seen in Xinjiang Attack'. *The Hindu*, 24 May 2014, p. 12.

91 Ananth Krishnan, 'Xinjiang Death Toll Close to 100: Officials'. *The Hindu*, 4 August 2014, p. 12. China's official Xinjiang toll: 37 civilians, 59 terrorists. *Times of India*, 4 August 2014, p. 14.

92 Ananth Krishnan, 'China Moves to Choke Funding of Terror Outfits in Xinjiang'. *The Hindu*, 18 January 2014, p. 13.

93 Ananth Krishnan, 'China Jails 55 in Rare Xinjiang Mass Trial'. *The Hindu*, 29 May 2014, p. 12.

94 Ananth Krishnan, 'China Plans Air and Rail Network to Boost Infrastructure'. *The Hindu*, 28 July 2010.

95 PRC State Council, *White Paper on Development and Progress in Xinjiang* (September 2009). Beijing, Beijing Language Press, 2009, p. 10.

96 Ibid., p. 8.

97 Ibid., p. 6.

98 Le Woke, 'Xinjiang Reportedly to Pilot 5% Tax on Gas, Oil'. *Global Times*, 27 May 2010.

99 Hu Yue, 'Hand in Hand'. *Beijing Review*, 10 June 2010, pp. 30–1.

100 *Dawn*, Karachi cited in *Times of India*, New Delhi, 7 March 1992.

101 Linda Benson, Justin Rudelson and Stenely W. Toops, 'Xinjiang in the Twentieth Century'. Woodrow Wilson Centre Occasional Paper – 65, p. 17.

16 Uyghur nationalism and the 5 July 2009 incident in Urumqi

Fu Jen-Kun

Introduction

Located in the northwest frontier of China, the area designated by the People's Republic of China (PRC) as 'the Xinjiang Uyghur Autonomous Region' has long been a contentious region. Indeed, from the many name changes the region has undergone, one can easily see vestiges of the political intrigue and struggle associated with this region during the past several hundred years as well as traces of the origin, development, setbacks and struggles of Uyghur nationalism.

Xinjiang as a political concept in historical discourse has been fluctuating (from *Xiyu* or western region, Xinjiang (province), East Turkestan (Islamic State to Republic), Doganstan, Khotan Emirate, the Three District Revolution, and the current Xinjiang Uyghur Autonomous Region), and these changes in naming Xinjiang represent the creation and development of modern Uyghur nation and nationalism. The policy priority for the People's Republic is the Chinese national unity and, therefore, the policy orientation in labelling and identifying the potential dissent produces inconsistency and confusion in coping with the minority issues. The crisis revealed in the disturbance in Urumqi on 5 July 2009 further confirms the tendency of mutual deprivation and voluntary apartheid between Uyghurs and Hans in Xinjiang and elsewhere in China. It also has the potential to progress to a more radical confrontation in the future without proper political and ethnic settlement.

The present Chinese strategy towards controlling Xinjiang incorporates many elements of the 'Great Game' played throughout Central Asia over the past three centuries. Political forces, both domestic and international, contend over various interests and hatreds; while these struggles are in the name of preserving Chinese sovereignty, their effect on everyday economic and social lives of local residents as well as working of the political system are such that they impede efforts to draw Uyghurs into the Chinese political process, an effort that constitutes part of the so-called 'national unity' (民族團結) policy.

Many days of violent civil unrest in Urumqi that began on 5 July 2009 made clear the failings of China's policies towards its minority groups as well as the long-hidden ethnic conflict in modern Chinese society. Using the concept of 'Xinjiang' as a point of departure, this chapter examines the background of contemporary

Chinese policy towards minority groups in Xinjiang and concisely reviews various consequences of the Chinese administrative policies in Xinjiang and the events of 5 July, thus outlining the contours of ethnic conflict in present-day Xinjiang.

'Xinjiang' as a discourse of Chinese political history

Two East Turkestan Republics

Designated as 'East Tujue' (東突厥) in historical records from the Sui-Tang period, Central Asia was typically referred to as 'East Turkestan' during the Warlord and Republican eras in the early twentieth century, a name that reflects the rise of nationalism in Central Asia during this period. The formal Chinese use of 'Xinjiang' (literally 'New Frontier') as the official name for this region can be traced to the Qianlong era of the Qing Dynasty, when it was referred to as 'Xiyu Xinjiang' (西域新疆; literally meaning New Frontier of the Western Region). Subsequently, the Ili General Song Yun's Work (伊犁總統事略) was changed by the Daoguang Emperor to Xinjiang Story (新疆事略); at this point, 'Xinjiang' became the commonly accepted designation of this region.

The beginning of the movement referred to by China as the 'Xinjiang Independence Movement' (疆獨) and seen in overseas exile Uyghur communities as an example of the successful revitalization of their country (nationalist revival?) can be traced to the First (1933–4) and the Second Eastern Turkestan Republic (1944–9) (erroneously referred to as the 'Three Districts Revolution' by the Chinese Communist Party).

Careful examination of the background of the leaders of the First Eastern Turkestan Republic suggests that there first existed a Khotan Emirate which thereafter was assimilated into Kashgar's East Turkestan Independence Organization; at this time, Khoja Niyaz, the leader of Hami who had just entered into alliance with the warlord Sheng Shicai, was selected as president. Despite the popularity of religious *Jadid* in Central Asia at that time the constitution and published materials of the First Eastern Turkestan Republic contained calls for educational and economic reforms – even democratic reforms – that did not accord with Islam. Although not internationally recognized, the passports of this country read 'Eastern Turkestan Republic'; the country's coinage, however, read 'The Republic of Ugyrstan'. During this period, the complex relation between ethnic identity and political struggle was especially chaotic. The ethnically-Hui general Ma Zhongying pledged to the Nationalist government in Nanjing that he would suppress the rebellion; he captured the old city of Hami and began a massacre of Uyghurs. After this, he no longer opposed Sheng Shicai's army; the remainder of the party entered and occupied the Khotan Emirate and established a regime called 'Doganstan'.

In contrast with the First Eastern Turkestan Republic, which was established in Hami and Khotan (Hetian) in southwest Xinjiang, the second 'Three District Revolution' occurred in Ili, Altay and Tarbagatay. The important figures in this second event can be roughly divided into two camps, namely those who advocated 'national independence' and those who favoured 'compromise with central government and ethnic autonomy'. The former group took Ahmedijan Qasimi as its leader and hoped ultimately to establish an independent state primarily composed of Turks. The latter group, on the other hand, saw independence as an overly idealistic goal, as it involved adjudicating between the interests and positions of revolutionary elites of Uyghur, Mongol, Kazakh, Kyrgyz and other ethnic groups. This second group – perhaps best represented by figures such as Masood Sabri Bayqozi and Isa Yusuf Aleptkin – was thus willing to compromise with China in order to gain a degree of autonomy.

Documents revealing the way in which the former Soviet Union led, used and ultimately brought an end to this second nationalist movement have already been verified. The Soviet leadership originally pushed East Turkestan and the Kuomingtang to establish a unified government. The independence-minded wing of the East Turkestan movement maintained a veneer of political comity with the former Soviet Union but in fact used this time both to expand its influence and more firmly establish itself. As part of this process, they established the Youth Corps of East Turkestan, propagated their message of independence in southern Xinjiang, and ceaselessly advocated that the army of Kuomintang withdraw completely from Xinjiang. However, due to international political developments, the Soviet Union eventually no longer needed East Turkestan to contain China; subsequently, the main leadership of East Turkestan was persuaded to enter into political negotiations with the Communist Party of China (CPC). According to reports published at the time, while flying from Almaty (Kazakhstan) to Beijing, China, the plane carrying the East Turkestani leadership crashed, killing all on board. Other rumoured explanations for these events are that because these leaders advocated national self-determination, they were either placed under house arrest or assassinated by the Soviets in order to avoid a potentially awkward political situation. Owing to the Cold War, the Second East Turkestan Republic disappeared quickly; but the lofty aspiration for national independence has long outlived those who participated in these events.

The creation of the 'Uyghur'

While Uyghurs constitute the majority of the population in Xinjiang, political power in the province has generally been held by Han Chinese. Indeed, the two attempts to establish an East Turkestan Republic demonstrate the complex relations that exist between various ethnic groups in Xinjiang, as seen in their various political dealings and their attempts to incriminate one another. Political struggle is not something to be overlooked, however, Sheng Shicai agreed to use Stalin's strategy for managing ethnic classification; in the highly symbolic task of choosing a name for an ethnic group, he agreed to compromise. The military governor of Xinjiang province Sheng Shicai, the Xinjiang provincial government Chairman Li Jun, and the Vice Chairman Khoja Niyaz (who was also the President of the First East Turkestan Republic) collectively announced in 1934 that henceforth the group previously called '*chan hui*' (纏回) would be known as 'Uyghur'. The original text is extremely interesting:

'The rulers of the Han and Tang Dynasties referred to the people who lived south of the Tianshan Mountains by a variety of names (for example, *hui ge*, *hui hu*, *wu hu*, etc.), while the Qing called them *chan hui*.' The Uyghur (*wei wu er* 威武爾 literally meant strong). Association of Education Promotion submitted a request. 'The provincial government examined various books written about Xinjiang, and they found that all of these writings use the word "Uyghur" (*wei wu er*) This name connotes the idea of "fearsome," or it originally referred only to a part of the group instead of the whole. To change a name of an ethnic group is nothing trivial. After the third conference of the government, the proposed new three characters (維吾爾) were passed. The name means, in a narrower sense, to protect our own group, and in a broader interpretation is to protect the state, which is in no conflict with the alternative name 威武爾. The chosen characters carry the notion of loving the state and the people. The sound of 維吾爾 is also more appropriate. Thus, the name is altered from 纏回 to 維吾爾, and 畏吾兒 (literally meaning son), 威武爾 and so on are all abolished. We hereby announce this to all Turkish people.'

This Mandarin translation 維吾爾 is already accepted everywhere, but it contains a confusing mix of concepts related to ethnicity, state and nation. The words (纏回, 畏吾兒, 維吾爾, 威武爾) and Turkish people, are all filled with particularly calibrated meaning; they must be carefully examined with regard to the question of ethnic identity. In the past, the sense of identity of peoples living in the oases surrounding the Tarim Basin extended only as far as their family, a phenomenon that scholars refer to as 'oasis identity'. 'Uyghur' is a fundamentally unclear concept – indeed, one might say that such a typology or category does not truly exist, and that it only came to have meaning after being officially recognized, bequeathed to local elites of the region, and subsequently used to develop a sense of Uyghur national identity. If one considers both its linguistic function and its political connotations, then 'East Turkestan' can be seen as the means by which modern China would imply the claim that Xinjiang was part of China 'since ancient times'.

Typology of Xinjiang Independence Movement/East Turkestan Movement

The sense of danger felt about Xinjiang stems from the development of nationalist revolutions perceived in East Tujuei/East Turkestan – terms which in historical explications and political discussions have had differing meanings. More specifically, the intermittent instances of violence and the way in which the media reports around the world embellish on and misread political Islam combine to create an atmosphere of terror. In reality, this movement is seeking a way in the current international political climate to reveal its true face; hints of this can be seen in recently published materials on Xinjiang.

Three evil forces theory

If one considers the historical development of imperial expansion as it has played out in Central Asia, the official Chinese policy towards the East Turkestan independence movement emphasizes the idea of 'three evil forces', namely religious extremism, ethnic splittism, and terrorism. Ma Dazhen lays this out in detail in his work *The Dream of East Turkestan Extinguished*. This type of categorization can also be said to have successfully drawn on the theory of the 'Clash of Civilizations' and international sentiment against terrorism to label negatively movements for an independent Xinjiang as the origin of instability in China. It also reveals the fact that the government requires a specific object on which it can exercise its power in order to maintain social 'stability'. Additionally, the threat that the Taliban poses has given rise to a similar sense of crisis among the leadership of five secular Central Asian nations. The Shanghai Cooperation Organization has thus become an important means of taking care of this transnational issue, as it has effectively allowed for the extradition of extremists associated with political Islam. Indeed, since the establishment of this organization, public activities of Uyghur nationalists in East Asia have ceased, with most activities now taking place underground. The utility of the Chinese policy of 'three evil forces theory' is not difficult to understand: it aims to completely subdue Uyghur opposition to the Chinese regime.

The official policy of 'national unity' – which is not limited to Han–Uyghur relations, but also encompasses Uyghur–Hui relations – has caused other issues to be either overlooked or politicized. This applies to the issues of human rights and self-governance, both issues fraught with political significance, but also to policies dealing with sanitation, environmental protection, drug trafficking, economic development, social equality, minority group literatures, religions and education. The scope of discussions of these topics has been reduced in such a way that they all must start with discussions of the same issues. In the publications of the overseas Uyghur community, apart from unrealistic dreams of national independence, one can also easily discern the anger and resentment these exiles feel towards various policies and their implementation.

Independence through violent revolt

'Stability trumps everything' is the framework of governance (overarching principle of Chinese governance). The government occasionally turns a blind eye to the civil or criminal cases, sometimes even exceeding the parameters of what the legal system will accept. However, as soon as these cases cross the line politically, the offender faces the prospect of losing everything and being forced into exile. The case of the prominent Uyghur Rebiya Kadeer is the most well-known example of this type of situation. When confronting this issue, the majority of Uyghur exiles confuse cause for effect; they simplify the 'question of Xinjiang' and attribute it to ethnic conflict and persecution, thus making national independence the only possible solution to this situation. This 'solution' is further divided into two possible routes, namely peaceful protest and violent revolution. The various groups of Uyghur exiles – including those who left during the early 1950s in the aftermath of the founding of the PRC and tended to go either to Southeast Asia or Turkey, those of the 'old generation' who left in the 1960s after the Sino-Soviet split, and the members of the 'new generation' who left after the period of Deng's Reform during the 1980s – began to collaborate and, eventually, manifest two tendencies. On the one hand, the 'old' and 'new' Uyghur nationalisms began to work together. These groups, which were primarily based in Europe and the United States, established the World Uyghur Congress in 2004. They emphasized the importance of using peaceful methods in their pursuit of national self-determination and stated their willingness to collaborate with the liberal Han people. Their initial efforts were largely directed towards obtaining international sympathy and support while at the same time aiding Uyghur refugees across the world. In contrast, the more radical groups of Uyghur nationalists living in Central Asia and the Middle East were hostile to Han Chinese, never giving up on the possibility of violent revolution. These groups were particularly active in 1990s following the break-up of the Soviet Union but have lately been subdued in their activities, as they are only able to engage in small-scale operations as opportunities present themselves.

Uyghurs of East Turkestan versus Hans of Xinjiang

One-party rule is the political reality in China. Overseas Uyghurs recognize that Han Chinese form the core of the party; they do not view the present situation as amenable to pursuing national self-determination through constitutional reform. The idea of the nation-state is a deep-seated one; China has since the founding of the PRC maintained the idea of a single officially recognized national identity. Because of this, some scholars believe that the former Soviet Union's policy of enforced ethnic separation and self-governance was a failed experiment; they suggest that the racial segregation that this type of system entails contains the seeds of national dissolution and, moreover, that discussing self-governance or cultural pluralism before inculcating a sense of loyalty to the nation is fundamentally misguided. If one considers, for example, the troubled history of the American government's relations with its native American population or the fact that the Japanese government only in June 2009 recognized the Ainu of Hokkaido as an aboriginal group, the direction and workings of China's policies towards its minority groups seem misguided.

5 July 2009 Urumqi incident and official response

There has been a host of explanations for the Han–Uyghur quarrel at a factory which mainly produces electronic toys in Shaoguan, Guangdong province. Chinese media reported that a disgruntled former female employee surnamed Zhu, who was upset because she was no longer employed, posted online the fabricated information that six Uyghur workers had raped two female Han employees. The resulting fight on the night of 25 June 2009 in the company dormitory left two Uyghur employees dead and 118 workers injured. While Chinese media described this incident as an 'ordinary problem of public safety', splittist elements – both domestic and abroad – recklessly exaggerated the incident, describing it as 'Han chauvinists' engaging in 'ethnic cleansing'. However, based on the reports of other foreign media, the security personnel on the scene at the time did not intervene to prevent the violence from occurring.

To summarize the information available online, the incident can be traced back to May 2009, when the toy factory in Shaoguan recruited 700 employees, both male and female, from the Kashgar region of Xinjiang. There was already a rumour that Uyghur employees were involved in several incidents of theft. And the first instance of rape is said to have occurred on 14 June 2009. After the victim reported the incident to the authorities, the Uyghurs who had committed the crime were laid off. After a few days, another rumour arose that a Han female employee was gang-raped in the company dormitory by several Uyghur workers. After the incident was reported to the police, the suspects were released after being held in custody for several days. It appeared that the authorities did not intend to pursue the matter. Unexpectedly, at this time, a third rape allegedly occurred; when the incident was reported to security officials and the police, they were seemingly reluctant to proceed investigation. Han workers in the factory were then furious and attacked Uyghurs. The fight began at 10 p.m. on 25 June 2009 and continued until 4 a.m. the next day. Han workers were holding steel bars and fought with the knife-wielding Uyghur employees. The enraged Han employees quickly grew in number, eventually swelling to a group of more than one hundred. According to fragmented reports, during the incident both male and female Uyghur employees were indiscriminately hacked to death. The Han employees subsequently went berserk in their pursuit of revenge. The chaos carried on until the early morning when anti-riot police, who are said to have arrived in 20 trucks and 30 police cars, fired in the air, thus bringing a stop to the violence. Among both the Han and Uyghur employees, there were many people who were seriously injured; additionally, several Uyghur employees died of their injuries. The windows of the four seven-storey dormitories in the factory complex were almost all broken. The fire extinguishers had all been taken and used in the riot. After the incident, more than 200 crowbars littered the ground of the factory, plus 200 fire extinguishers which were battered beyond recognition and concrete bricks used as weapons during the fight were also strewn about.

The gossip of 'rape of the female Han workers by Uyghur men' stirred up a strong reaction with racist terms and phrases which could be easily found in Chinese media and Internet online chat-rooms. The negative images towards Uyghurs were brought up and stereotyped by Han netizens. But the harsh scenario is that there was no authority to clarify the rumour and seriously tackle the ethnic conflict until the outbreak of the 5 July 2009 incident in Urumqi. The Guangdong local court of justice has already conducted investigation into the fight in Shaoguan factory and closed the case by sentencing those criminals in November 2009.

After the Shaoguan incident, the remains of the deceased Uyghurs were flown back to Xinjiang for funerals. At this point, a different version of the story began to circulate. Upon hearing the suggestion circulating in Urumqi that Han workers in the toy factory had seduced Uyghur women, several angry Uyghur youths set out to settle the score. There were even rumours saying that over 400 Uyghur women had been raped. On the Chinese website 'Uyghur Online', there appeared several postings implying that the Shaoguan incident had been orchestrated by the Chinese government, or that it was part of a campaign of ethnic cleansing.

One aspect of the Shaoguan incident that is beyond dispute and which led to a new round of vendetta killings are the film clips of the incident that were posted online. These videos were likely filmed by the mobile phones of Han workers at the Shaoguan factory from both the ground level and upper floors of the factory buildings. It is said that in the Shaoguan fight over 18 Uyghur workers perished, and the whole scenario of fighting and rape case was not clarified. Through Internet and telephone communications, unclear information regarding these incidents made its way not only to Xinjiang, but to overseas Uyghur communities in exile. According to information released by the government of the Xinjiang Uyghur Autonomous Region, starting on 4 July 2009, there came out some 'appeals for special caution' in communities, and on message boards and personal blogs. They also called for Uyghur communities to take to the streets on 5 July 2009 and hold demonstrations on the People's Square and the South Gate of Urumqi.

In just ten days, the Shaoguan Han–Uyghur brawl developed into a large-scale clash between Han Chinese and Uyghurs in Urumqi, Xinjiang. Beside the fact that the administration of Shaoguan was unable to promptly deal with the incident, facing peaceful student protests, the autonomous government located in Urumqi, Xinjiang did not react appropriately either. The social control in Xinjiang is indeed far tighter than the coastal areas in China, and the Xinjiang authority should have better experience in settling ethnic strife in contrast to its Guangdong counterpart. But, the 5 July incident exposed that the Xinjiang public security system seemingly ceased to function and finally contributed to the outburst of a large-scale conflict and killings. If one looks at the adequacy of the ethnic policy since Deng's reform era, it could be argued that the previously hidden tensions between Han Chinese and Uyghur have already reached a critical point that the antagonistic attitude between Han and minority people was obvious and can be triggered into fire right away.

Apart from the accusation of Hu Yaobang's ethnic policy, the failure of ineffective policy in governing Xinjiang over the last three decades is evident. Taking the approach to tackle the Xinjiang student movement as an example, there seems no improvement since the 1980s in the Xinjiang government. The government authority understands the significance of student movements which have been always initiated within the Xinjiang University. It is said that 'a quiet and pacified Xinjiang University indicates a peaceful Urumqi, and the analogy also applies to the importance of Urumqi to the whole Xinjiang'. But the Xinjiang University has always been out of control. As usual, the Xinjiang government announced that the 5 July incident was an attempt by external forces. They took the Shaoguan incident as an excuse to disseminate rumours, and thereby organize and set off the violent incident in Urumqi.

The Chinese government initially described the Xinjiang 5 July 2009 incident as a 'violent crime of terrorism' that resulted from the efforts of foreign forces to destroy ethnic unity in Xinjiang. In fact, they believed that this was an organized violent movement on the part of extremists and ethnic separatists, mainly because the methods employed in this particular incident were different from those used in previous incidents. In this case, the perpetrators drew the government's riot suppression team to the vicinity of Xinjiang University. Subsequently, they stirred up the crowd, which shouted violently and indiscriminately killed the Han Chinese. This bogged the police forces down; indeed, in some cases they were completely surrounded by protesters.

The CPC ordered that the following steps have to be taken in order to deal with the situation in Xinjiang. First, terrorist activities would be punished and suppressed, social stability in Xinjiang would be restored, and tourism would be reinstituted as soon as possible. Second, to maintain social stability in Xinjiang, the central government would use strategic reserves in order to provide for citizen's basic needs. Third, the government will effortlessly repair ethnic relations between Han Chinese and Uyghurs in Xinjiang. The high ranking officials of the provincial government in Xinjiang shall visit streets and villages in order to understand and alleviate complaints once and for all.

Wrong contextualization of 'Xinjiang Independence Movement'

The fact that the Chinese central government still recognizes Xinjiang as a locally administered entity would lead to a conflict of interests between the local and central governments and thus make possible political dissolution. However, to Uyghur dissidents, 'Xinjiang' is nothing more than a name forced upon the region by an external political power; politically, they seek 'East Turkestan Independence', that is the name intimately connected with the struggles between imperial powers for spheres of influence in Central Asia during the late nineteenth century, as well as with the contemporaneous efforts on the part of Turkey to promote Pan-Turkism.

The English 'East Turkestan', Turkish 'Doğu Türkistan' and even the modern Uyghur شىرقى تانؤت رکس are all relatively easy to grasp in the context of Western languages, as they differ merely in that they are written with different letters. After the break-up of the Soviet Union, the region known as 'West Turkestan' became several independent Central Asian states, while establishing an 'East Turkestan' turns out to be the goal of Uyghur exile dissidents. They create a new irredentist movement referring to the two instances of the 'Eastern Turkestan Republic' in the early twentieth century.

The Chinese government favours the alternate rendering of 'East Turkestan' as 'East Tujuie' which manifests the historical connection of Xinjiang to China and refutes the imposition of the Pan-Turkic nationalism. The term *Tujuie* in Chinese historical records indicates a group of people who resided in the north-western part of China and had been under China's political control through frequent interactions in cultural exchanges. The intention for manoeuvring the naming of Turkestan and *Tujuie* is to emphasize the closeness between Xinjiang and China, and to foreground the claim that China has exercised sovereignty over Xinjiang 'since ancient time'.

However, the idea of 'Xinjiang Independence Movement' (疆獨) is, if one considers it from its linguistic context, extremely confused unless 'Xinjiang' becomes a new potential object of political identity and evolves into a new ethnic name or sobriquet [which we temporarily refer to as 'an ethnic Xinjiang' (疆族"!)]. In line with the argument of 'Xinjiang Independence Movement', it thus refers to a non-Chinese identification that affiliates with land to which 'Xinjiang' locates. All those peoples who live in Xinjiang now – including Han, Uyghur, Hui, Kazakh and other ethnic groups – constitute the imagined collective entity of a Xinjiang nation which intends to separate from China and collectively seeks political independence.[1]

But there is no Xinjiang nation, and the problem is that all efforts to promote 'Xinjiang Independence' are unrealistic given the current situation in Xinjiang. The various names of Xinjiang actually have different political implications and needs. Selectively applying those naming concepts reflects different political aims and certainly it would be not helpful to address the actual situation; their accounts and descriptions lead merely to further confusion.

Elaborating the 5 July 2009 Urumqi unrest with 'Xinjiang Independence Movement' and other ethnic conflicts frequently cited in the global media, politicization emerges with false interpretation of Xinjiang's future. Xinjiang could be exaggerated as China's 'Balkan Gunpowder Chest', associated with the strife-ridden region of Palestine, or one could link the World Uyghur Congress[2] with the politically radical Taliban or Al Qaeda. Xinjiang then also could be argued more or less as a colony under Chinese occupation.

From ethnic mutual deprivation to voluntary segregation between Han and minority people in Xinjiang

The trend of sensationalism and tendency to unilaterally politicize the events reported in the media fabricate a framing effect. If politicians would truly take advantage of this development in media, it completely depends on whether they could comply with the expectation of the media and the taste of audience and readers. After the 5 July Urumqi unrest, as the media expected nothing from the Chinese authority, they turned to the Uyghur dissidents in exile. Nearly all liaisons to the World Uyghur Congress (WUC) in Washington, Munich and London were on standby and waited to be interviewed by major international media networks. The WUC then conducted an easy international propaganda campaign and demonstrated itself as the representative body for spelling out Uyghur grievances to the world. It is not certain whether the WUC have the wherewithal to organize a mass movement as such in Xinjiang. What would be beneficial or harmful to certain political leadership in Xinjiang can be speculated through the approach as well.

It is incredible that an incident of a brawl between Han and Uyghur workers at a toy factory in Shaoguag would escalate into a violent mass protest of Uyghurs who attacked police and massacred innocent Han people in Urumqi, Xinjiang. The incident developed later with the Han people preparing themselves to mount a mass retaliation. The Urumqi incident was different from those unrests in the past and no longer merely aimed at the Chinese government, but rather meted out violence directly at Han residents of Xinjiang. The incident comes as a watershed moment in the evolution of Han–Uyghur relations. Previously invisible tensions between Hans and Uyghurs have now been clearly transmitted through the lens of the media. A policy couched in terms of 'Uyghurs identifying with East Turkestan' versus 'Han Chinese identified with Xinjiang' has given rise to a demarcation of social identities between ethnic groups. Antagonistic relations have finally come to the fore.

With the platform of the Shanghai Cooperation Organization, China has successfully built an international alliance in Central Asia under the name of anti-terrorism and repressed Uyghur dissident activity in the Central Asian region. Given the proliferation of arrests, extraditions and assassinations, dissidents are unable to carry out activities to promote their irredentist claim on East Turkestan, and left for Turkey, or even further to Europe. Within the Chinese territory, with the slogan of 'national unity', China bans discussion of ethnic relations in almost any form with the 'three evil forces' theory. The Han–Uyghur relations then stall at the level of 'Uyghur dissidents' versus 'the Chinese government', and the Xinjiang society falsely assumes harmonious national unity.

Yet the 5 July 2009 Uyghur uprising in Urumqi broke out the conflict between the Hans and Uyghur people for the first time. The confrontation between two groups of people is rooted in the fabric of everyday life, and the incident is just an outcome. Regarding the issues such as hygiene norms of cleanliness and dirtiness, views concerning marriage and chastity, the usage of Mandarin and Uyghur in verbal discrimination, values deriving from Islamic religious beliefs, all contribute to strife in everyday practice and develop into numerous possibilities for conflict. Some minor factors accumulate into a big problem. Take the most common issue of eating pork in Xinjiang. Most Uyghur Muslims are extremely sick at the very sight of pork (perhaps comparable to the Han Chinese's reaction to a cockroach). When having meal together, to simply use different plates for pork and other dishes is not acceptable to the Uyghur Muslims. There is no way for them to dine while Han Chinese are enjoying their pig flesh nearby. Such minor things in everyday life result in the voluntary segregation of society in Xinjiang, so that there is no mutual respect and they even despise each other.

For the Han immigrants to Xinjiang, the government always indoctrinates them to develop a kind of righteous underdog solidarity in Xinjiang. As the Han people are the major ethnic group in China, they must cosy up with the local minority people, and tacitly agree to allow ethnic minorities certain forms of privileged treatment. The Han immigrants have not been treated equally when searching for job opportunities, promotion and education. Especially for those Hans located at the bottom of the society, they are at times sacrificed and made to share the sense of being unequal in Xinjiang.

As regards the Chinese ethnic minorities, so long as the Uyghurs in Xinjiang do not assemble or/and make trouble, the government treats them leniently. If they dared to agitate and crossed the line, then it comes in the form of another extremely harsh crackdown, which leads to regrettable instances of injustice and countless innocents perish. It means that if the Uyghurs are involved in usual civil and criminal case, the Han people believe that the government will be particularly lax in its punishment to ethnic minorities. A most cited scenario for Uyghurs living in China among the Han populated community is to describe the ubiquity of Uyghur thieves and pickpockets in large cities, or of outrageous instances of drug trafficking and theft. These stereotypes are abnormally deep-rooted in the mind of Han people. I once heard that when one encounters an Uyghur child pickpocket, there are surely to be several Uyghur men in pursuit as well. Even if this child pickpocket happens to be discovered, there is simply no way to punish him. For the Uyghur men will come up and argue for him, or go into a fight physically. Or, even if reporting to the police, they could not be of much assistance as the Uyghurs at most will be sent back to Xinjiang, without giving them a fair penalty. Thus they operate and take advantage of the presumption of impunity.

The mistaken impression that ethnic minority policy is beyond the law creates a sense of unfairness among Han people. It seems that when encountering the ethnic minorities, the government simply shrugs its shoulders in utter helplessness and is reluctant to provide assistance. The interest of Han people is evidently surrendered for the sake of pacifying the unfair treatment to minority people.

However, the indigenous Uyghurs in Xinjiang, especially those who serve as the labour force at the bottom of society, believe that the Chinese government is often more generous in word than in deed. The development of the socio-economic structure has made it difficult for them to compete equally and fairly with their Han peers, and most of the resources in Xinjiang are controlled by the Han officials who favour the Han people instead of fairly providing opportunities to ethnic minority people. If the Uyghurs dare to oppose collectively in any form of mass resistance, the government would throw them into jail immediately. The Uyghurs believe that there is no channel to facilitate their grievance. Under the circumstances, the sense of ethnic mutual deprivation exacerbates the segregation between Hans and Uyghurs. Both sides are turning to be resentful and there is no sign that the vicious ethnic tension will reach an end.

Conclusion

With the false unilateral politicization in the elaboration of ethnic relations in contemporary Xinjiang, it will easily lose in the speculation of nationalist discourses in criticizing the Han chauvinism or local ethnic nationalism. The naming of Xinjiang and East Turkestan is evident example to provide two opposite contexts for each side to take what they need for mass mobilization, and the problem persists.

When ethnic conflict escalates to a crisis, the government unavoidably goes to tighten control and suppress not only the dissidents but hurt the innocent people who then lose their faith in the authority. Affirmative action and preferential treatment actually offers no easy solution to the ethnic hatred built up in the violent confrontation, but contributes to the making of ethnic mutual deprivation and voluntary segregation. Chinese government needs to adopt a more pragmatic attitude to deal with the Xinjiang question. There is a simple solution to the social issues in Xinjiang. The approach to tackle possible ethnic strife in everyday life is crucial, and reducing the income gap and equal distribution of resources between the Hans and Uyghurs is just part of the story. How to reorient a perspective that would be acceptable to future development and thus reshape a common identity for both Han and ethnic minorities in Xinjiang are decisive for the successful integration of China's northwest region.

Notes

1 The declaration of the establishment of the World Uyghur Congress in 2004 announced that: 'Any ethnic groups who believe in any religion, communicate with any language and now reside in East Turkestan shall be treated equally and entitle to have the right to promote their culture.' 'In pursuit of independence movement, religious belief is separated from politics.' 'Democracy and Peaceful means are approach to pursue political independence. Dictatorship and other violent terrorist activity are not permitted.'
2 A lot of analyses appeared in Chinese TV and newspapers in Taiwan, Hong Kong and Singapore. Xinjiang as China's Palestine is depicted by Wong Lixiun's book, *My Xinjiang and Your East Turkistan*.

Bibliography

Amnesty International, *People's Republic of China: China's Anti-Terrorism Legislation and Repression in the Xinjiang Uighur Autonomous Region* (ASA 17/10/2002). London, Amnesty International, March 2002.

Bai Zhensheng *et al.*, *Xinjiang xian dai zhengczhi she hui shi lue, 1912–49* (*Brief History of Contemporary Xinjiang*). Beijing, 1992.

Barnett, Doak A., *China's Far West: Four Decades of Change*. Boulder, Westview, 1993.

Benson, Linda, *The Ili Rebellion: The Moslem Challenge to Chinese Authority in Xinjiang, 1944–1949*. New York and London, M.E. Sharpe, 1990.

Benson, Linda and Svanberg, Ingvar, *China's Last Nomads: The History and Culture of China's Kazakhs*. London and New York, M.E. Sharpe, 1998.

Betta, Chiara, *Xinjiang or Eastern Turkistan? The Conundrum of Chinese Central Asia*. Occasional Papers, Athens, Institute of International Economic Relations, 2001.

Bovingdon, Gardner, *Autonomy in Xinjiang: Han Nationalist Imperatives and Uyghur Discontent*. Washington, East West Centre, 2004.

Bush Jr., Richard C., *The Religion in Communist China*. Nashville and New York, Abingdon, 1970.

Chen, Jack, *The Sinkiang Story*. New York, Macmillan, 1977.

China Islamic Association, *The Religious Life of Chinese Moslems*. Peking, 1956.

China State Council, *White Paper, National Minorities Policy and its Practice in China*. Beijing, September 1999.

China State Council, *White Paper, China's National Defence in 2002*. Beijing, 9 December 2002.

China State Council, *White Paper, History, Development of Xinjiang*. Beijing, May 2003.

China State Council, *White Paper, Regional Autonomy for Ethnic Minorities in China*. Beijing, 2005.

China State Council, *White Paper on China's Ethnic Policy and Common Prosperity and Development of all Ethnic Groups*. Beijing, 2009.

China State Council, *White Paper on Development and Progress in Xinjiang*. Beijing, 2009.

China Statistical Year Book 1998, Beijing, China Statistics Bureau, 1998.

Dabbs, Jack Autrey, *History of the Discovery and Exploration of Chinese Turkestan*. The Hague, Mouton, 1963.

Dawamat, Tomur, *Xinjiang – My Beloved Home*. Beijing, China Today Press, 1993.

Debata, Mahesh Ranjan, *China's Minorities: Ethnic-Religious Separatism in Xinjiang*. New Delhi, Pentagon, 2007.

Dillon, Michael, *Xinjiang: Ethnicity, Separatism and Control in Chinese Central Asia*. Durham East Asian Paper I, Durham, Department of East Asian Studies, University of Durham, 1995.

Dillon, Michael, *China's Muslim Hui Community: Migration, Settlements and Sects*. London, Curzon, 1999.

Dillon, Michael, *Xinjiang – China's Muslim Far Northwest*. London and New York, RoutledgeCurzon, 2004.

Dreyer, June Teufel, *China's Forty Million: Minority Nationalities and National Intergration in the People's Republic of China*. Cambridge, MA, Harvard University Press, 1976.

Dwyer, Arienne M., *The Xinjiang Conflict: Uyghur Identity, Language Policy, and Political Discourse*. Washington, East West Centre, 2005.

Fletcher, Joseph, 'Ch'ing Inner Asia *c*.1800'. In Denis Twitchett and John K. Fairbank (eds), *The Cambridge History of China*, Vol. No. 10. London, Cambridge University Press, 1978.

Forbes, Andrew D., *Warlords and Muslims in Chinese Central Asia: A Political History of Sinkiang, 1911–1949*. Cambridge, Cambridge University Press, 1986.

Forsyth, Thomes Douglas, *Report of a Mission to Yarkand in 1873*. Calcutta, 1875.

Gladney, Dru C., *Muslim Chinese: Ethnic Nationalism in the People's Republic*. Harvard, Harvard University, 1996.

Gladney, Dru C., *Dislocating China: Reflections on Muslims, Minorities, and Other Subaltern Subjects*. London, Hurst & Company, 2004.

Harrell, Steven, *Cultural Encounters on China's Ethnic Frontiers*. Seattle, University of Washington Press, 1990.

He, Baogang and Guo, Yingjie (eds), *Nationalism, National Identity and Democratization in China*. Aldershot, Brookfield, Singapore and Sydney, Ashgate Publishing Ltd., 2000.

Heberer, Thomas, *China and its National Minorities: Autonomy or Assimilation*. Armonk, M.E. Sharpe, 1989.

Hodong, Kim, *Holy War in China: The Muslim Rebellion and State in Chinese Central Asia, 1864–1877*. Stanford, Stanford University, 2004.

Hopkirk, Peter, *Foreign Devils on the Silk Road: The Search for the Lost Cities and Treasures of Chinese Central Asia*. Amherst, University of Massachusetts Press, 1980.

Hsu, Immanuel C.Y., *The Ili Crisis: A Study of Sino-Russian Diplomacy 1871–1881*. Oxford, Clarendon Press, 1965.

Jelavich, Charles and Jelavich, Barbara (eds), *Russia in the East 1876–1880: The Russo-Turkish War and the Kuldja Crisis As Seen Through the Letters of A.G. Jomini to N. K. Giers*. Leiden, E.J. Brill, 1959.

Kim, Hodonge, *Holy War in China: The Muslim Rebellion and State in Chinese Central Asia, 1864–7877*. Stanford, Stanford University Press, 2004.

Lattimore, Owen, *Pivot of Asia, Sinkiang and the Inner Asian Frontiers of China and Russia*. Boston, Little Brown Publishers, 1950.

Lattimore, Owen, *Inner Asian Frontiers of China*. Oxford and New York, Oxford University Press, 1988.

Lipman, J., *Familiar Strangers: A History of Muslims in Northwest China*. Washington, Washington University Press, 1997.

Mackerras, Colin, *The Uighur Empire According to the Tang Dynastic Histories: A Study in Sino-Uighur Relations 744–840*. Canberra, Australian National University Press, 1972.

Mackerras, Colin, *China's Minorities: Integration and Modernization of 20th Century*. New York, Oxford University Press, 1994.

Mackerras, Colin, *China's Ethnic Minorities and Globalisation*. London and New York, RoutledgeCurzon, 2003.

Mackerras, Colin and Clarke, Michael, *China, Xinjiang and Central Asia: History, Transition and Crossroads Interaction into the 21st Century*. USA and Canada, Taylor & Francis, 2009.

McMillen, Donald H., *Chinese Communist Power and Policy in Xinjiang, 1949–1977*. Boulder, Westview Press, 1979.

Manz, Beatrice Forbes (ed.), *Studies on Chinese and Islamic Inner Asia*. Hampshire and Vermont, Variorum, 1995.

Millward, James, *Violent Separatism in Xinjiang: A Critical Assessment*. Washington, East West Centre, 2004.

Millward, James, *Eurasian Crossroads: A History of Xinjiang*. New York, Columbia University Press, 2007.

Moseley, George, *A Sino-Soviet Cultural Frontier: The Ili Kazakh Autonomous Chou*. Cambridge, MA, Harvard University Press, 1966.

Norins, Martin, *Gateway to Asia: Sinkiang: Frontier of the Chinese Far West*. New York, John Day, 1944.

Patterson, George N., *The Unquiet Frontier: Border Tensions in the Sino-Soviet Conflict*. Hong Kong, International Studies Group, 1966.

Rashid, Ahmed, *Taliban: Islam, Oil and the New Great Game in Central Asia*. London and New York, I.B. Tauris, 2001.

Rashid, Ahmed, *Jihad: The Rise of Militant Islam in Central Asia*. New Haven, Yale University Press, 2002.

Rossabi, Morris, *China and Inner Asia: From 1368 to the Present Day*. London, Thames & Hudson Ltd., 1975.

Rudelson, Justin Jon, *Oasis Identities – Uyghur Nationalism along China's Silk Route*. New York, Columbia University Press, 1997.

Schwarz, Henry G., *The Minorities in Northern China: A Survey*. Bellingham, Western Washington University, 1984.

Skrine, C.P., *Chinese Central Asia*. London, Methuen, 1926 (reprinted in 1971).

Skrine, C.P. and Nightingale, Pamela, *Macartney at Kashgar: New Light on British, Chinese and Russian Activities in Sinkiang, 1890–1918*. London, Methuen, 1973.

Snow, Edgar, *The Battle for Asia*. Cleveland and New York, World Publishing Company, 1944.

Soucek, Svat, *A History of Inner Asia*. Cambridge, Cambridge University Press, 2000.

Starr, S. Frederick, *Xinjiang: China's Muslim Borderland*. New York, M.E. Sharpe, 2004.

Statistics Bureau of Xinjiang Uyghur Autonomous Region, *Xinjiang Statistical Yearbook 1989*. Beijing, China Statistics Press, 1989.

Statistics Bureau of Xinjiang Uyghur Autonomous Region, *Xinjiang Statistical Yearbook 2002*. Beijing, China Statistics Press, 2002.

Syroezhkin, K.L., *Myths and Reality of Ethnic Separatism in China and Security of the Central Asia*. Almaty, Daik Press, 2003.

Toops, Stanley, *Demographics and Development in Xinjiang after 1949*. Washington, East West Centre, May 2004.

Twitchett, Denis and Fairbank, John K., *The Cambridge History of China*. London and New York, Cambridge University Press, 1978.

Tyler, Christian, *Wild West China: The Taming of Xinjiang*. London, John Murray, 2003.

Wang, David D., *Under the Soviet Shadow: The Yining Incident, Ethnic Conflicts and International Rivalry in Xinjiang, 1944–49*. Hong Kong, Chinese University Press, 1999.

Warikoo, K., *Central Asia and Kashmir: A Study in the Context of Anglo-Russian Rivalry*. Delhi, 1989.

Warikoo, K. (ed.), *Afghanistan Factor in Central and South Asian Politics*. New Delhi, Trans Asia Informatics, 1994.

Warikoo, K. (ed.), *Central Asia: Emerging New Order*. New Delhi, Har Anand, 1995.

Warikoo, K. (ed.), *Society and Culture in the Himalayas*. New Delhi, Har Anand, 1995.

Warikoo, K. (ed.), *Bamiyan: Challenge to World Heritage*. New Delhi, Bhavna Books, 2002.

Warikoo, K. (ed.), *The Afghanistan Crisis: Issues and Perspectives*. New Delhi, Bhavna Books, 2002.

Warikoo, K. (ed.), *Afghanistan: The Challenge*. New Delhi, Pentagon Press, 2007.

Warikoo, K. (ed.), *Himalayan Frontiers of India: Historical, Geo-Political and Strategic Perspectives*. London and New York, Routledge, 2009.

Warikoo, K. (ed.), *Religion and Security in South and Central Asia*. London and New York, Routledge, 2011.

Warikoo, K. (ed.), *The Other Kashmir: Society, Culture and Politics in the Karakoram Himalayas*. New Delhi, IDSA, Pentagon, 2014.

Warikoo, K. and Norbu, D. (eds), *Ethnicity and Politics in Central Asia*. New Delhi, South Asian Publishers Pvt. Ltd., 1992.

Warikoo, K. and Umarov, Khojamahamad (eds), *Tajikistan in the 21st Century: Society, Politics and Economy*. New Delhi: Pentagon, 2015.

Whiting, Allen S. and Shih-ts'ai, Sheng, *Sinkiang: Pawn or Pivot*. Michigan, Michigan State University Press, 1958.

Winters, C.A., *Mao or Muhammad: Islam in the People's Republic of China*. Hong Kong, Asian Research Service, 1979.

Wu, Aitchen K., *Turkistan Tumult*. Hong Kong, Oxford University Press, 1940. (Reprinted in 1984).

Yee, Robert S., *Ethnic Relations in Xinjiang: A Survey of Uyghur-Han Relations in Urumqi*. London, Taylor & Francis, 2003.

Yin, Ma (ed.), *Questions and Answers about China's National Minorities*. Beijing, New World Press, 1985.

Zhang, Yonojjin and Azizian, Rouben (eds), *Ethnic Challenges Beyond Borders: Chinese and Russian Perspectives of the Central Asian Conundrum*. London, Macmillan, 1988.

Index

Taylor & Francis eBooks

Helping you to choose the right eBooks for your Library

Add Routledge titles to your library's digital collection today. Taylor and Francis ebooks contains over 50,000 titles in the Humanities, Social Sciences, Behavioural Sciences, Built Environment and Law.

Choose from a range of subject packages or create your own!

Benefits for you

>> Free MARC records
>> COUNTER-compliant usage statistics
>> Flexible purchase and pricing options
>> All titles DRM-free.

REQUEST YOUR FREE INSTITUTIONAL TRIAL TODAY

Free Trials Available
We offer free trials to qualifying academic, corporate and government customers.

Benefits for your user

>> Off-site, anytime access via Athens or referring URL
>> Print or copy pages or chapters
>> Full content search
>> Bookmark, highlight and annotate text
>> Access to thousands of pages of quality research at the click of a button.

eCollections – Choose from over 30 subject eCollections, including:

Archaeology	Language Learning
Architecture	Law
Asian Studies	Literature
Business & Management	Media & Communication
Classical Studies	Middle East Studies
Construction	Music
Creative & Media Arts	Philosophy
Criminology & Criminal Justice	Planning
Economics	Politics
Education	Psychology & Mental Health
Energy	Religion
Engineering	Security
English Language & Linguistics	Social Work
Environment & Sustainability	Sociology
Geography	Sport
Health Studies	Theatre & Performance
History	Tourism, Hospitality & Events

For more information, pricing enquiries or to order a free trial, please contact your local sales team:
www.tandfebooks.com/page/sales

 Routledge
Taylor & Francis Group

The home of
Routledge books

www.tandfebooks.com